Data Management's Concepts & Terms

Michael M. Gorman

Whitemarsh Information Systems Corporation
2008 Althea Lane
Bowie, Maryland 20716
Tele: 301-249-1142
Email: Whitemarsh@wiscorp.com
Web: www.wiscorp.com

Designations used by companies to distinguish their products are often claimed as trademarks. In all instances where Whitemarsh Press is aware of a claim, the product names appear in initial capital or all capital letters. Readers, however, should contact the appropriate companies for more complete information regarding trademarks and registration.

©2009 by Whitemarsh Information Systems Corporation
All rights reserved.

This publication is designed to provide accurate and authoritative information in regard to the subject matter covered. It is sold with the understanding that the publisher is not engaged in rendering legal, accounting, or other professional services. If legal advice or other expert assistance is required, the services of a competent professional person should be sought. FROM A DECLARATION OF PRINCIPLES JOINTLY ADOPTED BY A COMMITTEE OF THE AMERICAN BAR ASSOCIATION AND A COMMITTEE OF PUBLISHERS.

Reproduction or translation of any part of this work beyond that permitted by section 107 or 108 of the 1976 United States Copyright Act without the permission of the copyright holder is unlawful. Requests for permission or further information should be addressed to Whitemarsh Press.

ISBN   978-0-9789968-6-4

Printed in the United States of America

Table of Contents

Preface	xxix
4GL	1
Abnormal Termination	1
Abstract Data Type	1
Access Control	1
Access Method	1
Access Path	2
Access Strategy	2
Action Type	2
After Image Recovery	2
Aggregate	2
Alias	2
ANSI	2
ANSI Database Standards	3
ANSI NDL	6
ANSI SQL	6
Application Database	6
Application Optimization	6
Application Type	6
Archival Database	6
Area	6
Array	7
Assertion	7
Assigned Task:	7
Atomic	7
Attribute	7
Attribute Assigned Meta Category Values	8
Attribute Assigned Value Domain	8
Attribute Name	8
Audit Trail	8
Authorization Identifier	8
Automatic Backout	8
Automatic Restart	8
B-Tree	9
Backup	9
Backus Naur Form (BNF)	9
Backward Recovery	9
Base Line	9

Data Management's Concepts & Terms

Base Line Staff 10
Base Line Work Environment Factor 10
Base Relation 10
Before Image Recovery 10
Benchmark Test 10
Blocking Factor 10
Buffer 10
Buffer Flush 11
Business Calendar Cycle 11
Business Cycle 11
Business Domains: 11
Business Event 11
Business Event Assigned Business Information System 11
Business Event Cycle 12
Business Event Cycle Structure 12
Business Event Cycle Structure Type 12
Business Event Model 12
Business Function 12
Business Function Assigned Business Event 12
Business Function Assigned Document 13
Business Function Assigned Form 13
Business Information System 13
Business Information System Model 14
Business Information System Resource Life Cycle Node Assignment ... 14
Business Information System Database Object Information System
    Assignment 14
Business Information System and View 14
Business Information System Generators 14
Business Information System Plan 15
Business Information System Plan Characteristic: Maintainable 15
Business Information System Plan Characteristic: Quality 15
Business Information System Plan Characteristic: Reproducible 16
Business Information System Plan Characteristic: Timely 16
Business Information System Plan Characteristic: Useable 16
Business Organizations 16
Business Process 16
Business Rule 17
Business Term 17

Table of Contents

CALC 17
Calendar Cycle 17
Calendar Cycle Structure 17
Calendar Cycle Structure Type 17
Candidate Key 17
Cardinality 17
CASE 18
Central Version 18
Chain 18
Character 18
Character Fill 18
Characteristic 18
Characteristic Type 18
Check Clause 19
Checkpoint 19
Client-Server 19
Clarion 19
CODASYL 20
CODASYL Model 20
CODASYL Set 21
Collating Sequence 21
Collection Data Type 21
Column 22
Column Assigned Data Integrity Rule 23
Column Assigned Meta Category Values 23
Column Assigned Value Domain 23
Command 23
Commit 23
Communications Link 23
Complex Fact 23
Complex Row 24
Complex Table 24
Compound Data Element 24
Compound Data Element Assigned Data Element 24
Compound Data Element Structure 24
Compound Data Element Structure Type 24
Compression 24
Computer Program 24

Concatenate 24
Concatenated Key 25
Concept Structure 25
Concept Structure Type 25
Concepts 25
Conceptual Data Model 25
Conceptual Schema 26
Conceptual Value Domain Structure 27
Conceptual Value Domain Structure Type 27
Conceptual Value Domains 27
Concurrent Operations 27
Consistency 28
Contention 28
Contract 28
Contract & Organization 28
Contract Resource 29
Contract Role 29
Cursor 29
Data Administration 30
Data Administrator 30
Data Aggregate 30
Data Analysis 30
Data Architecture Reference Model 30
Data Architecture Class 34
Data Definition 35
Data Definition Language (DDL) 35
Data Dictionary/Directory System (DD/DS) 36
Data Driven Methodology 36
Data Element 36
Data Element Assigned Data Element Classification 37
Data Element Assigned Data Integrity Rule 37
Data Element Assigned Derived Data Element 38
Data Element Assigned Meta Category Value 38
Data Element Classification Structure 38
Data Element Classification Structure Type 38
Data Element Classifications 38
Data Element Concepts 38
Data Element Concept Structure 39

Table of Contents

Data Element Concept Structure Type	39
Data Element Concept Assigned Data Integrity Rule	39
Data Element Concept Assigned Meta Category Value	39
Data Element Length	39
Data Element Model	39
Data File	41
Data Flow	41
Data Flow Diagram	41
Data Independence	41
Data Integrity	42
Data Integrity Rule	42
Data Item	43
Data Manipulation Language (DML)	43
Data Model	44
Data Resource Management	52
Data Security	53
Data Storage Description Language (DMCL or DSDL)	53
Data Storage Structure	53
Data Store	53
Data Structure	53
Data Type	53
Data View	53
Data Volatility	53
Data Warehouse	53
Database	53
Database Administrator (DBA)	54
Database Domain	54
Database Domain Assigned Database Object	54
Database Key (DBKEY)	54
Database Management	54
Database Management System (DBMS)	55
Database Management Systems (DBMS) History	57
Database Nature	60
Database Object Assigned Property Class	60
Database Object Class	61
Database Object Data Structure	61
Database Object Information System	61

Data Management's Concepts & Terms

Database Object Information Systems Assigned Database Object Table Process 61
Database Object Model 61
Database Object Resource Life Cycle Node Assignment 62
Database Object State 63
Database Object State and Database Object Information System 63
Database Object Table 63
Database Object Table Process 63
Database Object Table Process Column 63
Database Production Status 64
Database Recovery 64
Database Update 64
Database View 64
Database View column 64
DBMS 64
DBMS Column 64
DBMS Column Assigned Column 65
DBMS Column Assigned Meta Category Values 65
DBMS Column Assigned Value Domain 65
DBMS Column Constraint 65
DBMS Data Type 65
DBMS Data Type Picture 66
DBMS Environment 66
DBMS Record 66
DBMS Schema 66
DBMS Subschema 67
DBMS Table 67
DBMS Table Assigned Assertion 67
DBMS Table Assigned Stored Procedure 67
DBMS Table Assigned Trigger 68
DBMS Table Candidate Key 68
DBMS Table Candidate Key Assigned DBMS Column 68
DBMS Table Constraint 68
DBMS Table Foreign Key 68
DBMS Table Foreign Key Assigned DBMS Column 69
DBMS Table Primary Key 69
DBMS Table Primary Key Assigned DBMS Column 69
DBMS Table Secondary Key 69

Table of Contents

DBMS Table Secondary Key Assigned DBMS Column 69
Deadly Embrace 70
Degree (Of a Relation) 70
Delimiter 70
Deliverable 70
Deliverable Template 70
Deliverable Template Type 70
Derived Data 71
Derived Data Element 71
Derived Data Element Assigned Compound Data Element 71
Derived Data Element Assigned Data Element 71
Determinant 71
Device Media Control Language (DMCL) 71
Dictionary (Storage Structure Component) 71
Discrete and Release Development Environments 72
Distributed Database 72
Division 72
Document 72
Document Cell 72
DOS 72
Dynamic Backout 72
Dynamic Relationship 73
Element 73
Embedded Pointer 73
Encode/Decode Tables 73
End-User 73
Enterprise 73
Enterprise Architecture 74
Enterprise's Architecture Class 74
Enterprise Database 74
Enterprise Resource Planning (ERP) 74
Entity 75
Entity Candidate Key 75
Entity Candidate Key Assigned Attribute 75
Entity Foreign Key 76
Entity Foreign Key Assigned Attribute 76
Entity Primary Key 76
Entity Primary Key Assigned Attribute 76

Entity Relationship Diagram 76
Environment Type 76
Error Recovery 77
Exclusive Control 77
Extent 77
External Document 77
Fact 77
Fact Name 79
Fail Soft 79
Field 79
Field Length 79
File 79
File Block 80
File Cell 80
FIPS 80
Fixed Length Fact 80
Fixed Length Record 80
Foreign Key 80
Form 80
Form Cell 80
Framework 80
Fully Functionally Dependent 80
Function 80
Functional Decomposition 81
Group 81
H2 81
HASH/CALC Logical 83
HASH/CALC Physical 83
Heuristics 84
Hierarchical Data Model 84
Hierarchical Index 85
Home Address 85
Host Language Interface 85
Implemented Data Model 85
Implemented Data Model Relationship 87
Independent Logical File Data Model 87
Index 88
Inferential Relationship 88

Table of Contents

Information	88
Information Engineering	88
Information Need	88
Information Need Analysis Model	89
Information Need Characteristic Assignment	90
Information Need Type	90
Information Resource Management	90
Insertion	90
Installation and Maintenance	90
Instance	90
Integrity	90
Integrity Constraints (DBMS Enforced)	90
Internal Schema	91
Interrogation	91
Inverted Access	91
ISO	91
Job Title	91
Join	91
Journal File	91
Justify	91
Keeplist	92
Key	92
Key Value	92
Knowledge Worker Framework	93
Language	93
Line	93
List	93
List Processing	93
Load (Data)	94
Lock	94
Log File	94
Logging	95
Logical Data Model	95
Logical File	95
Logical Record Facility	95
Logical Reorganization	95
Logical User View	95
Management Level	95

Many-to-Many Relationship 95
Member 96
Membership Rationale 96
Message Processing 96
Messages 96
Meta Category Value Type 96
Meta Category Value Type Classification 96
Meta Category Values 97
Meta Language 97
Metabase System Business Event Process 98
    Accomplish Business Information System Database Object Assignments
    98
    Accomplish Business Information System View Assignment 98
    Create, Modify or Delete Application Types 98

        Create, Modify or Delete Business Event Cycle Structure Types 98
    Create, Modify or Delete Business Event Cycle Structures 98
    Create, Modify or Delete Business Information System 98
    Create, Modify or Delete Business Events 98
    Create, Modify or Delete Business Event Cycle 98
    Create, Modify or Delete Business Information System Level 98
    Create, Modify or Delete Business Information System View Role 99
    Create, Modify or Delete Calendar Cycle Structures 99
    Create, Modify or Delete Calendar Cycle 99
    Create, Modify or Delete Calendar Cycle Structure Types 99
    Create, Modify or Delete DBMS Environment Types 99
    Create, Modify or Delete Predominant User Type 99
    Create, Modify or Delete [Application] Environment Types 99
Metabase System Business Term Process 99
    Accomplish Business Term Assignment 99
    Accomplish Business Term Interrelationship 99
    Create Business Term from a Candidate Business Term 99
    Create, Modify, or Delete Business Term 100
    Discover Business Terms 100
Metabase System Concept Process 100
    Accomplish Data Element Concepts to Concept Reassignments 100
    Accomplish Data Elements to a Compound Data Element Assignments
    100

> Create, Modify or Delete Concept Structure Types 100
> Create, Modify or Delete Concept Structures 100
> Create, Modify or Delete Concepts 100
> Metabase System Conceptual Value Domain Process 100
> > Accomplish Data Element Concepts to Conceptual Value Domain Reassignments 100
> > Accomplish Value Domain to Conceptual Value Domain Reassignments
.... 100
> > Create, Modify or Delete Conceptual Value Domain Structure Types . 101
> > Create, Modify or Delete Conceptual Value Domains 101
> > Create, Modify or Delete Conceptual Value Domain Structures 101
> > Accomplish Data Element Classifications to Data Element Assignments
.... 101
> Metabase System Data Element Classification Process 101
> > Create, Modify or Delete Data Element Classification Structure Types
.... 101
> > Create, Modify or Delete Data Element Classification Structures 101
> > Create, Modify or Delete Data Element Classification 101
> Metabase System Data Element Process 101
> > Accomplish Data Element Classifications to Data Element Assignments
.... 101
> > Accomplish Data Element Concepts to Concept Reassignments 102
> > Accomplish Data Element Concepts to Conceptual Value Domain Reassignments 102
> > Accomplish Data Elements to a Compound Data Element Assignments
.... 102
> > Accomplish Data Elements to Business Domain Reassignments 102
> > Accomplish Data Elements to Data Element Concept Reassignments . 102
> > Accomplish Data Elements to Value Domains Reassignments 102
> > Accomplish Derived Data Elements to Compound Data Element Assignments 102
> > Accomplish Derived Data Elements to Data Element Assignments ... 102
> > Create, Modify or Delete Compound Data Element Structures 102
> > Create, Modify or Delete Compound Data Element Structure Types .. 102
> > Create, Modify or Delete Compound Data Elements 103
> > Create, Modify or Delete Data Element Classification 103
> > Create, Modify or Delete Data Element Classification Structures 103

Create, Modify or Delete Data Element Classification Structure Types 103
Create, Modify or Delete Data Element Concept 103
Create, Modify or Delete Data Element Concept Structures 103
Create, Modify or Delete Data Element Concept Structure Types 103
Create, Modify or Delete Data Elements 103
Create, Modify or Delete Derived Data Elements 103
Promote Data Element Concept to Concept 103
Promote Data Element to Data Element Concept 103
Reallocate Business Domains 104
Remove Data Element Concept Meta Category Value Assignments ... 104
Metabase System Data Integrity Rule Process 104
Accomplish Data Integrity Rule Assignment 104
Accomplish Data Integrity Rule Interrelationship 104
Create, Modify, or Delete Data Integrity Rule 104
Metabase System Database Domain Process 104
Create, Modify, or Delete Database Domain and Database Object Association 104
Create, Modify, or Delete Database Domain 104
Reallocate Database Domains 104
Metabase System Database Object Process 105
Accomplish Database Object Information Systems to Database Object Table Process Assignment 105
Accomplish Database Object Information Systems to Database Object Table Process Reassignment 105
Accomplish Database Object State to Database Object Information System Assignments 105
Accomplish Database Object State to Database Object Information System Reassignment 105
Accomplish Database Object Table Process to Column Reassignment 105
Accomplish Database Object Table Process to Column Assignment ... 105
Accomplish Database Object to Database Domain Reassignment 105
Accomplish Database Object to Schema Reassignment 105
Accomplish Database Object to Table Reassignments 105
Create, Modify or Delete Database Object Information Systems 106
Create, Modify or Delete Database Object Table Assignment 106
Create, Modify or Delete Database Object 106

Table of Contents

- Create, Modify or Delete Database Object Table Membership Rationale ... 106
- Create, Modify or Delete Database Object Table Process ... 106
- Create, Modify or Delete Database Object State ... 106
- Metabase System Environment ... 106
- Metabase System Function Process ... 107
  - Accomplish Mission-organization and Function Assignments ... 107
  - Create, Modify or Delete Functions ... 107
  - Reallocate Functions ... 107
- Metabase System Implemented Data Model Process ... 107
  - Accomplish Assign Columns to Column Reassignments ... 107
  - Accomplish Assign Columns to Data Elements Reassignments ... 107
  - Accomplish Assign Columns to SQL Data Types Reassignments ... 107
  - Accomplish Assign Columns to Attribute Reassignments ... 107
  - Accomplish Columns to Table Reassignments ... 107
  - Accomplish Tables to Schema Reassignments ... 107
  - Accomplish Tables to Tables Reassignments ... 108
  - Create Many Columns ... 108
  - Create, Modify or Delete Allocation of Columns to the Candidate Key ... 108
  - Create, Modify or Delete Allocation of Columns to the Primary Key ... 108
  - Create, Modify or Delete Candidate Key ... 108
  - Create, Modify or Delete Tables ... 108
  - Create, Modify or Delete Foreign Keys ... 108
  - Create, Modify or Delete Primary Key ... 108
  - Create, Modify or Delete Schema ... 108
  - Create One Column ... 108
  - Create SQL Data Types ... 108
  - Export SQL DDL ... 109
  - Import Attribute from Specified Data Model ... 109
  - Import Entity Set from Specified Data Model ... 109
  - Import Entity Tree from Specified Data Model ... 109
  - Import SQL DDL ... 109
  - Maintain Column Meta Category Values ... 109
  - Maintain Column Value Domains ... 109
  - Maintain Columns ... 109
  - Promote Column to Attribute ... 110
  - Promote Column to Data Element ... 110

Data Management's Concepts & Terms

- Promote Implemented Data Model Table to Specified Data Model Entity ... 110
- Promote Implemented Data Model to Specified Data Model ... 110
- Remove Column Attribute Assignments ... 110
- Remove Column Data Element Assignments ... 110
- Remove Column Meta Category Values ... 110
- Report Column Data Hierarchies ... 110
- Synchronize Local Columns Definitions ... 111

Metabase System Information Needs Analysis Process ... 111
- Accomplish Mission-Organization-Function Ranked Information Need Assignment ... 111
- Create, Modify or Delete Information Need Type ... 111
- Create, Modify or Delete Ranking ... 111
- Create, Modify or Delete Information Need ... 111
- Create, Modify or Delete Characteristic ... 111
- Create, Modify or Delete Association Between Information Need and Characteristic ... 111
- Create, Modify or Delete Characteristic Type ... 111

Metabase System Information Systems Plan Process ... 112
- Accomplish Association Between Business Information System and Database Object Information System ... 112
- Accomplish Association Between Business Information System and Business Event ... 112
- Accomplish Association Between Business Information System and Resource Life Cycle Node ... 112
- Accomplish Association Between Business Information System and View ... 112
- Create, Modify or Delete Application Types ... 112
- Create, Modify or Delete Business Information System Levels ... 112
- Create, Modify or Delete Business Information System ... 112
- Create, Modify or Delete Construction Methods ... 112
- Create, Modify or Delete DBMS Environment ... 112
- Create, Modify or Delete Environment Type ... 113
- Create, Modify or Delete Predominant User Class ... 113
- Create, Modify or Delete Programming Language ... 113
- Create, Modify or Delete Status ... 113

Metabase System Meta Category Value Process ... 113
- Create, Modify or Delete Data Element Meta Category Values ... 113

Table of Contents

- Create, Modify or Delete Data Element Concept Meta Category Values 113
  - Create, Modify or Delete Meta Category Value 114
  - Reallocate Meta Category Value Types 114
  - Reallocate Meta Category Values 114
  - Remove Data Element Concept Meta Category Value Assignments .. 114
  - Remove Data Element Meta Category Value Assignments 114
- Metabase System Meta Category Value Process 114
  - Create, Modify or Delete Meta Category Value Type 114
  - Create, Modify or Delete Meta Category Value Type Class 114
- Metabase System Mission Process 114
  - Create, Modify or Delete Missions 114
  - Reallocate Missions 115
- Metabase System Operational Data Model Process 115
  - Accomplish DBMS Column to DBMS Table Reassignment 115
  - Accomplish DBMS Columns to DBMS Data Type Reassignment 115
  - Accomplish DBMS Columns to DBMS Column Reassignment 115
  - Accomplish DBMS Tables to DBMS Schema Reassignment 115
  - Accomplish DBMS Tables to DBMS Table Reassignment 115
  - Allocate DBMS Columns to the Candidate key 115
  - Allocate DBMS Columns to the Primary Key 115
  - Allocate DBMS Columns to the Secondary Key 115
  - Create DBMS Columns 115
  - Create, Modify or Delete Candidate Key 116
  - Create, Modify or Delete Primary Key 116
  - Create, Modify or Delete Secondary Key 116
  - Create, Modify or Delete Foreign Keys 116
  - Create, Modify or Delete DBMS Table Candidate Key 116
  - Create, Modify or Delete DBMS Tables Primary Key 116
  - Export SQL DDL 116
  - Import Column from Implemented Data Model 116
  - Import SQL DDL 116
  - Import Table Set from Implemented Data Model 116
  - Import Table Tree from Implemented Data Model 117
  - Maintain DBMS Column Value Domains 117
  - Promote DBMS Table Column to Implemented Data Model 117
  - Promote DBMS Table to Implemented Data Model 117
  - Promote Operational Data Model to Implemented Data Model 117

- Remove DBMS Table Column to Column Assignments 117
- Report DBMS Column Data Hierarchies 117
- Synchronize Local DBMS Columns Definitions 118

Metabase System Organization Process 118
- Accomplish Mission and Organization Assignments 118
- Create, Modify or Delete Organizations 118
- Reallocate Organizations 118

Metabase System Position and Person Process 118
- Create Mission-Organization-Function and Position 118
- Create, Modify, or Delete Position-Person Association 118
- Create, Modify or Delete Person 118
- Create, Modify or Delete Management Level 118
- Create, Modify or Delete Position 118

Metabase System Resource Life Cycle Process 119
- Accomplish Resource Life Cycle Node Business Information Systems Assignments 119
- Accomplish Resource Life Cycle Node Mission Assignments 119
- Accomplish Resource Life Cycle Node Information Need Assignments 119
- Accomplish Resource Life Cycle Node Database Object Assignments 119
- Create, Modify or Delete Resource Type 119
- Create, Modify or Delete Resource 119
- Create, Modify or Delete Resource Life Cycle Node 119
- Create, Modify or Delete Resource Life Cycle Node Structure 119
- Create, Modify or Delete Resource Life Cycle Node Structure Type ... 119

Metabase System Specified Data Model Process 119
- Accomplish Attributes to Data Element Reassignments 119
- Accomplish Attributes to Entity Reassignments 120
- Accomplish Entities to Entity Reassignments 120
- Accomplish Entity to Subject Reassignments 120
- Accomplish Subject to Subject Reassignments 120
- Allocate Attributes to the Primary Key 120
- Allocate Attributes to the Candidate Key 120
- Create Many Attributes 120
- Create, Modify or Delete Foreign Keys 120
- Create, Modify or Delete Candidate Key Definition 120
- Create, Modify or Delete Subjects 120

    Create, Modify or Delete Entities 121
    Create, Modify or Delete Primary Key Definition 121
    Create One Attribute 121
    Export SQL DDL 121
    Import SQL DDL 121
    Maintain Attribute Meta Category Values 121
    Maintain Attributes 121
    Maintain Value Domains 121
    Promote Attribute to Data Element 121
    Remove Attribute Data Element Assignment 122
    Remove Attribute Meta Category Value Assignments 122
    Report Data Hierarchies 122
    Synchronize Local Attribute Definitions 122
Metabase System 122
Metabase System Value Domain Process 123
    Accomplish Data Elements to Value Domains Reassignments 123
    Accomplish Value Domain to Conceptual Value Domain Reassignments
    123
    Accomplish Value Domain Value to Value Domain Reassignments .. 123
    Create, Modify or Delete Value Domain Value Structures 123
    Create, Modify or Delete Value Domain Values 123
    Create, Modify or Delete Value Domain Value Data Types 123
    Create, Modify or Delete Value Domain Structures 123
    Create, Modify or Delete Value Domain Structure Types 123
    Create, Modify or Delete Value Domain Value Structure Types 124
    Create, Modify or Delete Value Domains 124
Metabase System View Data Model Process 124
    Accomplish DBMS Columns to View Column Assignments 124
    Accomplish View Column to Compound Data Element Assignments
    124
    Accomplish View Column to Derived Data Element Assignments ... 124
    Create, Modify or Delete View Columns 124
    Create, Modify or Delete View Column Structure Type 124
    Create, Modify or Delete View Column Structure Process 124
    Create, Modify or Delete View Column Structure 124
    Create, Modify or Delete Views 124
    Generate View Columns 125
    Generate Views 125

Data Management's Concepts & Terms

Metadata	125
Metadata Management System	125
Metric	126
Mission Assigned Business Term	126
Mission Assigned Database Domain	126
Mission	126
Mission-Organization Assigned Business Function	127
Mission-Organization-Function	127
Mission-Organization-Function Position Assignment	127
Mission-Organization-Function Position Role	127
Mission-Organization-Function-Position-Assignment Model	127
Mission-Organization-Functional Ranked Information Need	128
Mission Resource	129
Mission versus Function	129
Module	129
Multi-User Mode	130
Multiple Database Processing	130
Multiset	130
Multithread	130
Multivalued Dependency	130
Natural Language	130
Navigate	131
NDL Data Language Standard	132
Network	132
Network Data Model	132
Nested Repeating Group	132
Next Key (Next Pointer)	132
Non Procedural Language	133
Normal Forms	133
Normalize	137
Normalized Data	138
Null	138
ODBC	138
O/S File	138
OLAP	138
OLTP	138
One-to-One Relationship	138
One-to-Many Relationship	139

Table of Contents

Open Database Connectivity (ODBC) 139
Operational Data Model 139
Operational Data Model Relationship 141
Order 141
Ordered 141
Organization 141
Outer Join 141
Overflow 142
Owner 142
Owner Key (Owner Pointer) 142
Owner-multiple Member 142
Owner-Single Member Relationship 142
Packed Decimal 142
Padding 142
Page 143
Parameter 143
Password 143
Person 143
Phone 143
Phone Type 143
Physical Attribute 143
Physical Data Model 143
Physical Database 144
Physical Record 144
Physical Reorganization 144
Physical Schema 145
Pointer 145
Populate 145
Position 145
Precedence Vector 145
Precision 145
Predominant User 146
Primary Key 146
Prior Key (Prior Pointer) 146
Privacy 146
Privacy Key 146
Privacy Lock 146
Procedural Language 146

Procedure Oriented Language 146
Process Driven Methodology 146
Program 147
Project 147
Project Management Model 147
Project Template 149
Project Template & Deliverable Template 149
Project Template & Task Template 149
Project Template Type 150
Projection 150
Property Class 150
Pure Alphabetic 150
Pure Numeric 150
Qualification 150
Quality Assurance 150
Query Update Language 151
Queue 151
RAM 151
Random Access 151
Ranking 151
Record 151
Record Check 151
Record-Element 151
Record Layout 151
Record Length 151
Record Type 151
Recovery 151
Recovery File 152
Recursive Relationship 152
Referential Integrity 153
Relation 153
Relational Algebra 153
Relational Calculus 153
Relational Database 153
Relational Data Model 153
Relational View 154
Relationships 154
Relative Addressing 156

Table of Contents

Reorganization 156
Repeating Group 156
Report 157
Report Writer 157
Representation 157
Resource 157
Resource Life Cycle 157
Resource Life Cycle Analysis 157
Resource Life Cycle Analysis Model 157
Resource Life Cycle Analysis Node 159
Resource Life Cycle Characteristics 159
Resource Life Cycle Characteristic: Basic 159
Resource Life Cycle Characteristic: Centralized 159
Resource Life Cycle Characteristic: Complex 159
Resource Life Cycle Characteristic: Enduring 159
Resource Life Cycle Characteristic: Shareable 159
Resource Life Cycle Characteristic: Structured 160
Resource Life Cycle Characteristic: Valuable 160
Resource Life Cycle Node Business Information Systems Assignment 160
Resource Life Cycle Node Database Object Assignment 160
Resource Life Cycle Node Information Need Assignment 160
Resource Life Cycle Node Matrix 160
Resource Life Cycle Node Structure 161
Resource Life Cycle Node Structure Type: 161
Resource Type 161
Restore 161
Retention 161
Retrieval 161
Ring Structure 161
RJE 162
Robust 162
Role 162
Rollback 162
Role Type 162
ROM 162
Root Segment 162
Row 162
Run-Unit 162

Data Management's Concepts & Terms

Save 163
Savepoint 163
Scale 163
Schema 163
Schema Assigned Database Object 163
Secondary Key 164
Security and Privacy 164
Segment 165
Selection 165
Semantics 165
Sequential Search 165
Serial Search 165
Serial Storage 166
Serializability 166
Set 166
Simple Fact 166
Simple Row 166
Simple Table 166
Single Thread 166
Single User Mode 166
Singular, Multiple Member Relationship 166
Singular Set 166
Singular, Single Member Relationship 167
Skill 167
Skill Level 167
Skill Level Type 167
Snapshot 167
Specified Data Model 167
Specified Data Model Relationship 169
SQL Data Language Standard 170
SQL Data Type 177
Staff 178
Staff Skill Level 178
State 178
Static Relationship 178
Status Type 178
Storage Structure 179
Stored Procedure 179

Table of Contents

Subject	179
Subschema (External Schema or User Schema)	179
Subschema Data Definition Language	179
Subschema Record Type	179
System	179
System Control	179
Systems Analysis	179
Table	180
Table Candidate Key Assigned Column	181
Table Foreign Key Assigned Column	182
Table Look up	182
Table Primary Key	182
Table Primary Key Assigned Column	182
Task	182
Task & Work Environment Factor	182
Task Skill Level Requirement	183
Task Template	183
Teleprocessing Task	183
Temporary View Table	183
Time Charges	183
Top-Down versus Bottom-up Modeling	183
Topology	185
Transaction	185
Transaction Backout	185
Transaction Processing Monitor	185
Transitive Dependency	185
Tree Structure	185
Trigger	185
Truncate	185
Tuple	186
Unload	186
Unordered	186
Update (Data)	186
User	187
User Interface	187
User Schema (Subschema)	187
User View	187
Valid, Invalid, and Range Value Tables	187

Value Domain Data Type 187
Value Domain Structure 187
Value Domain Structure Type 187
Value Domain Value 187
Value Domain Value Structure 188
Value Domain Value Structure Type 188
Value Domains 188
Variable Length Data Element 188
Variable Length Record 188
Vector 188
View 188
View Column 189
View Column Assigned Compound Data Element 189
View Column Assigned DBMS Column 190
View Column Assigned Derived Data Element 190
View Column Structure 190
View Column Structure Process 190
View Column Structure Type 190
View Data Model 190
Virtual Data Element 192
Virtual Relation 192
Volatility 192
Warehouse Database 192
Where Clause 192
Where Expression 192
Work 193
Work Environment Factor 193
Work Environment Factor Type 193
Work Environment Multiplier Type 193
Work Environment Factor 194
X3H2 194
Zachman Framework 194
INDEX 195

Figures

Figure 1. Contemplating the need for a Concepts and Terms book. xxix
Figure 2. Business Information Systems Model. 13
Figure 3. Data Architecture Classes. 29
Figure 4. Five data model generalization levels. 32
Figure 5. Data Element Model. 40
Figure 6. Data Model Engineering. 49
Figure 7. Tabulation of features for data models. 50
Figure 8. DBMSs by data model type. 52
Figure 10. Database Object Model. 62
Figure 11. Implemented Data Model. 86
Figure 12. Information Needs Analysis Model. 89
Figure 13. Mission-organization-function Position Assignment Model. . . . 128
Figure 14. Pre-Normal Form. 133
Figure 15. First Normal Form. 133
Figure 16. Second Normal Form. 134
Figure 17. Third Normal Form. 134
Figure 18. Fourth Normal Form. 135
Figure 19. Operational Data Model. 140
Figure 20. Project Management Model 148
Figure 21. Resource Life Cycle Model. 158
Figure 22. Specified Data Model. 169
Figure 23. View Data Model. 191

Tables

Table 1. Data Model and Relationships. 46
Table 2. Legend for Eight Data Model Relationship Types. 46
Table 3. Relationship Operations 47
Table 4. The Data Models Legend. 51
Table 5. Lineage of H2 Database Language Standards – 1978 through 1996.
.... 83
Table 6. Lineage of H2 Database Language Standards – 1996 through 2014.
.... 84
Table 7. Comparative 1986 through 1992 SQL Data Language Standard
  Features. 172
Table 8. SQL:1999 support of Simple and Complex Facts. 175
Table 9. SQL:1999 Relationships. 176

Preface

I remember thinking that a discipline "came of age" once it needed a glossary. The fact that this book of concepts and terms is more than 245 printed pages including a table of contents and index and has almost 900 entries says something, just not sure what.

Synonyms are identified by citing them and pointing to a root concept or term. An index is also included and serves as a way of interrelating entries.

Are these concepts and terms along with their definitions universally held? Absolutely not. In any intellectual discipline, terms, concepts and their definitions are forever in *discussion*. Just ask 10 data people what are the definition for Conceptual, Logical, and Physical and you will get 15 different answers.

Figure 1. Contemplating the need for a Concepts and Terms book.

Just ask 10 people if they know what a Data Element is. All will say yes, but none will agree. So, while this book does not settle any arguments, it has been constructed to represent the most common data management terms, the Whitemarsh data management terms, and hopefully their common sense definitions.

In this book, and in data management in general, there are often pairs of words that correspond to types and instances. Before "relational" there was the pair: record type and record. Since "relational" the corresponding type-instance pair is table and row. Table generally means record type. Row generally means record. In this book, regardless of data model (i.e., Network, Hierarchical, Independent Logical File, Relational, or SQL), table and row are deployed instead of record type and record. Column is a type-based word to represent a well-defined and partitioned data field. There is however no commonly accepted instance-based word for column other than value. In this book a data element is not a synonym for column. Rather, a data element is a type-based word and it is exclusively reserved for the ISO Standard, 11179, Data Element metadata.

While a primary purpose of this book is to provide definitions of terms commonly found in data management, this book also serves as the basis for all Whitemarsh terms. For example, the terms, Conceptual, Logical, and Physical are clearly data management terms, while the terms, Specified Data Model, Implemented Data Model, and Operational Data Model which are somewhat analogous, but are different in significant ways, are Whitemarsh terms. This book contains both cross walks between these two term trios and also an explanation why Whitemarsh chooses to use its own terms instead. This book should be employed as the "definitive" source of Whitemarsh terms for all its books, papers, courses, and methodologies.

A good many of the terms in this book are Whitemarsh product-base terms. The terms, for example, Specified Data Model, Implemented Data Model, and Operational Data Model are the proper metadata-based products defined, created, reported, and maintained within the Whitemarsh metadata management system, Metabase System.

I want to thank Hank Lavender for a careful review of these concepts and terms. Not only did he find all the usual culprits, his questions regarding the SQL standard, SQL-based DBMSs, the relational data model, and ANSI SQL standards were very insightful. Hank also suggested that I make my observations about process-driven methodologies more pointed.

Please feel free to disagree with any contained term and send me an email at Whitemarsh@wiscorp.com. Additionally, if you find any conflict with a term in this book and within a Whitemarsh product, please let me know. It will be fixed. I look forward to hearing from you. Who knows, your term and its definition might settle an ages-long argument. If your contributed term is included in a future edition, you, as its source will be cited, assuming you want to be cited.

Note: In this book, all data model relationships are one-to-many, and are shown as a line with a single arrowhead. See for example, Figure 2 on page 13.

Michael M. Gorman
September 2009

Concepts & Terms

4GL: Fourth Generation Language--A broad class of computer languages that are simpler, easier to use than third generation languages such as COBOL or Fortran. Prior to ANSI SQL/CLI (call level interface), 4GLs were commonly bound to particular DBMSs. For example, FORMS with Oracle. Since SQL/CLI, 4GLs can invoke DBMS engine functions through calls, ODBC, or JDBC.

Abnormal Termination: An Abnormal Termination is an unplanned cessation of processing such that user control is not returned to the processor that was being used at the time the error occurred.

Abstract Data Type: An Abstract Data Type is described by an abstract data type descriptor which, in turn, specifies a set of columns whose values represent the value of an abstract data type instance, the operations that define the equality and ordering relationships of the abstract data type, and the operations that implement the behavior of the abstract data type.

When the abstract data type name, Address, contains multiple columns such as Street, City, State, and Zip, it acts as a group of facts.

When a collection data type (e.g., set, list, or multiset) is the abstract data type, Address, the Address can have multiple occurrences and it acts as a repeating group of facts.

An abstract data type can contain an abstract data type. For example, the table EMPLOYEE has a list abstract data type, Dependents. It in turn, has the columns Dependent SSN, Dependent First Name, Dependent Last Name, and the contained abstract data type Medical Conditions. That, in turn, contains the columns: Condition Name, Date of Onset, and Date of Resolution. This example represents a nested repeating group of facts.

There are three abstract data type cases, group, repeating group, and nested repeating group. In this book these are all complex fact types.

Access Control: See Security and Privacy.

Access Method: An Access Method is a data processing strategy used to obtain data from or to place data onto a mass storage device; usually this refers to operating system software capability provided by mainframe manufacturers. Common access methods are B-Trees (balanced binary trees), BDAM (basic direct access method), ISAM (Indexed sequential access method), Hash, Calc, and Sequential.

Access Path: See View.

Access Strategy: An Access Strategy is a process that represents a set of DBMS routines that analyze storage structure constructs to determine the access path in the database to find, retrieve, store, or modify any of the data contained in any of the storage structure components under the control of the DBMS. The access strategy typically involves DBMS vendor software and O/S vendor access methods.

Action Type: An Action Type signifies a type of action that can take place such as:

    SELECT – viewing or reading data
    DELETE – removing data from the database
    INSERT – placing new data into the database
    UPDATE – change data from one value to another

After Image Recovery: See Backup and Recovery.

Aggregate: See Fact.

Alias: An Alias is an alternate identifier for a column or table name. Aliases are typically employed in different programming languages to avoid naming illegalities. For example, CODE-NAME is legal in COBOL, but means CODE minus NAME in Fortran. Consequently, an alias, CODNAM, would be required. In Clarion there can be aliases for tables. This enables multiple cursors to operate against the same table from within a Clarion procedure.

ANSI: ANSI is an acronym for the American National Standards Institute. It was founded in 1918. ANSI acts as the United States organization for standards and conformity assessment.
    ANSI oversees the creation, promulgation and use of thousands of norms and guidelines that directly impact businesses in nearly every sector: from acoustical devices to construction equipment, from dairy and livestock production to energy distribution, and many more. ANSI is also actively engaged in accrediting programs that assess conformance to standards – including globally-recognized cross-sector programs such as the ISO 9000 (quality) and ISO 14000 (environmental) management systems.

With respect to Information Technology ANSI has a large quantity of technical committees that standardize many areas including data and information processing. INCITS (International Committee for IT Standards) is a standard's development organization (SDO) that hosts the development of voluntary IT standards. The INCITS committee that addresses database standards is H2, the Committee on Database Languages.

ANSI Database Standards: ANSI Database Standards efforts started in the early 1970s through study groups. The first "official" database languages standards group, X3H2 was established in 1978.

During the 1970s, the database standards study effort was accomplished by the ANSI SPARC. It was the **S**tandards **P**lanning **a**nd **R**equirements **C**ommittee. Actually, ANSI/SPARC was the committee's "local" name. Its proper name was ANSI/X3/SPARC. X3 was the coded name for the IT standard's committee under ANSI. X3 was hosted by an IT association in Washington, D.C., called CBEMA (Computer and Business Equipment Manufactures Association).

X3 managed the standards' development for languages such as COBOL, Fortran, C, and C++. It also managed the development of hardware specifications such as SCSI (Small Computer Systems Interface).

During the middle 1980s, X3's name was changed to NCITS (National Committee for IT Standards). CBEMA's name was also changed to ITIC (Information Technology Industry Council). It was during this "name change" period that the SPARC committee's name and functions were changed to be accomplished by the Standards Policy Board and the Standards Development Board of the new NCITS management structure. In the late 1990s, the name, NICTS was changed to INCITS for the **In**ternational Committee for IT Standards. As a consequence of X3 changing its name to INCITS, X3H2 became just H2.

In the middle 1960s, the Systems Committee of CODASYL (**C**ommittee **o**n **D**ata **S**ystems and **L**anguages) undertook two surveys of existing DBMSs. Among the reports produced by the CODASYL Systems committee was the Feature Analysis of Generalized Data Base Management Systems. It was published in 1971.

In 1969, the effort to specify standards for common DBMS facilities was started. The first of these efforts were by CODASYL. Starting in the early 1970s, ANSI/X3/SPARC began an effort to standardize DBMS facilities by developing a framework from which sprang two standards: NDL, and SQL. NDL is for network databases and up until 1999, SQL was for relational databases. Today, the SQL language supports features from all the four traditional data models, that is, network, hierarchical, independent logical file and relational.

The ANSI standards process did not fix features. Rather, it standardized interfaces. The real value of ANSI database standards is that the days of being locked in by a vendor are now over. For example, a company can purchase a sophisticated menu-driven report writer that produces interactive SQL data manipulation language. This SQL is read by the DBMS, which obtains the rows and passes them across the standard interface for final formatting by the report writer.

In 1972, ANSI/X3/SPARC established the ad hoc study committee on data base languages. One of the documents from the ad hoc group was the ANSI/X3/SPARC DBMS Framework.

The 1975 ANSI/X3/SPARC committee created an overall data base management system architecture report. Note that there was a "space" at that time between "data" and "base." This ad hoc study group did not intend their three schemas (conceptual, external, and internal) to be definitive, but illustrative, as these three schemas were merely the committee's shorthand way of discussing the three different sub groupings of the 42 different interfaces (schemas) it had identified. As support for that statement, consider that each ANSI standard consists of five main components: conformance statements, field of applicability, (syntax) format, general rules, and syntax rules.

The ANSI/X3/SPARC study group produced, at best, the field of applicability section. If the remaining sections of this database management systems architecture report had been completed, it would have covered many hundreds of pages.

During this overall 1970s time frame, the CODASYL organization created several committees to develop specifications for a network data model DBMS. The results of the CODASYL efforts were called JODs (Journals of Development). These were not standards. They were large scale language specifications. ANSI accomplished standards from the CODASYL JODs. Key JODs were the 1969, 1973, and 1978. The 1978 JOD was the last published by CODASYL.

When the CODASYL JODs for database languages were published, they were being reviewed by the ANSI/X3/SPARC ad hoc database languages' study group. Since the 1975 ANSI/X3/SPARC committee was never created to produce standards, SPARC, in 1975, dissolved its ad hoc subcommittee and recommended to ANSI that it create an ANSI committee, X3H2, with the expressed purpose of creating database language standards.

The first X3H2 meeting was in April 1978, and its initial charter was to develop a network data language (NDL) standard based on the 1978 CODASYL JOD. In 1981, X3H2's charter was expanded to include the development of a relational data language (RDL) standard. In 1984, the RDL standard name was changed to SQL. In addition to standardizing the data definition language (DDL) and the data manipulation language (DML) for NDL and SQL, X3H2 has standardized the use of these database languages from within the ANSI standard languages: COBOL, Fortran, PASCAL, PL/I, Ada, and C.

In summary, the ANSI database standards process began with ANSI/X3/SPARC, which identified the need for database standards through the definition of a draft reference model (1975). SPARC recommended the establishment of a database standards committee (X3H2) to draft the standards NDL and SQL. To ensure that these standards work together, X3H2 maintains liaisons with the various language development committees, such as PL/I (X3J1), BASIC (X3J2), Fortran (X3J3), COBOL (X3J4), Pascal (X3J9), and C (X3J11).

During this time there was also all-out warfare to determine the "one true" data model. ANSI/X3/SPARC, in 1972, addressed the battle over data models with the following statement:

> There is continuing argument on the appropriate data model: e.g., relational, network, hierarchical. If, indeed, this debate is as it seems, then it follows that the correct answer to this question of which data model to use is necessarily *all of the above.*

The 1975 ANSI/X3/SPARC committee saw, as confirmed by the IEC/ISO/JTC1 reference model committee in 1988, that a data model is merely a formalized method of defining tables, columns, the relationships among the tables, and the operations that are allowable on those columns, tables, and relationships.

During the database languages standardization time frame from 1978 through 1999, the only data model that gained significant market share was the relational data model, as expressed by the ANSI database language SQL.

Data Management's Concepts & Terms

The remaining 1960s and 1970s popular data models, Network, Hierarchical, and Independent Logical File lost both market share and vendors.

In the end it seems that the ANSI/X3/SPARC committee was correct because starting with SQL:1999 and more recent SQL standards have now embraced all the best features of not only the relational data model but also the network, hierarchical, and independent logical file data models into just one data model: the SQL Data Language Standard.

See Database Management Systems

ANSI NDL: See NDL Data Language Standard.

ANSI SQL: See SQL Data Language Standard.

Application Database: An Application Database is an organized collection of data designed to support only a collection of closely related functions.

Application Optimization: Application Optimization represents a set of DBMS facilities for determining the overall performance characteristics of an installed database against a set of benchmark database operations. The DBMS application optimization facilities produce statistics that indicate such performance indicators as I/Os, CPU time, overlay processing, and the like.

Application Type: Application Type represents a classification of the application such as distribution, finance, human resources and the like.

Archival Database: See Backup.

Area: An Area is a CODASYL data model concept to identify a collection of rows. A particular row is assigned to a single area and may not migrate between areas. For all CODASYL DBMSs, an area may contain occurrences from one or more tables. For some CODASYL DBMSs, a table may have instances stored in more than one area. In other CODASYL DBMSs, all the instances from a table may be restricted to just one area. In CODASYL DBMSs, the relationship between an area and an O/S file varies. Because of these great differences in the AREA concept, the ANSI NDL does not contain a specification for AREA because to do so would require picking one vendor definition over all the others.

SQL based DBMSs such as Oracle and DB2 have all developed facilities similar to areas.

Array: See Fact.

Assertion: An Assertion is a set of independently defined procedure code that, when executed, must test true when no updating is occurring. An action that causes a violation to an assertion is rejected. An assertion is the same as a table constraint except that it is independently named and defined.

Assigned Task: An Assigned Task is a work task that has a role type and a staff skill level. For example, Defining the Mission Model by Gary Duchesneau, a Business Analyst at the Expert level.
See Project Management Model.

Atomic: Atomic is a characteristic of a fact indicating that it was not derived from within the context in which the fact is employed.

Attribute: Attributes are the manifestation of the semantics of a data element within an entity of a subject contained in the Whitemarsh Specified Data Model. Attributes may have additional semantics that further refines it within the context of the data element. An attribute is intended to be a data-value based partial descriptor of an entity.
There are four classes of attributes within an entity: content, instance, and metadata, and relationships. The first, content, represents the entity's content. For example, if the entity is Customer Address, the content attributes would be Customer Street-1, Customer Street-2, Customer City, Customer State, and Customer Zip.
The second, instance, is the set of attributes that have a combined value such that only one row from the entity is found. This set of attributes is commonly called the entity's primary key.
The third, metadata, are the attributes that represent the metadata about the entity such as who created in an instance of the entity, who updated it, what project caused the row to be added or changed, and finally, what was the date of the add or change.
The fourth, relationships, represent the attributes that, when valued, provide the uniqueness value for a different row in the same entity (recursive relationship) or a different entity (parent entity for a parent-child

relationship). In this later situation, the uniqueness column is often called the parent entity's primary key.
See the Specified Data Model.

Attribute Assigned Meta Category Values: An Attribute Assigned Meta Category Values is a meta category value that has been assigned to an attribute. An assigned meta category value, whether a semantic or data use modifier, is a "meaning" constraint on the attribute. The assigned meta category value cannot be the same as that assigned to the data element. Nor can a meta category value be more expansive than that assigned to the data element.
See the Specified Data Model.

Attribute Assigned Value Domain: An Attribute Assigned Value Domain is a value-based constraint on the attribute. The assigned value domain cannot be the same as that assigned the data element. Nor can a value domain be more expansive than that assigned to the data element.
See the Specified Data Model.

Attribute Name: See the Specified Data Model.

Audit Trail: An Audit Trail is a log of all database activity in a format such that the audit trail rows are reportable through the various interrogation languages of the DBMS.

Authorization Identifier: An Authorization Identifier represents a character string that designates a set of privilege descriptors.

Automatic Backout: Automatic Backout is the process through which all the updates performed within unsuccessfully completed transactions are automatically removed without outside intervention.

Automatic Restart: Automatic Restart is a process by which any inconsistency in the database caused by the partial execution of an update command during a previous session is resolved, typically through automatic backouts.

B-Tree: A B-Tree, balanced binary tree, is a storage structure and access strategy that maintains its order by continually dividing the possible choices into two equal parts and reestablishing links (pointers) to the respective parts but not allowing more than two levels of difference to exist concurrently.

Backup: A Backup is a copy of the database. The inverse of backup is recovery. A database backup is also called a "save," or archival database. The database backup contains all the information necessary to transport a database from one computer site to another. A database is restored to operational status by recopying the database backup onto mass storage. A database backup is normally not accomplished through a database record unload, unless that is the only process that is available to accomplish a backup. Normally, the backup is instigated through a DBMS command or utility.
 See also Recovery.

Backus Naur Form (BNF): Backus Naur Form (BNF), synonymous with Backus Normal Form, is a meta-language used to specify or describe the syntax of a language in which each symbol, by itself, represents a set of strings of symbols. The two sentences preceding this one are "language." A meta language for these two sentences would begin with the definitional assertion: "Sentence::=." This is followed with a syntactically correct combination of nouns, verbs, commas, periods, prepositions, capital letters and small letters. The meta-language is thus a definitional mechanism of a correct construction over the domain of that construction.

Backward Recovery: See Backup and Recovery.

Base Line: A Base Line is a representation of a fixed task work effort that is subsequently employed as a basis for comparing the accumulation of actual work in the Work table. This represents staff hours that are affected by work environment factors. For example, 7500 hours represents 5750 hours multiplied by an overall work environment factor of 1.304.
 See Project Management Model.

Base Line Staff: The Base Line Staff is the quantity of staff hours that are allocated without being affected by the base line work environment factors. For example 5,750 staff hours to develop the Exchange Student Management System.
   See Project Management Model.

Base Line Work Environment Factor: The Base Line Work Environment Factor is the quantity of staff hours that have been affected by base line work environment factors.
   See Project Management Model.

Base Relation: A Base Relation is a relation that is not completely derivable (independent of time) from other relations in a relational database.

Before Image Recovery: See Backup and Recovery.

Benchmark Test: A Benchmark Test is a test that uses a representative set of programs, procedures and data designed to evaluate the performance of the DBMS over a range of configurations.

Blocking Factor: A Blocking Factor is the ratio between rows and DBMS record instance sizes. For example, if a DBMS record instance size is 20,000 bytes, and every row is 200 bytes, the blocking factor is 100.
   The effective blocking factor is the actually experienced ratio between needed rows contained in one DBMS record instance. For example, while the blocking factor may be 100, if through a sequential search (see Sequential Search), the rows are found only 10 to the DBMS record instance, the effective blocking factor is 10, not 100.

Buffer: A buffer is an allocation of computer memory or of a temporary area of disk into which data can be stored. Buffers are normally defined within the context of the DBMS and are under the total control of the computer's operating system (O/S) that is acting as the writer-reader controller of the DBMS. DBMS buffers can almost always be "sized," located, and specialized to store one class of DBMS information such as a database's dictionary, indexes, relationships or DBMS records.

Buffer Flush: Buffer Flush is a process in which all updated DBMS record instances in memory are written out to the database.

Business Calendar Cycle: A Business Calendar Cycle is a set of recurring calendar-based dates of interest to the enterprise. Examples are quarterly, biweekly, monthly, daily, and the like. Business Calender cycles are linked to Business Events so that the timing of business event triggering can be known.
   See the Business Information Systems Model.

Business Cycle: A Business Cycle is a cycle during which business activities occur such as sales, manufacturing, reporting, distribution, and inventory may occur. A business cycle may be simple or complex. If complex, the business cycle actually consists of other business cycles as represented in the business cycle structure.
   See the Business Information Systems Model.

Business Domains: Business Domains are the parents of one or more data elements, that enable same-named data elements which may be named the same to be distinguished by the business domain that becomes their context.
   See the Data Element Model.

Business Event: A Business Event is an event representation intersection between a business information system and a business function. A business event is a triggering event. It is invoked by the business function. The business information systems that execute are a response. Business events may be set within business event cycles and calendar cycles, or both.
   See the Business Information Systems Model.

Business Event Assigned Business Information System: A Business Event Assigned Business Information System is a business information system that is assigned to a business event. As the business event occurs, one or more business information systems execute to completely accomplish the intended purpose of the business event.
   See the Business Information Systems Model.

Business Event Cycle: A Business Event Cycle is a cycle during which an identified collection of business events occurs such as financial reports, holidays, business planning and the like. A business event cycle may be simple or complex. If complex, the business event cycle actually consists of other business event cycles as represented in the business event cycle structure.
See the Business Information Systems Model.

Business Event Cycle Structure: A Business Event Cycle Structure is a collection of business event cycles, for example, a Summer cycle may also consist of an End of School cycle, Back to School Cycle, Vacation Cycle, and a Holiday Cycle.
See the Business Information Systems Model.

Business Event Cycle Structure Type: A Business Event Cycle Structure Type represents a classification of a set of business event cycle structures.
See the Business Information Systems Model.

Business Event Model: The Business Event Model is a collection of database tables from the Whitemarsh Metabase System that relate to events within a business. Included in this collection, as depicted within the Business Information Systems Model presented in Figure 2, is business event, business event cycle, business event cycle structure, business event structure type, calendar, calendar structure, and calender structure type.

Business Function: A Business Function is an activity or process. It is described through a set of hierarchically organized text that describes the activities performed within an organization. Business functions are entirely human-based and if support is needed from a business information system, a business event is the triggering mechanism. Business functions are independent of organizations and may be allocated to more than one business organization.
See the Mission-Organization-Function-Position-Assignment Model.

Business Function Assigned Business Event: A Business Function Assigned Business Event is a business event that is assigned to a business function. In order to completely accomplish a business function, one or more business events must occur.

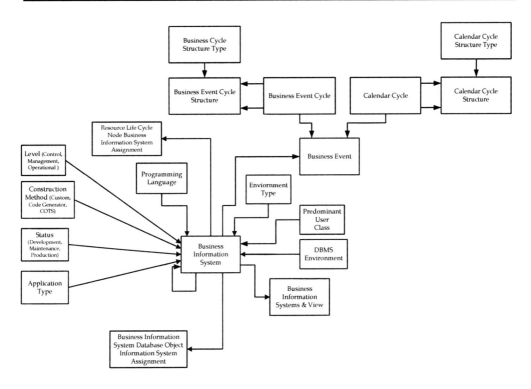

Figure 2. Business Information Systems Model.

Business Function Assigned Document: A Business Function Assigned Document represents the association of one or more documents with a business function.

Business Function Assigned Form: A Business Function Assigned Form represents the association of one or more forms with a business function.

Business Information System: Business Information System is a generic term for an information system that most commonly employs a database management system and a database. Simply put, a business information system is an application of IT technology in support of the business functions of a collection of end users. The term is distinguished for example, from a computer's Operating System such as Windows or Unix, or a Database Management System (DBMS) such as Oracle, or "office" systems like Microsoft's Word, Power Point or Excel.

The business language specifications of the business information system are managed through the Metabase System. It is known by its characteristics, its operation cycles (business event and calendar), subordinate business information systems, employed databases, views, and associated resource life cycle nodes.

See the Business Information Systems Model.

Business Information System Model: The business information system model contains a collection of database tables that identify and define the specifications of a business information system. Included are business information system, programming language, level, construction method, status, application type, data architecture class, environment type, predominant user class, DBMS environment, and business information systems and view. See Figure 2.

Business Information System Resource Life Cycle Node Assignment: The Business Information System Resource Life Cycle Node Assignment is an association between the business information system with one or more resource life cycle nodes.

See the Resource Life Cycle Assignment Model.

Business Information System Database Object Information System Assignment: A Business Information System Database Object Information System Assignment records the database object information systems invoked by the business information system.

Business Information System and View: A Business Information System and View are an association between a view and a business information system. This enables the business information system to know of the DBMS columns and DBMS tables accessed by the business information system.

Business Information System Generators: A Business Information System Generator imports the database's design and creates a first-cut business information system that has menus, browse lists, and update windows. The first-cut business information system is in a design-metadata form that users can "tune-up" without compromising the ability to generate the actual program code that gets compiled, linked and bound into an executing module. Business information system generators dramatically improve programmer productivity, and enable these tools to be used in prototyping. Whole business information systems can be created in a week or two. Iterations can be created in just days. This is ideal for prototyping. Prototyping is the critical ingredient for iterating toward valid database and business information system requirements.

Business Information System Plan: The Business Information Systems Plan is a highly organized strategy for the development of database and business information systems throughout the enterprise to cause maximum reuse and to accomplish the building and evolution of databases and business information systems in a business-rationale-based and highly ordered fashion.

The business information system data that defines the plan includes the business information systems interconnected through resource life cycle nodes. The resource life cycle nodes and their supporting resource life cycle node interrelationships enable the correct sequencing of business information system project work. Supporting metadata for a business information system plan includes database object classes, information needs, missions, functions, and organizations.

Business Information System Plan Characteristic: Maintainable: The Business Information Systems Plan must be maintainable. New business opportunities, new computers, business mergers, etc., all affect a business information systems plan. The business information systems plan must support quick changes to the estimates, technologies employed, and possibly even to the fundamental project sequences. Once these changes are accomplished, a new business information systems plan should be just a few computer program executions, or at most, a few days away.

Business Information System Plan Characteristic: Quality: While a Business Information Systems Plan must be a quality product, no business information systems plan is ever perfect on the first try. As a business information systems plan is executed, the metrics employed to derive the individual project estimates become refined as a consequence of new hardware technologies, business information system generators, techniques, or faster working staff. As these changes occur, their effects should be installable into the data that supports business information systems plan computation. In short, a business information systems plan is a living document. It should be updated with every technology event, and certainly no less often than quarterly.

Business Information System Plan Characteristic: Reproducible: The Business Information Systems Plan must be reproducible. That is, when its development activities are performed by any other staff, the business information systems plan produced should essentially be the same. The business information systems plan should not significantly vary as a consequence of the assigned staff.

Business Information System Plan Characteristic: Timely: The Business Information Systems Plan must be timely. A business information systems plan that is created long after it is needed is useless. In almost all cases, it makes no sense to take longer to plan work than to perform the work planned.

Business Information System Plan Characteristic: Useable: The Business Information Systems Plan must be useable. It must be so for all the projects as well as for each project. A business information systems plan should exist in sections that once adopted can be parceled out to project managers and immediately accomplished.

Business Organizations: A Business Organization is an organizational unit within an enterprise. It is hierarchical so any quantity of organizational levels can be represented. It is a unit within a business that has a charter to perform a certain class of business functions or activities.
  See the Mission-Organization-Function-Position Assignment Model.

Business Process: A Business Process is a collection of interrelated tasks that accomplish a particular goal. A business process begins with a customer's need and ends with a customer's need fulfillment. In Whitemarsh terms, a business process is generally equivalent to a very key business function.
  A business process can be decomposed into several sub-processes, which have their own attributes, but also contribute to achieving the goal of the super-process. The analysis of business processes typically includes the mapping of processes and sub-processes down to activity level.
  Business Processes should be designed to add value and should include only necessary activities. The outcome of a well-designed business process is increased effectiveness (value for the customer) and increased efficiency (lower costs for the company).

Business Rule: A Business Rule is an explicit rule that is able to be unambiguously tested. The rule often consists of data selection, ordering, calculations, and the like. The objective of a business rule is that it tests true. If a false condition is determined, specific actions occur.
    See Data Integrity Rule.

Business Term: A Business Term is a name that has a special meaning to the business. The term may be subject matter or computer related. A subject matter related term might be, for example, remaining balance. A computer term would be DBMS, the abbreviation name for the database management system.
    See Data Element Model.

CALC: See Hash.

Calendar Cycle: A Calendar Cycle is a set of recurring calendar-based dates of interest to the enterprise. Calendar cycle examples are: quarterly, biweekly, monthly, daily, and the like. Calender cycles are linked to business events so that the timing of business event triggering can be known.
    See the Business Information Systems Model.

Calendar Cycle Structure: A Calendar Cycle Structure is a collection of calendar cycles, for example, a financial report cycle may consist of a second week of the month, the last Friday of the month, and the first day of the quarter.
    See the Business Information Systems Model.

Calendar Cycle Structure Type: A Calendar Cycle Structure Type represents a classification of a set of calendar cycle structures.
    See the Business Information Systems Model.

Candidate Key: See Key.

Cardinality: Cardinality represents the quantity of rows (tuples) in a table (relation). In data modeling the cardinality is represented figuratively: that is, zero, one or more than one.

CASE: CASE, or Computer Assisted System Engineering, is a discipline along with computer software support that both the engineering and the developing business information systems. Commonly, there is UpperCASE and LowerCASE. UpperCASE focuses on requirements analysis and design. LowerCASE focuses on the actual generation of software systems. The Whitemarsh Metabase System is an example of UpperCASE. Softvelocity's Clarion is an example of LowerCASE. What results is I-CASE, or Integrated CASE. The output of the Whitemarsh Metabase System can be fed into SoftVelocity's Clarion.

Central Version: A Central Version represents an executing DBMS instance that allows multiple user access to one or more databases. See also concurrent operations.

Chain: A Chain is a linked list of rows that may be physically dispersed. Each link, representing a row, typically contains a next row pointer, a prior row pointer, and an owner row pointer.

Character: A Character is a letter, digit, punctuation mark, or other symbol. Each character is uniquely represented in the computer by a series of bits (1's & 0's). Characters that are patterns of 3-bit groupings are represented by octal numbers. Characters that are patterns of 4-bit groupings are represented by hexadecimal numbers.

Character Fill: Character Fill is the process of inserting, as often as necessary, into a storage medium, the representation of a specified character (normally a blank) that does not itself convey data. A character fill process displaces any other data already present.

Characteristic: A Characteristic is an [information need] collection of properties of an information need type that can be assigned to an information need. For example, if the characteristic type is media of production, the probable set of characteristics might be hard-copy or on-line access.

Characteristic Type: A Characteristic Type is a collection of characteristics that applies to one or more [information need] characteristic. Examples include: cut-off, media of production, distribution, and the like.

Check Clause: Check Clauses restrict data characteristics such as length, type (such as a numeric or alphabetic character), editing and validation rules, and the like. If check clauses are assigned to data elements, they are inherited by attributes of entities in the Specified Data Model, by columns of tables in the Implemented Data Model, and by DBMS columns of DBMS tables in the Operational Data Model. Check clauses can also be defined within attributes, columns, DBMS columns, and view columns.

The three types of check clauses are: type, null, and valid/invalid values. Once these clauses are installed, only conforming data values are accepted by the DBMS for database loading/update.

See also Data Integrity Rule, Assertion, and Trigger.

Checkpoint: A Checkpoint is a snapshot of all currently active data and processes, such that in the event of a failure, processing can recommence once the snapshot is restored. In database processing, a checkpoint is a special transaction placed on the journal file that indicates that once a database is restored to that transaction, the database is consistent.

Client-Server: Client-Server is an expression that refers to a source computer on one end of a transaction and a target computer on the other end of the connection. The source computer, which instigates the transaction is called the client. The target computer, which processes a significant target computer-based activity of the transaction is called the server.

Clarion: Clarion is a software development tool set from the SoftVelocity Corporation. Their website is: www.SoftVelocity.com.

Whitemarsh has been employing Clarion as its application development tool set for over 20 years. The Whitemarsh metadata management system, Metabase System, is completely developed in Clarion. The Metabase System greatly exceeds 16,000 function points in size.

The following is a description of Clarion from the SoftVelocity website. Whitemarsh agrees with this characterization.

Clarion is a software development tool to help you get your business applications completed up to 10 times faster. Clarion features a Template driven Code Generator that automates the creation of complete Database Applications. Clarion features round-trip Code Generation, which means that it preserves all of your hand-written code while still allowing you to make changes and regenerate your application, or any part of your application, as often as needed. Clarion can help you create higher-quality, more consistent database applications in less time.

At the core of the Clarion IDE is the Data Dictionary -- a metadata repository which stores table definitions, business rules, attributes for defaults on how columns should be displayed on Windows and Reports, and user-defined options.

In Clarion, developer productivity doesn't mean just a code editor and some wizards. Clarion extends your productivity with its focus on application templates and underlying business class framework. Clarion enables you to tackle new business problems while decreasing the total cost of building applications.

The Clarion IDE provides a unified tool set for developing native code Win32 applications and pure ".Net" managed code applications for the desktop, web and mobile platforms, taking advantage of a common set of tools including rich Template sets, Visual Designers, Drag and Drop controls, and Code Completion. Templates enable developers to solve complex business problems while reducing the total cost of development.

CODASYL: CODASYL is an acronym for the organization, Conference of Data Systems and Languages. CODASYL was an Information technology industry consortium formed in 1959 to guide the development of programming language that could be used on many computers. This effort led to the development of COBOL.

CODASYL's members were individuals from industry and government involved in data processing activity. Its larger goal was to promote more effective data systems analysis, design, and implementation. The organization worked on various languages over the years such as COBOL and Fortran.

It is critical to understand that CODASYL was never constituted to develop standards. ANSI develops standards. The catch phrase to describe the relationship between CODASYL and ANSI was "CODASYL proposes and ANSI disposes."

See CODASYL Model.

CODASYL Model: The CODASYL Model is a form of the network database model that was originally defined by the **Database Task Group (DBTG)** of the COnference of DAta SYstem Language (CODASYL) organization. Development of the CODASYL Model was stopped in 1980. The CODASYL data model, after significant simplification, was standardized by the ANSI

INCITS H2 Technical Committee on Database Languages as the network data model (NDL).

See the NDL Data Language Standard and ANSI.

CODASYL Set: A CODASYL Set is a named and defined relationship of a collection of rows that may exist within a single table, or between a table and one or more rows from other tables. For example, the Employee Family set might consist of an employee row from the employee table and one or more rows from the dependents table. Static relationships bind the rows together into the set. It is called a CODASYL set because it was the CODASYL organization that first defined it.

See Relationships. See CODASYL. See CODASYL Model. See NDL Data Language Standard.

Collating Sequence: A Collating Sequence is a specified ordering sequence based on values, that is, numeric (1, 2, etc.), alphabetic (a, b, c, etc.), and special (!, ", #, etc.). Typically the concern is whether numbers sort higher or lower than letters, and where the special characters fall in the sort sequence, that is, high, low, or where?

Collection Data Type: A Collection Data Type is a class of data type that defines certain collections such as sets, multi-sets, and lists. Collection data types are a different name for complex facts.

All collection data types are complex facts that contain zero or more values. An example is a list of telephone numbers for an employee. A set is a collection data type in which the values are unique. In the case of an employee phone numbers, no two may be the same.

A multi-set list-type is similar to a set list-type except that the multi-set type allows duplicate values. An example of a multi-list type is the set of UPC codes for a set purchased products such as four cans of tomato soup.

The list collection type is the same as a multi-set list-type except that the values are ordered. An example is an alphabetical listing of the product names in the purchased collection of products such as chicken noodle soup, tomato soup, and vegetable beef soup.

Each component in a collection data type may be either a traditional data type such as character, integer, and decimal, or it can be an abstract data type such as weight, volume, and square feet. In these cases the abstract data type has been further defined. SQL:1999, 2003 and 2008 have specified collection data types.

Column: Columns are the manifestation of the semantics of an ISO 11179 data element from the Data Element Model of the Whitemarsh Metabase System within a table of a schema of the Implemented Data Model. Additionally, a column is a deployment of the semantics of an attribute from an entity within the Specified Data Model. Columns may have additional semantics that further refine the column within the context of either the attribute or the data element.

The order of processing additional semantics is that the column must first be a subset of the attribute, which in turn must be a subset of the data element. Not all the columns of a table must map to attributes from a single entity. A column, like an attribute of an entity, is intended to be a data-value based partial semantic descriptor of a table.

Columns can represent complex facts, and thus, represent arrays, groups, repeating groups, and nested repeating groups.

Like attributes, there are four classes of columns: content, instance, and metadata, and relationship. The first, content, represents the table's content. For example, if the table is CustomerAddress, the content columns would be CustomerStreet-1, CustomerStreet-2, CustomerCity, CustomerState, and CustomerZip.

The second, instance, are the set of columns that have a combined value such that only one row from the table is found. This is commonly called the table's primary key.

The third, metadata, are the table's columns that represent metadata needs such as who created in an instance of the table, who updated it, what project caused the row to be added or changed. Finally, what was the date of the add or change?

The fourth, relationships, represent the columns that, when valued, provide the uniqueness value for a different row in the same table (recursive relationship) or a different table (the parent table of a parent-child relationship). In this later situation, the uniqueness column is often called the parent table's primary key.

See Implemented Data Model.

Column Assigned Data Integrity Rule: A Column Assigned Data Integrity Rule is a data integrity rule that is assigned to one or more columns. The role played by the column within the data integrity rule is defined in the metadata of the association. See Data Integrity Rule.
  See Implemented Data Model.

Column Assigned Meta Category Values: A Column Assigned Meta Category Values is a meta category value that has been assigned to a column. An assigned meta category value, whether a semantic or data use modifier, is a "meaning" constraint on the column. The assigned meta category value cannot be the same as that assigned the data element or an attribute. Nor can a meta category value be more expansive than that assigned the data element or the column.
  See Implemented Data Model.

Column Assigned Value Domain: A Column Assigned Value Domain is a value domain that is assigned to one or more columns. An assigned value domain is a value-based constraint on the column. The assigned value domain cannot be the same as that assigned the data element or the attribute. Nor can a value domain be more expansive than that assigned the data element or column.
  See Implemented Data Model.

Command: A Command is an order or trigger for an action or permissible action to take place.

Commit: A Commit is a process through which changes to a database are flushed from all memory buffers and placed within the appropriate database storage structure components such that these data can no longer be canceled or rolled back.

Communications Link: A Communications Link is a named and described link between two or more processing nodes.

Complex Fact: See Fact.

Complex Row: A Complex Row is a tuple that consists of a collection of facts in which one or more are complex.

Complex Table: See Table.

Compound Data Element: Compound Data Elements consist of multiple data elements in a specific sequence. For example, Full Name is a compound data element that may consist of a Salutation, First Name, Middle Name, Last Name, and Suffix. Compound data elements may also consist of other compound data elements which too, appear in a specific sequence.
See Data Element Model.

Compound Data Element Assigned Data Element: A Compound Data Element Assigned Data Element is one or more data elements that participate within a compound data element.
See Data Element Model.

Compound Data Element Structure: A Compound Data Element Structure represents a collection of compound data elements that are, in turn, a compound data element.
See Data Element Model.

Compound Data Element Structure Type: A Compound Data Element Structure Type represents a classification of a set of compound data element structures.
See Data Element Model.

Compression: Compression is the process of removing trailing blanks from alphanumeric fields and leading zeros from numeric field.

Computer Program: See Program.

Concatenate: Concatenate is a process through which two strings of characters are linked or connected together, generally for the purpose of using them as a single value.

Concatenated Key: A Concatenated Key is a representation of the concatenation of two or more values from columns that are used together as a single key.

Concept Structure: Concept Structures represent a collection of concepts that are related and are, in turn, represented by a collective concept.

Concept Structure Type: A Concept Structure Type represents a classification of a set of concept structures.

Concepts: Concepts represent sets of ideas, abstractions, or things in the real world that are identified with explicit boundaries and meaning and whose properties and behavior follow the same rules. Concepts are used as a basis for specifying the conceptual scope of data elements. Concepts are identified, described, and interrelated. Concepts are the root-semantic source for all data elements.

Concepts may be complex in their relationships with other concepts forming either hierarchies, networks, or both. An example might be resources, of which an example might be a materiel resource such as equipment, or supplies. There also might be a nonmaterial resource such as intellectual property or intelligence.

The concept model within the Whitemarsh Data Element Model consists of concepts that are identified, described, and interrelated.

The Whitemarsh Specified Data Model represents collections of data models of concepts. In this situation, however, the concept is a "container" just like a table or DBMS table. In the Specified Data Model, this container is called an entity. It has attributes, a primary key, and when there are relationships among entities, foreign keys exist. A collection of all the entities, attributes, and relationships represent the data model of that concept. Concept data models naturally exist about persons, organizations, locations, customers, purchase orders, and invoices. Collections of concept data models are organized into subjects.

See Data Element Model. See Specified Data Model.

Conceptual Data Model: A Conceptual Data Model is a data model in its conceptual form. Subsequently, this conceptual data model may be refined into a logical data model, and finally refined into a physical data model. In both transformations, that is, from conceptual to logical to physical, the domain boundaries are the same. It's the content that is refined. The content, in fact, does not increase. Rather it becomes refined to the extent that it can be deployed through a DBMS.

A conceptual data model may be missing some features, or contain features that are not fully refined or developed. Some conceptual data models are just collections of entities and relationships without attributes.

In Whitemarsh, the Specified Data Model is not a conceptual data model. Rather, the Whitemarsh Specified Data Model is a collection of data models of concepts.

The Whitemarsh Specified Data Model is different from a conceptual data model in these respects. First the Specified Data Model is a complete model in all respects except for the specification of data types.

Second, the purposes of the Specified Data Models are to be data models of concepts, not data models in a conceptual form.

Third, a Specified Data Model exists as data structure templates that can be used as a basis for creating data structures within the Whitemarsh Implemented Data Model. Thus, there can be many-to-many relationships between Specified Data Models and Implemented Data Models. In contrast, with a traditional conceptual data model, there is a one-to-many relationship between the content domain of a conceptual data model and the logical data model. The logical data model's domain is either the same or a subset of the conceptual data model.

Finally, the Specified Data Model's data models of concepts are not the same as the concepts that are the root semantics of data elements defined in the Data Element Model. The former represents full data models. The later represent the semantic concepts that are the foundation for data elements.

Conceptual Schema: A Conceptual Schema is a term popularized by the ANSI/X3/SPARC architecture. From SIGMOD Record (Volume 15 No 1, March 1986), the conceptual schema "*serves as an information model of the enterprise which the database is to serve, and as a control point for further database development. Information of interest to the enterprise is described in terms of relevant entities, their properties, and their interrelationships, together with various integrity, security, and other constraints.*" The data representing the specifications of the conceptual schema is metadata and is stored in a metadata management system.

It is unfortunate that most data modeling tools do not retain separate and mappable instances of the conceptual schema because, in all essence, the conceptual schema is the enterprise's collective data model of all concept data models. Consequently, the total set of concept data models within the Whitemarsh Specified Data Models represent a more true implementation of the ANSI/X3/SPARC conceptual schema.

Conceptual Value Domain Structure: Conceptual Value Domain Structures represent a collection of conceptual value domains that are related and are, in turn, represented by a collective conceptual value domain.
   See Data Element Model.

Conceptual Value Domain Structure Type: A Conceptual Value Domain Structure Type represents a classification of a set of conceptual value domains.

Conceptual Value Domains: Conceptual Value Domains are identified, described, and interrelated. Conceptual value domains are the concepts behind value domains from which both data element concepts and value domains are derived. An example of a concept behind a value domain might be numbers, and within that, integers, floating point. Another might be descriptions, text and codes. Conceptual value domains can be either simple, or complex. If complex, they can be networks or hierarchies.
   See Data Element Model.

Concurrent Operations: Concurrent Operations are operations that can occur concurrently. Within a DBMS, concurrent operations permits multiple run-units to operate against a single database--at the same time--in a manner that preserves consistency and integrity.
   The following definitions apply to the different classes of concurrent operations within a DBMS environment.
   A single database DBMS is one that permits commands to access only the single database that is under its control.
   A multiple database DBMS is one that permits commands to access different databases that are under the control of the single instance of the DBMS.
   A multi-user DBMS is one that can process commands from multiple run-units.
   A single-threaded DBMS is a multi-user DBMS that can execute only one command at a time and cannot service another command until the processing is finished for the first command.

A multi-threaded DBMS is a multi-user DBMS that can concurrently execute the multiple commands from the multiple run-units against a database.

A multiple database processing DBMS is one that can concurrently access multiple databases during a single executing instance of a run-unit.

A single-threaded, multiple-database DBMS is one that can execute only one command at a time while serving multiple users against multiple databases.

A multi-threaded, multiple database DBMS is one that can concurrently execute multiple commands from multiple run-units against multiple databases.

Consistency: Consistency represents a database state in which there are no partially completed updates, nor are there any partially complete updates to any component of a database's storage structure.

Contention: Contention represents a condition in which a user attempts to access a row of a table that has already been locked by another user. Contention may be at the row level, or higher, that is, at the DBMS record level or even at the database level, depending upon the capabilities or options of the DBMS. If the lock is at a high level, more users are locked out. However, the locking process is simpler to manage. It the lock is at a lower level, fewer users are locked out. However, the locking process is very complicated to manage.

Contract: A contract is a legal instrument through which work is accomplished. For example, a contract to re-engineer the Rental Units Collections Management System.
See Project Management Model.

Contract & Organization: A Contract & Organization is the association between Contract and Organization. For example, the Membership Management System contract with National Chemical Society.
See Project Management Model.

Data Management's Concepts & Terms

Contract Resource: A Contract Resource is the assignment of a given staff member to be a resource on the contract to accomplish work. For example, Hank Lavender as the Functional Data Administrator.
See Project Management Model.

Contract Role: A Contract Role is a named activity type that is performed within a contract through an organization. For example, a Project Manager, Data Modeler, or Programmer.
See Project Management Model.

Cursor: A Cursor is an indicator that designates a current position relative to the ordering of the rows in a table for relational DBMSs, or rows from an independent logical file DBMS table. For hierarchical data model DBMSs, the

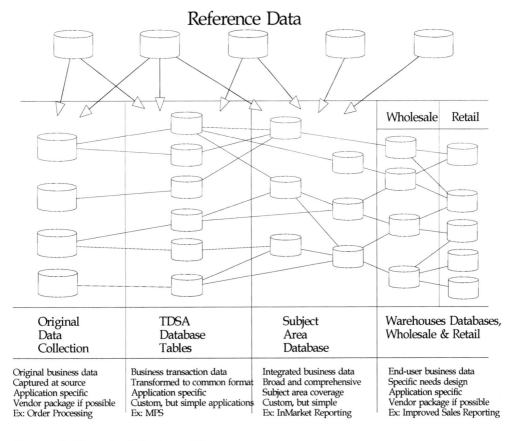

Figure 3. Data Architecture Classes.

cursor designates the current position relative to the ordering of each row within the accessed hierarchical row structure.

For the ANSI NDL Data Language Standard DBMSs, the cursor designates the current table, row, and position within the set of rows that are "current" to the run-unit.

For the ANSI SQL Data Language Standard, a cursor represents the nth row of a row-set that is the consequence of a SELECT. In SQL, cursors have names such as CustomerSelect. If the cursor value was 10, the retrieved customer would be the 10th row in the selected set.

Data Administration: Data Administration is an organization within a company that is charged with the definition, organization, management and control of data, not with its processing.

Data Administrator: A Data Administrator is a member of a data administration group. The role of the data administration is to either oversee and/or manage the development of at least the enterprise's Data Element Model and the Specified Data Model. Commonly, the data administration group oversees the development and evolution of the Implemented Data Model and the Operational Data Models as those are the purview of database projects.

Data Aggregate: See Fact.

Data Analysis: Data Analysis is the study of the definition and characteristics of data, and the relationships between distinct categories/classes of data. The emphasis is on data's structure, not the data's flow.

Data Architecture Reference Model: The Data Architecture Reference Model of Whitemarsh has two dimensions. The first dimension, data architecture classes, is the classes of data implemented across the enterprise. Each data architecture class is most often represented as a database of a specialized design and operated under the control of a DBMS.

There are five discrete data architecture classes. These, as illustrated in Figure 3, proceed from left to right with respect data flow with exception of reference data that is employed across all the data architecture classes. These are Original Data Capture, Transaction Data Staging Area, Subject Area

Database, Data Warehouse (Wholesale and Retail (also called Data Mart)), and Reference Data.

The second Data Architecture Reference Model dimension, data model generalization levels, are: Data Elements, Specified Data Models, Implemented Data Models, Operational Data Models, and View Data Models. These data models are depicted in Figure 4.

The Data Element Model captures the once-only identification, specification, semantic supporting infrastructure, and definition of data elements, which, in turn, may have its semantics represented within attributes of one or more entities of Specified Data Models.

The Specified Data Models, that is, the data models of concepts, can be deployed in one or more Implemented Data Models, which, in turn, can be operationally deployed in one or more DBMS specific Operational Data Models. Operational Data Models are best intersected with business information systems through View Data Models.

Each of these five data model classes serves a special purpose and is interrelated with the other data models in some integrity-enhancing and work-saving manner.

Figure 4 shows a left-side set of one-to-many relationships going "down." Each of these four one-to-many relationships support two meanings. The first is the mapping of an individual component of a model, and the second is the mapping of a whole collection from within that data model generalization level.

In the Data Element Model there can be individual data elements such as Person First Name, and there can be collections of data elements within a specific data element concept collection, for example, Person Related Information such as Person Identifier, Person Birth Date, Person First Name, Person Middle Name, and Person Last Name.

In the first type of left-side one-to-many relationship, the individual data element, Persons First Name, would be semantically mapped to zero, one, or more attributes within different entities. For example the mapping to Employee First Name, to Customer Contact First Name, or to Causality Insurance Contract First Name.

In the second type of "left-side" relationship, a whole collection of data elements can be mapped to a whole collection of attributes across one or more entities. For example, all the Data Elements within a Data Element Concept collection called Biographic Data Elements might be mapped to the entity, Person Information, or to the entity, Customer Contact Information. In this case, the mapping of the data elements, Person Identifier, Person First Name, etc., is mapped to a corresponding set of attributes within one or more entities.

It is important to remember that data elements from different collections can be related to different attributes within the same entity. Similarly, different attributes within different entities can be related to different columns of the same table. Finally, different columns of the same table can be related to different DBMS columns of the same DBMS table.

On the right-side of Figure 4, there also is a set of one-to-many relationships. This time, the relationships proceed upwards from the Operational Data Model to the Implemented Data Model to the Specified Data Model, but not to the Data Element Model. This set, like the left-side one-to-many relationships, has two meanings: individual component, and

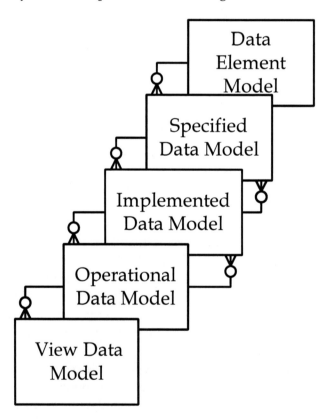

Figure 4. Five data model generalization levels.

whole collections. The meanings of the right-side one-to-many relationship are however different from the left-side one-to-many relationships.

The first type of right-side relationship, individual component, represents the mapping of a single individual component, for example from a DBMS Column within an Operational Data Model DBMS table to a Column within an Implemented Data Model table. This relationship is not one-to-many, but one-to-one. That is because an individual DBMS Column, for example, EmpFrstNam, can be inherited from only one higher level component, for example, the single column, EmployeeFirstName.

The second type of right-side relationship, the mapping of collections can be one-to-many. That is, one collection of DBMS Columns from a DBMS table in the Operational Data Model can map to one set of columns within one table of a single Implemented Data Model while a different DBMS Columns collection from the same Operational Data Model DBMS table (but not the same DBMS Columns, of course) could be mapped to a different column collection within a different Implemented Data Model. Hence, the collections can be seen as "from" one Operational Data Model table to zero, one, or more Implemented Data Model tables.

This is quite common within the Data Architecture Class, data warehouse. There may be, for example, an Operational Data Model DBMS table, Monthly Sales Statistics, that might consist of columns drawn from multiple Implemented Data Model tables such as Customers, Product Shipments, Product Returns. On a monthly basis, the sales data computed for the different Operational Data Model DBMS table columns might be:

- Customer Gross Sales Amount
- Customer Gross Sales Profit Percent
- Average Customer Quantity
- Average Product Shipment Dollar Value
- Average Product Shipment Shipping Costs
- Average Product Return Amount

The first three DBMS columns would likely come from a Customer Implemented Data Model table. The fourth and fifth DBMS columns might come from a Product Shipments Implemented Data Model table, and the sixth and seventh DBMS columns might come from a Shipment Returns Implemented Data Model table.

Analogous right-side relationship descriptions apply to the Implemented Data Model to the Specified Data Model but not to the Data Element Model. It does not apply to the Data Element Model because a data element is not a container concept such as an entity, table or DBMS table. Rather, a data element represents the semantics of a fact.

These Figure 4 data model generalization levels address enterprise-wide data semantics management from enterprise-wide data elements down to Operational Data Models and View Data Models. These generalization levels enable enterprises to engineer data definitions and semantics that are integrated, non-redundant and semantically harmonious. Data definitions and semantics not engineered this way give rise to stove-pipe databases which, in turn, result in stove-pipe business information systems and ultimately stove-pipe data across the enterprise. Elimination of stove-pipes is essential to a well ordered and managed information technology environment. Each data model generalization level is defined in this glossary.

See Data Architecture Class. See Data Element Model. See Specified Data Model. See Implemented Data Model, See Operational Data Model. See Enterprise Architecture.

Data Architecture Class: A Data Architecture Class is a recognizable style of database design that generally has a special purpose. The five data architecture classes are: Original Data Capture, Transaction Data Staging Area, Data Warehouse (wholesale and retail), and Reference Data. These are depicted in Figure 3, above. The data generally proceeds from left to right except for reference data which serves all the other data architecture classes.

The first data architecture class, Original Data Capture, represents originally collected data, and is the set of data structures appropriate for the application package such as order processing, personnel management, or invoicing.

The second data architecture class, Transaction Data Staging Area, represents transaction-based data that is retrieved from Original Data Capture databases that is transformed into enterprise-based semantics, granularity, and precision, and is placed it into Transitional Data Storage Areas on a daily or more frequent basis so that other database applications throughout the enterprise may use it.

The third data architecture class, Subject Area Database, addresses the needs of multiple applications across broad subject areas. This type of data represents the business data such as invoices, contracts, products manufactured, operational, tactical, and strategic business plans, and employees. Subject area databases often contain complete histories of the captured data.

The fourth data architecture class is data warehouse data. A data warehouse database contains longitudinal, broad context summaries of operational database transactions that are enriched with external-to-the business data so businesses can research the past in preparation for planning and simulating the future. Data warehouse databases are not updated in the traditional sense. Rather, rows are added or deleted. Summary data is of course updated.

Data warehouses can be either wholesale or retail. A wholesale warehouse database is one in which the data structures can be highly normalized so that either it favors no particular class or type of reporting, or somewhat denormalized to favor a general reporting orientation. A retail warehouse database is a subset of a wholesale warehouse database and its data structures are highly designed to favor one class of reporting. A common form of a retail data warehouse, also called a data mart, is a star schema. At the center of the star is a table that mainly contains facts or measurements. The "points" of the star are the dimensions or major sorting criteria through which fact subsets are selected and summarized. Often the dimensions are highly denormalized inverted hierarchies.

The fifth class of data is reference data. Reference data contains the commonly used data codes and other types of data special to the business to provide fact data its context. For example, units of measure codes might be "mm," "cm," and "m" which, to the business, might mean millimeters, centimeters, and meters. Reference data is standard throughout the enterprise and employed by all databases. Reference data can also contain whole collections of stable, seldom changing data such as manufactured parts and their descriptions, distribution locations, and corporate facilities. This type of reference data is called master data.

Data Definition: Data Definition is the process that creates a data file of data definition language commands.

Data Definition Language (DDL): A Data Definition Language (DDL) is a DBMS processable language that consists of statements that provide the syntax for of the data model generalization levels: Specified, Implemented, Operational, and View.

Data Dictionary/Directory System (DD/DS): See Metadata Management System.

Data Driven Methodology: A Data Driven Methodology is a data-centric versus process-centric approach to business information system and database development. Thus, it is a methodology that centers its analysis and design on enterprise missions, database domains, database object classes, and finally, tables and columns. Thereafter, business information systems are identified and engineered to create and maintain business data. Studies have shown that this approach is cleaner, easier and far more efficient.
See Process Driven Methodology.

Data Element: A Data Element is a fact that is independent of its contextual use. Contexts may be entities, tables, screens, files, and reports. A data element may be represented in many different contexts. When the semantics of a data element are represented within an entity, the data element's semantics representation is called an attribute. When the semantics of a data element is represented within a table, its semantics representation is called a column. When the semantics of a data element is represented within a DBMS table, the data element's semantic representation is called a DBMS column. When the semantics of a data element is represented within a View, the data element's semantic representation is called a view column.

Similarly, when the semantics of a data element is represented within a file, screen, document, or form, the data element's semantic representation is called a data field, a screen fields, a document cell, or a form cell, respectively. In all these cases, what does the value actually represent? Simple. It is a value-based surrogate for the data element's semantics from within the context of the attribute, a column, a DBMS column, a view column, a form cell, etc.

It should therefore be obvious that a data element is not an attribute, column, DBMS column, view column, data field, a screen fields, a document cell, or a form cell. Rather, it is a generic name applied to the semantic representation of a data field, a screen field, a document cell, or a form cell within any of the corresponding contexts of entity, table, DBMS table, view, screen, document, or form. Thus, there is a semantic hierarchy or parentage from a data element to an attribute to a column to a DBMS column to a view column.

Simply put, Data Elements are context independent business fact semantic templates. The complete sets of semantics for a data element are those that are explicitly assigned, that is, the assigned: meta category values, data element concepts, data element classifications, and business domains. A data element's inherited semantics includes those assigned to its containing data element concept and value domains. The value domains of the data element can be specifically assigned. Data Element Concepts inherit semantics from Concepts and Conceptual Value Domains. Value domains inherit semantics from Conceptual Value Domains.

Data elements within the Whitemarsh context are defined according to the requirements of the ISO 11179 standard for data element metadata. Additionally, data elements include semantic and data use modifiers that enable automatic name construction, automatic definitions, and automatic abbreviations. There is a one-to-many relationship between data elements and attributes of entities from the Specified Data Models. There is a one-to-many relationship between Data Elements and columns of the tables from the Implemented Data Model. Finally, Data Elements are defined within the context of their data element concepts and their assigned value domain.

A key feature of the Whitemarsh Data Element Model approach is that data element semantics are inherited by attributes within entities in the Specified Data Model, columns within tables in the Implemented Data Model, DBMS columns within DBMS tables in the Operational Data Model, and view columns in views in the View Data Model. Consequently, there can be automatic data naming, definitions, and abbreviations. All semantics, that is, meaning modifiers, data use modifiers, and value domains assigned to a data element must be a subset of any previously assigned to a data element concept.

See Data Element Model.

Data Element Assigned Data Element Classification: A Data Element Assigned Data Element Classification is the assignment of one or more data elements to one or more data element classifications.

See Data Element Model.

Data Element Assigned Data Integrity Rule: A Data Element Assigned Data Integrity Rule represents the assignment of one or more data integrity rules to a data element. The role played by the data element within the data integrity rule is defined in the metadata of the association.

See Data Element Model.

Data Element Assigned Derived Data Element: A Data Element Assigned Derived Data Element represents one or more data elements assigned within a derived data element. Each data element plays a role in the derivation of the value represented by the derived data element.
See Data Element Model.

Data Element Assigned Meta Category Value: A Data Element Assigned Meta Category Value represents the assignment of a data element to one or more meta category values.
See Data Element Model.

Data Element Classification Structure: Data Element Classification Structures represent a collection of data element classifications that are related and are in turn represented by a collective data element classification.
See Data Element Model.

Data Element Classification Structure Type: A Data Element Classification Structure Type represents a classification of a set of data element classifications.
See Data Element Model.

Data Element Classifications: Data Element Classifications are a way to assign data elements to certain classification schemes. A data element may be assigned to more than one classification scheme.
See Data Element Model.

Data Element Concepts: Data Element Concepts are identified, described, and interrelated. Data element concepts are the common concepts of a data element collection. A Data Element Concept is the joining of a Concept and a Conceptual Value Domain that, in turn, is a generalized representation of a collection of data elements. An example of a Data Element Concept Is Real Property Characteristics. The Data Element Concept contained Data Elements that would result would be a Real Property Name, Description, Dimensions, Valuations, and the like. Data Element Concepts can be either simple, or complex. If complex, they can be networks or hierarchies. Data element concepts are able to be assigned one or more semantics and data use modifiers to specialize their general nature. Together, these enable automatic data naming, definitions, and abbreviations.

See Data Element Model.

Data Element Concept Structure: A Data Element Concept Structure represents a collection of related data element concepts that, in turn, are represented by a collective data element concept.
See Data Element Model.

Data Element Concept Structure Type: A Data Element Concept Structure Type represents a classification of a set of data element concepts.
See Data Element Model.

Data Element Concept Assigned Data Integrity Rule: A Data Element Concept Assigned Data Integrity Rule represents the assignment of one or more data integrity rules to a data element concept. The role played by the data element concept within the data integrity rule is defined in the metadata of the association.
See Data Element Model.

Data Element Concept Assigned Meta Category Value: A Data Element Concept Assigned Meta Category Value represents the assignment of a data element concept to one or more meta category values.
See Data Element Model.

Data Element Length: A Data Element Length represents a measure of length (size) of a data element usually expressed in units of characters, words, or bytes.
See Data Element Model.

Data Element Model: The Whitemarsh Data Element Model consists of the following components: Concepts, Conceptual Value Domains, Value Domains, Data Element Concepts, and Data Elements. The model conforms to the core of the ISO 11179 Data Element metadata standard. Figure 5 depicts the meta entities for the Whitemarsh Data Element Model.
Data element models provide the basis and engineering for all business facts and semantic elements deployed throughout the various Whitemarsh Metabase System models that form data structure templates (Specified Data Model), or database models (Implemented and Operational Data Models).

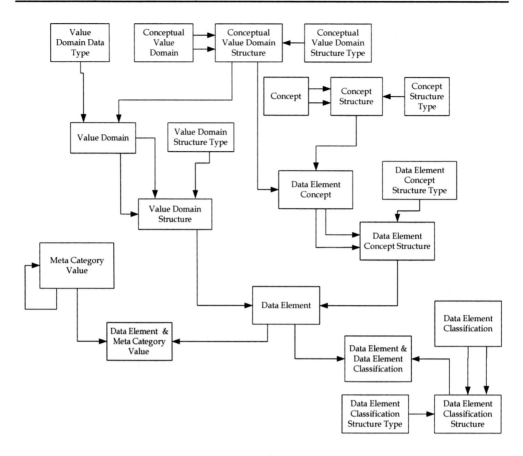

Figure 5. Data Element Model.

Data elements are key to understanding and administering data across the enterprise. It is common for a business fact, regardless of what it is called, to be reused between 30 and 100 times across a collection of database data models. It would clearly be a waste to require that each and every reuse be redefined. Data elements are thus both integral and critical to the proper management of enterprise data.

Data types for data elements are defined from the ISO standard for language independent data types. A data element can be assigned both semantic and data use modifiers as can attributes of entities from Specified Data Models and columns of tables from Implemented Data Models. Data elements can also be assigned a value domain.

As with the Implemented and Specified Data Models, if an attempt is made to assign a semantic that is either the same, or that is not a proper subset of an already assigned semantic, the assignment is disallowed. Thus, there is a proper hierarchy of semantic modifiers, data use modifiers, and value domains enforced across the Data Element Model and the Specified, Implemented and Operational Data Models.

Data File: A Data File is an instance of data used in a procedural manner to arrive at some result or conclusion. Data files can be either manual or automated. If automated, they can be controlled by DBMSs or by defined strategies contained in a computer program. A data file could be a computer system for testing Data Integrity Rules, programs, modules, for training, and the like.

Data Flow: A Data Flow is a named representation of data that is passed between processes.

Data Flow Diagram: A Data Flow Diagram is a graphic depicting processes and data flows. Each "page" of a data flow diagram has sibling processes. The processes are interconnected through data flows. Each process can be decomposed into subordinate processes that are represented on their own diagram page. In data flow diagrams, data is read from or written to data stores. Data that is input to a process is transformed in some way and can be output from that process. A data flow process many have many inputs and a fewer quantify of outputs, or vice versa.

Data Independence: Data Independence is a measure of the independence between a DBMS schema and a business information system. Changes in the DBMS schema model that do not relate to the business information system's data selection or processing should not require the business information system's programs to change. Changes in the physical storage structure of a database should not require changes to the DBMS schema. Changes to the DBMS schema should only affect the business information system's programs that are directly affected by the DBMS schema change.

Data Management's Concepts & Terms

Data Integrity: Data Integrity is a quality characteristic of data that exists as long as accidental or malicious destruction, alteration, or loss of data does not occur. Data quality implies that the data is correct, timely, accurate, complete, relevant, and accessible for the uses for which it was intended.

Data Integrity Rule: A Data Integrity Rule is a statement that must test true when no database updating is taking place. A data integrity rule may relate to columns within the same or different tables. A data integrity rule may also state a condition that must be true in a row instance before an action can take place, for example, all columns must be valued before the row is accepted into the database.

The seven classes of data integrity rules are:

- Single table, single column.
- Single table, multiple column.
- Single table, single column, multiple row.
- Single table, multiple column, single row derived data.
- Single table, single column, multiple row derived data.
- Multiple table derived data.
- Multiple table, multiple column (referential integrity).

Each data integrity rule consists of a "truth assertion" and a "false reaction." The data integrity rule statement is the truth assertion. If it is determined to be true, no subsequent action is taken. If the rule tests false, the reaction process executes. In some cases, the reaction process rejects a row add/modify/delete, or a process invokes a user-displayed message, or a process invokes another whole activity.

An example of the first is "row not added, or birthdate is blank." An example of the second is "employee middle initial not provided." An example of the third is "parts resupply activated as current inventory is now too low."

An example of the second is the reordering of a product because the inventory has gotten to or fallen below a reorder point. In this case, the truth assertion would be Quantity-on-hand GT <x>, where <x> is the minimum allowed quantity. If the truth assertion is false, the quantity-on-hand is too low and the reorder process is executed.

Many data integrity rules related to only one column. Others can also relate to a discrete subset of columns, such as a person's name parts. Data integrity rules can also be "before" or "after" an action is allowed or disallowed.

Referential Integrity is the last class of a data integrity rule. Referential integrity is what its name implies: an integrity of the reference between rows of different or the same tables. Generally, the reference is the primary key value of a source table to the foreign key value of the target table. The integrity of the reference means that the values must be identical. If the referential integrity truth assertion is false, the referential integrity clause syntax dictates an action after an update is attempted. The two referential integrity actions are [CASCADE] DELETE, and SET NULL (or SET DEFAULT). By implication, if the conditions do not exist that permits either of those two actions to occur, the initial action (ADD, DELETE, or MODIFY) is itself rejected. The types of MATCH that are examined are MATCH ALL or MATCH NONE.

While referential integrity is explicitly defined in ANSI/NDL and the ANSI/SQL, it also exists implicitly in varying forms in other data models such as the hierarchical or independent logical file data models.

ANSI/NDL referential integrity exists through the use of the INSERTION and RETENTION clauses in the schema set clauses that are specified on behalf of a member table.

ANSI/SQL referential integrity exists through the specification of the REFERENCES clause within the definition of a "child" table. The clause identifies a column within the "child" table that is referred to as a "foreign key," and a table name and a column name of another table that is acting as the "parent" of the referential action. If no parent row column is specified, its primary key is the default specification.

Data Item: See Fact.

Data Manipulation Language (DML): A Data Manipulation Language (DML) is a DBMS recognized syntactic representations of commands that access data within a database. The commands are broadly divided into the following three categories: row, relationship, and combination.

The row commands include FIND, GET, STORE, and DELETE. The relationship commands for static relationships include GET OWNER, GET NEXT, GET MEMBER, CONNECT (a row to a relationship), and DISCONNECT (a row from a relationship). The relationship commands for dynamic relationships include PROJECT, DIVIDE, JOIN, etc. Combination commands include FETCH (FIND and GET), or MODIFY (FIND, GET, change, STORE).

Data Model: A Data Model is a term that has several different definitions. The two key definitions relate to Database Management Systems (DBMS), and the information engineering discipline called data modeling.

With respect to DBMS, a data model consists of three components: Data Structure, Relationships, and Operations. Collectively these three components are defined within either a data definition language (DDL) or a data manipulation language (DML).

The first data model component, data structures, are either simple or complex. Data structures are defined within the data definition language. Simple data structures conform to simple facts. Complex data structures conform to complex facts.

Simple facts are single valued columns that have a single intent, single data type, and single instance. An example is Person First Name. A value example is: George.

Complex facts can be arrays, groups, repeating groups, or nested repeating groups. Arrays have multiple values but a single data type. An example is Telephone Numbers. Value examples: 1-717-648-5913, 1-215-428-3982, 1-540-297-1297.

Groups can have multiple contained facts in which each fact can have a different data type but only a single value instance. An example is Address. The contained facts in this case might be House Street Number, Street Name, Street Type, City, State, Postal Code, and Country. A value example is: 5, South Rock, Street, Shamokin, PA, 19172, US.

A repeating group is a group but with the possibility of multiple value-set instances. An example is Dependents with the contained facts of First Name, Middle Name, Last Name, Birth Date, Birth City, and Birth State. A single value example is: <Karen Elizabeth Shannahan, 4/30/1952, Philadelphia, PA>, <Edward Albert Shannahan, 10/15/1956, Shamokin, PA>. There could be multiple dependents

A nested repeating group is a repeating group with the possibility that one or more of its contained facts can also be a group and possibly a repeating group. An example would be Employee Dependents with nested structures of addresses, telephone numbers, and skills. A value example is: <<<Karen Elizabeth Shannahan, 4/30/1952, Philadelphia, PA, <5, South Rock ,Street,

Shamokin, PA , <1-717-648-5913, 1-717-428-3982, 1-540-297-1297>, <soccer, basketball, baseball> > >

The second data modeling component, relationships, has eight different types. These are: Owner and single Member, Owner and multiple Member, Owner and single Member, Owner and multiple Member, Recursive, Many-to-many, Inferential, and One to One. Each is defined in this book. These eight relationships and a legend for the abbreviations are set out in Tables 1 and 2. Note in the SQL columns of Table 1 that the ANSI SQL language substantively conformed to the relational data model from 1986 through 1999. Thereafter, SQL conformed to its own data model.

How these relationships are both defined and bound into the rows is probably the most distinguishing characteristic among DBMSs. Fundamentally, relationships are created either at load and/or update time, or are dynamically discovered at retrieval time.

Static relationships are made a part of the source row of the relationship. In this case, the actual mechanism of a relationship between and among rows is static. To accomplish this, the relationship definition language must be part of the DDL.

	Data Model				
	DDL Declaration		DML or Simulation		
Relationship Type	ANSI Network	Hierarchy	ILF	Relational SQL: 1986 - 1992	ANSI- SQL: 1999 onward
Owner and 1 Member	DS	DS	DD	DD	DD
Owner and >1 Member	DS	No	No	No	No
Singular and 1 Member	DS	No	No	SK	SK
Singular and >1 Member	DS	No	No	No	No
Recursive	DS	ID	DD	ID	DML
Many-to-many	IS	ID	DD	ID	DD

Data Management's Concepts & Terms

Relationship Type	Data Model				
	DDL Declaration		DML or Simulation		
	ANSI Network	Hierarchy	ILF	Relational SQL: 1986 - 1992	ANSI- SQL: 1999 onward
Inferential	ID	NO	DD	DD	DD
One to One	DS	ID	DD	DD	DD

Table 1. Data Model and Relationships.

	Relationship Code Meaning
DS	Direct, static relationships. Most often represented by DBMS generated embedded pointers.
IS	Indirect, static relationships. Most often represented by DBMS generated embedded pointers.
DD	Direct, dynamic relationships. Most often represented by column values supported by primary key and foreign keys.
ID	Indirect, dynamic relationships. Most often represented by additional tables.
No	No means no practical method.
SK	Secondary key. Here all the key selected rows share the same key-volume based value.
DML	Data Manipulation Language. Special SQL-defined syntax to accomplish the relationship

Table 2. Legend for Eight Data Model Relationship Types.

In contrast, if relationships are expressed at retrieval time, the rows that participate in the relationship can only be discovered through DBMS software execution. Under these circumstances, the relationship between and among rows is said to be dynamic. To accomplish this run-time relationship hypothesis and discovery strategy, the relationship definition language must be part of the DML.

The third data model component, operations, are two types: row based and relationship based. A row-based operation causes the creation, update or deletion of a row. A relationship-based operation sets one row into a relationship with another row. Table 3 sets out the different kinds of relationship operations that are present in static and dynamic data models. Notice that there are no overlaps.

Operation	Relationship Type	
	Static	Dynamic
Connect	Add to a Named RELATIONSHIP in Specific Order	N/A
Disconnect	Delete From RELATIONSHIP	N/A
Get Owner	Obtains the Parent of the Row That is Current	N/A
Get Member	Obtains the First Child of the Owner for the Named Relationship	N/A
Get next	Obtains the Next Row Within the Named Relationship	N/A
Intersect	N/A	Find and Keep Only the Common
Difference	N/A	Find and Keep Only the Not Common
Join	N/A	"Append" Relations to Each Other
Divide	N/A	Subset
Product	N/A	Cross-Product
Union	N/A	Merge and Drop Duplicates

Table 3. Relationship Operations

When these three data model components, data structures, relationships, and operations are taken together according to a commonly recognized style, a DBMS data model arises. It must be said, however, that there never was an overall "conspiracy" or universal DBMS technology model that details, in advance, the DBMS characteristics of data structures, relationships and operations. Such a universal DBMS technology has evolved however and can be employed to classify the DBMSs according to data model.

The four most commonly existing data models are Network, Hierarchical, Independent Logical File, and Relational. Most textbooks in the 1970s and 1980s only describe Network, Hierarchical, and Relational. That leaves out about 75% of all the DBMS that existed at time. The remaining DBMSs are generally described as "others." Notwithstanding the textbooks at the time, an examination of Figures 7 and 8 clearly shows that the Independent Logical File data models based DBMSs were quite robust and widely implemented.

Figure 6 brings together four points. The first point (row 1 from Figure 6) is that every DBMS data model consists of table structures, inter-table relationships, and operations.

The second row indicates that there are only two broad languages for defining these three components: Data Definition Languages (DDL), and Data Manipulation Languages (DML). The key issue here is where to place relationship definition and binding, that is, in the DDL or in the DML. Rows three and four address that issue by distinguishing two fundamentally different types of data models, dynamic and static.

From row three, if the relationships are defined as part of the DDL, the data model class is static. From row four, if relationships are defined as part of the DML, the data model class is dynamic.

Rows three and four set out very different DBMS classes: Static and Dynamic. Different DBMSs classes support fundamentally different data structures.

Figure 7 presents a tabulation of the features of the most common data models. The data models are identified below the Data Models header. The characteristics of the five data models are identified below the Data Model Characteristics header. The legend for this figure is provided in Table 4.

The second row of Figure 7 identifies the table organization for each data model. The third row identifies the types of relationships. The fourth row identifies the types of record operations and types of relationship operations within each data model. The fifth row identifies the components of the data model's DDL, and the sixth row identifies the components of the data model's DML.

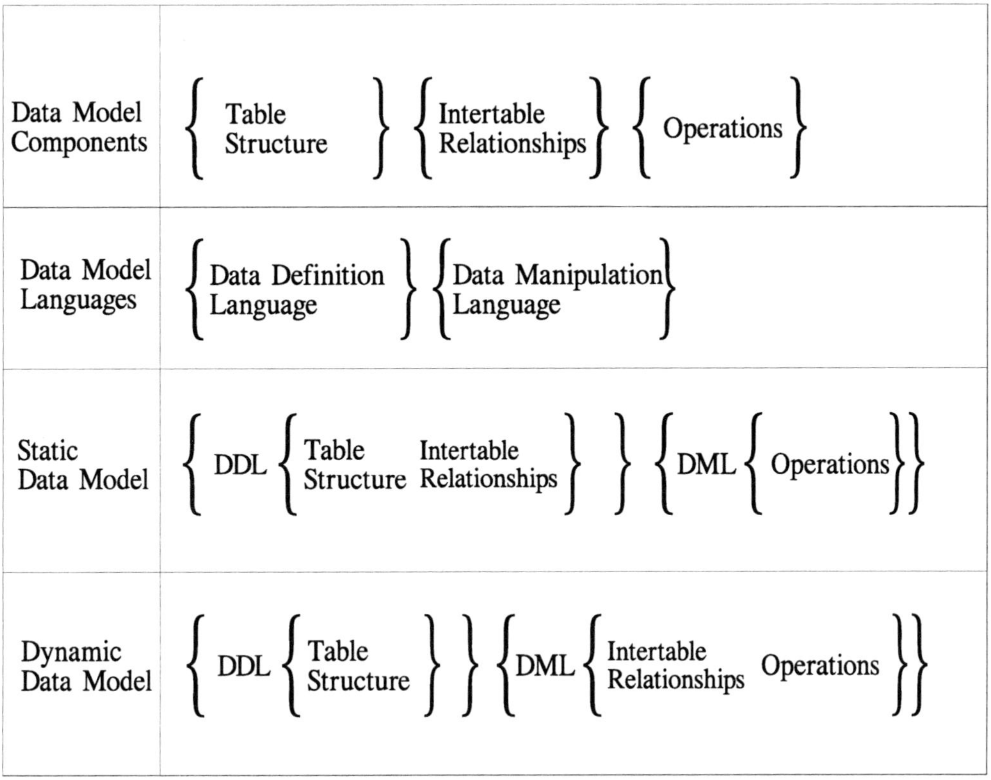

Data Model Components	{ Table Structure } { Intertable Relationships } { Operations }
Data Model Languages	{ Data Definition Language } { Data Manipulation Language }
Static Data Model	{ DDL { Table Structure Intertable Relationships } } { DML { Operations } }
Dynamic Data Model	{ DDL { Table Structure } } { DML { Intertable Relationships Operations } }

Figure 6. Data Model Engineering.

When DBMS first started in the late 1950s, and into the middle 1960s, all the DBMSs were static. The two data models were Network and Hierarchical. Starting in the late 1960s, a third data model that represented a collection of DBMSs came into existence. This was the Independent Logical File data model. Finally, in the late 1970s and early 1980s, the relational data model became popular. ANSI-SQL was the most common language for relational data model DBMSs. Figure 8 depicts these data models and identifies the DBMSs that generally conformed to each.

The trek to ANSI data model standards started in 1978. The first data model standard, ratified in 1986 was the ANSI Network Data Model (NDL). The second data model standard, also ratified in 1986 was the ANSI SQL Data Language Standard that generally conformed to the relational data model.

Data Model Characteristics		Data Models				
		Network	Hierarchic	Independant Logical File	Relational SQL: 1986, to 1992	SQL: 1999 onward
Table Organization		SF, A, G, RG NRG	SF Segments of Columns	SF, A, RG	SF	SF, A, G, RG NRG
Relationship (REL)		A—B / C	A / B C	A B C / D E F	A B C / D E F	A B D / C E F
Operations (OPS)	Record	A, D, F, M	A, D, F, M	A, D, F, M	A, D, F, M, P	A, D, F, M, P
	Relationships	C, D, GO, GM, GN	GO, GM, GN	J, INT DIV, UN DIF	J, INT, DIV, UN PR, DIV	J, INT, DIV, UN PR, DIV
DDL		REL, RO	REL, RO	RO	RO	RO
DML		OPS	OPS	REL & OPS	REL & OPS	REL & OPS

Figure 7. Tabulation of features for data models.

The successor SQL standards, i.e., 1989, and 1992 also generally conformed to the relational data model. As a consequence of market pressures, the 1999 SQL Data Language Standard broke away from being relational, and is shown on the bottom of Figure 8 as its own data model and included features from the Network, Hierarchical, Independent Logical File, and Relational data models. The SQL 2003 and SQL 2008 standard both conformed to and expanded these SQL proprietary features.

With respect to the data modeling discipline, there are traditionally three refinement scenarios for data models: Conceptual, Logical, and Physical. These terms are subject to much debate. Simply put, there's no consensus on the meaning of these terms. One person's conceptual is another person's logical, and another person's logical is a different person's physical. These three terms, conceptual data model, logical data model, and physical data model are defined in this book.

Data Model Component Legend Supporting Figure 5.			
Data Model Component	Legend for the Data Model Component		
Table Organization	SF = Simple Fact		
	A = Array		
	G = Group		
	RG = Repeating Group		
	NRG = Nested Repeating Group		
Operations	Record	A = Add	
		D = Delete	
		M = Modify	
		P = Project	
		F = Find	
	Relation-ship	C = Connect	Dis = Disconnect
		P = Project	J = Join
		DIV = Divide	GO = Get Owner
		GM = Get Member	GN = Get Next
		INT = Intersection	PR = Product
		UN = Union	DIF = Difference

Table 4. The Data Models Legend.

Because of a lack of a consensus, Whitemarsh chose to disengage from this irreconcilable battle that borders on choosing the "one true religion." Instead, Whitemarsh chose to identify and very precisely define its five data model generalization levels, that is, Data Element Models, Specified Data Models, Implemented Data Models, Operational Data Models, and View Data Models.

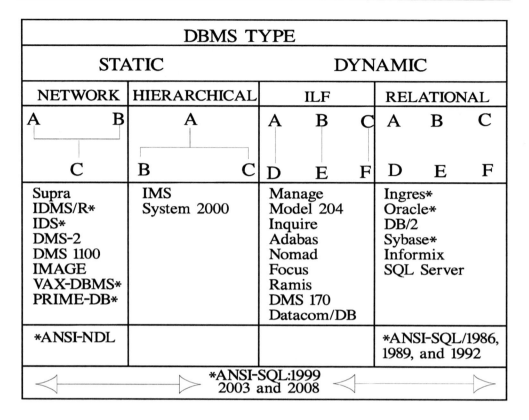

Figure 8. DBMSs by data model type.

These models are precise, unambiguous, employ different data component terms, and are thoroughly integrated end to end.

See Information Engineering. See NDL Data Language Standard. See SQL Data Language Standard. See ANSI Database Standards. See Static Relationships. See CODASYL Data Model. See Dynamic Relationships. See Fact. See Specified Data Model. See Implemented Data Model. See Operational Data Model. See Data Type. See SQL Data Type. See Table. See Column.

Data Resource Management: See Data Administration.

Data Security: See Security and Privacy.

Data Storage Description Language (DMCL or DSDL): See Physical Schema.

Data Storage Structure: A Data Storage Structure is the data component of a database's storage structure that contains rows. The complexity of the data storage component ranges from one operating system (O/S) file for each table to one O/S file for all the occurrences of all the tables.
   Whenever the DBMS allows flexibility of storing more than one table's rows per O/S file, or storing just a subset of one or more of a table's rows per O/S file, the concept of an AREA is needed. An AREA is a definition construct that indicates which rows (from one or more types) are stored in the same O/S file.

Data Store: A Data Store is a general term for a data file. These are often used often within the creation of data flow diagrams.

Data Structure: A Data Structure is an organized collection of data that may map onto a complete or a collection of columns within a table.
   See data model.

Data Type: See Fact.

Data View: See View.

Data Volatility: Data Volatility represents the rate of change of the column values stored within a row, or the rate of change of row adds and deletes.

Data Warehouse: A Data Warehouse is one of the five commonly seen Data Architecture Classes.
   See Data Architecture Classes.

Database: A Database is a collection of interrelated data stored according to a schema. The data is stored such that it is independent of programs that use it. At a minimum, a database must contain information about its own data structure, and of course, data. A database may optionally include mechanisms for fast access, that is, indexes. Finally, databases may contain relationships, implicit or explicit between rows and among rows of the same or different tables.

A database is able to be accessed by a DBMS, that is, loaded, unloaded, updated, backed up, and restored independently from those same activities that may be occurring to another database operating under the control of the same executing DBMS.

Database Administrator (DBA): A Database Administrator (DBA) is a person who is given the responsibility for the definition, organization, protection, efficiency, and evolution of databases for an organization.

Database Domain: A Database Domain is a hierarchically organized set of noun-intensive descriptions associated with a mission leaf. Analyzed database domains lead to the identification of database object classes, enterprise data elements, and property classes. Property classes, in turn, often lead to database tables.

Database Domain Assigned Database Object: A Database Domain Assigned Database Object represents one or more database objects that have been assigned to a database domain.

Database Key (DBKEY): A Database Key (DBKEY) is a DBMS created mechanism used by the DBMS's access strategy to access a row. While in all cases, DBKeys function as a table's primary key, some primary keys are not DBKeys. In that case, the value of a primary key is created by the user.

Database Management: Database management is a discipline for the management of databases. Involved in this discipline are strategies, policies, procedures that support the definition of databases including data modeling, data integrity, and data quality.

Database management from a technical viewpoint defines the underlying engineering for data models including table structures, relationships among rows of data, and the operations allowed for both rows and relationships.

When database management technology is implemented in software, a database management system (DBMS) is created.

Data Management's Concepts & Terms

Database Management System (DBMS): A Database Management System provides functional components in four areas: logical database, physical database, interrogation, and system control. The enumeration of the DBMS components in each of these four areas is presented in Figure 9.

The logical database component enables the definition of data structures

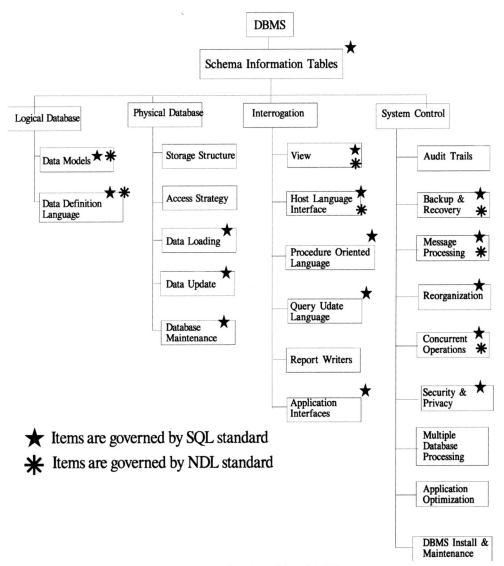

Figure 9. DBMS Components Standardized by ANSI.

with a data definition language (DDL) according to the capabilities of the DBMS's data model.

The physical database component enables the definition of the physical structures (dictionary, indexes, relationships, and data) according to the scheme set down by a data storage definition language (DSDL). The physical database also encompasses the processes that enable data loading, data update, and database maintenance (backup).

The interrogation component includes two main types of data access languages, host and natural. The host languages provide DML verbs that allow data access through COBOL, Fortran, etc.

The natural languages are of three varieties: Procedure oriented (like C++), query-update (single sentence oriented), and report writers that support control breaks, subtotals, etc.

Natural languages are also called Fourth Generation Languages (4GL). The 4GL term is imprecise since there is no ISO/ANSI specification for this language as exists for SQL. Further, the term 4GL is misleading as some natural languages were created prior to some the third generation languages such as C.

The system control component includes facilities for backup and recovery, security and privacy, concurrent operations and the like.

Despite the near 40 years of effort to standardize database management systems, as described in the ANSI Database Standards entry above, it is instructive to understand just what has been standardized. This is shown in Figure 9, above. The items with an "asterisk" are the NDL components that have been standardized by ANSI. The "star" components are the SQL standardized components. The components that provide a DBMS its performance are its storage structure and access strategy. Neither is standardized as these components can dramatically change depending on operating system and computing hardware capabilities.

Standardized but not fully developed has been the procedure oriented language that can be employed for the process specification of assertions, triggers, and stored procedures. The ANSI standardization lacks any real presentation layer. Thus, it could be more fully developed and be employed to dramatically assist in the portability of database applications from one DBMS to the next. The main problem with the SQL stored procedure language (ANSI SQL PSM (Persistent Stored Modules)) is that it has been roundly ignored by most the DBMS vendors. IBM has implemented it as has

MIMER (Sweden). The other DBMS vendors such as Microsoft, and Oracle have not. This fact alone cripples most database application portability.

The query language, while this too has been standardized, has been greatly extended by most DBMS vendors to give it a presentation layer and sophisticated report-writing like functions.

As a consequence of not standardizing components, not implementing standardized components, or by employing significant extensions to standardized components, most database applications cannot be considered portable between DBMSs.

To achieve database application portability, database applications must only safely employ the following from DBMS vendors: data models, data definition language, views, host language interface, message processing, concurrent operations, and security and privacy. The remaining components, that is, Query Update, Report Writers, and Procedure Oriented Languages have to be procured from other vendors who have developed DBMS independent versions of these tools. The way this is accomplished is by using ODBC or JDBC.

The remaining components, Storage Structure, Access Strategy, Audit Trails, Multiple Database Processing, Application Optimization, and DBMS Installation and Maintenance are all highly dependent on the fundamental nature of the database application, the deploying DBMS, and the operating system and hardware on which the database application operates.

Database Management Systems (DBMS) History: The following is a very brief history of database management systems (DBMS). It is explained along two tracks: Generations, and Mergers.

First, there are the generations. There have been three broad generations of DBMS. The first generation of DBMSs consisted of three general classes: National Defense Systems, Commercial Systems, and File Oriented Systems. This time span for this generation was between 1955 and 1970.

The national defense systems were created mainly by the U.S. Department of Defense (DoD) under contract to FFRDC organizations. FFRDC stands for Federally Funded Research & Development Centers. The most notable among these organizations is Rand, Lincoln Labs, the MITRE Corporation, and the Institute for Defense Analysis. Both Lincoln Labs and MITRE were founded out of MIT (The Massachusetts Institute of Technology) in Boston, MA.

Starting in the middle 1950s, there was a very real threat of a strategic attack from the Soviet Union. In response, the DoD realized the importance of computers in terms of threat identification, threat analysis, and threat response. Intense analysis at that time showed that under severe stress, humans are most capable of dealing with 1) hierarchical data structures, 2) a natural language for asking questions, and 3) an inverted process for seeking and accessing data. These three characteristics became the preeminent design criteria of a computer-software-based system that would assist the DoD in countering the strategic threat posed by the Soviet Union.

Inverted access was clearly a criterion because at the time, the only mode of data processing was record-access. That is, get a record and search for a value. If the value was not there, get the next record. Clearly such a type of access was not very immediate or precise. Invented during that time was a "full concordance" strategy that enabled users to discover records based on direct access through value. This was a Value then Record access. That strategy is *inverted* to the traditional approach of Record then Value.

The first DBMS was called ADAM. It was started in the very early 1960s and was operational by early 1965. ADAM was created by the MITRE Corporation. ADAM was a generalized DBMS that allowed for database design, loading, reporting, and update. It ran on the IBM 7030 Stretch computer that had 64K words and a 4 million word disk.

From ADAM, a whole lineage of DoD-based DBMSs arose through development at other FFRDCs. The System Development Corporation (SDC), a spin off from Rand, created the last of the FFRDC DBMSs, TDMS, which was a Time-Shared Data Management System. It was operational by the middle 1960s. RFMS of the University of Texas was derived from TDMS and was operational in the late 1960s. System 2000, a commercially available DBMS that operated on CDC, IBM, and Univac computers was derived from RFMS and was operational by 1969.

Characteristic of the National Defense Systems were hierarchical data structures, natural languages for query, update, and reporting, and inverted access. There was no access to these databases from traditional languages such as COBOL of Fortran. The ultimate objective was to support the protection of the U.S. from the Soviet Union.

The second class of DBMSs in the first generation was the commercial DBMSs. The ultimate objective of these systems was to protect the investment in massive quantities of business information systems built in COBOL. A critical element of COBOL, as with other 3GLs such as Fortran, was that each file structure had to be defined within the computer program. If there was a need for a file structure change and 100 programs included that file structure,

100 programs had to be changed and recompiled. Needed was a data independence layer that existed in between the database and the program. That was and is a very key role of the DBMS. The most popular DBMSs of this type was IBM's IMS (hierarchical with simulated network data structures), IDMS, and Total.

Since the software applications at the time were almost entirely for commercial applications, their three key characteristics were: network data structures, interface through COBOL, and record processing. These are very different from the National Defense DBMS characteristics. Consequently, a single organization was unable to procure a DBMS for both types of database applications.

The third class of DBMS was the file-oriented DBMSs. These focused on providing DBMS support to existing stand-alone file-based applications. DBMSs such as RAMIS, Adabas, Model 204, Inquire, and Focus. These file-based DBMSs supported simple two level file structures, had interfaces through COBOL, had record then value access, and record access through the use of indexes. Relationships existed from one file to the next through "join-like" operations. Every one of these DBMSs had a similar data model but very different storage structure and access strategy. Whitemarsh asserts that all these file-oriented DBMSs conform to the data model, Independent Logical File.

The second generation of DBMSs started with the creation of the relational model and with IBM's popularity of it through System R, SQL-DS, and finally SQL. DBMSs that immediately implemented competitive systems to IBM's relational implementation were Oracle, Informix, and Sybase.

The third generation of DBMSs started with ANSI SQL:1999. That standardization brought into the SQL data structures features from the Network, Hierarchical and Independent Logical file DBMSs. Figures 7 and 8, above, identify this data model's characteristics and enumerate the names of the DBMSs that have implemented this data model.

As to "mergers" there have been two significant ones. The first occurred in the middle 1970s with the merger of the capabilities of the host language DBMSs and the self-contained language DBMSs. The resulting DBMSs were almost all based on embedded, inter-table relationship mechanisms, known in this book as static relationships. Then, there arose the dynamic relationship mechanism DBMSs (shared column values in different table instances). The first such systems were servicing hundreds of production databases in the late 1960s, years before the first papers *discovering* the relational data model were published. Throughout the late 1960s and 1970s, static and dynamic relationship DBMSs were installed and used with great success.

The second merger began around 1984. Some DBMS vendors discovered that the majority of the facilities contained in their respective products were independent of data model and independent of technology. Thus, they made their products support both network (static) and relational (dynamic) facilities and also implemented on a variety of hardware types, that is, microcomputers, minicomputers, and mainframes.

This author first encountered a DBMS, TDMS, in 1969. It was an inverted access, hierarchical data model, natural language DBMS that became operational in the middle 1960s. This DBMS's maximum database size was about one million characters. It supported between 50 and 100 concurrent users and the computer required to support it filled a room. Today's room-sized computers support databases 10,000 times larger and service thousands of concurrent users. Today's desk top computers support databases 10 to 25 times larger than the 1969 database and service from 20 to 30 concurrent users.

In many ways, DBMSs are the same today as they were years ago. The same data models still exist, as do the types of natural and host language interfaces. Today, however, it is even more necessary to have storage efficient databases that can load, update, and retrieve data rapidly because database sizes have grown from millions to billions to trillions of characters. And, it is even more necessary to provide security, audit trails, and multiple user access.

See ANSI Database Standards. See NDL. See SQL. See Database Management Systems.

Database Nature: Database Nature is a general classification of the business type and use of the database. Value examples would include operational, control, management.

Database Object Assigned Property Class: A Database Object Assigned Property Class represents one or more property classes assigned to a database object.

See Database Object Model.

Database Object Class: A Database Object Class is a type of data structure that proceeds through predefined states according to embedded process transformations. The database object class, the specification of database objects, is defined in four parts: database object data structure, database object process, database object information system and database object state. An instance of a database object class is a database object.
   See Database Object Model.

Database Object Data Structure: A database object class data structure is the set of data structures that map onto all the different value sets for real world database objects such as an auto accident, vehicle and emergency medicine incident. A database object class data structure's set of columns may be drawn from one or more tables, all of which must be semantically related through primary and foreign key relationships.
   See Database Object Model.

Database Object Information System: A Database Object Information System is a set of specifications that controls, sequences, and iterates the execution of various database processes that cause changes in database objects to achieve specific value-based states in conformance to the requirements of business policies. For example, the reception and database posting of data from business information systems activities (screens, data edits, storage, interim reports, etc.) that accomplish entry of the auto accident information.
   See Database Object Model.

Database Object Information Systems Assigned Database Object Table Process: A Database Object Information Systems Assigned Database Object Table Process represents one or more Database Object Table Processes that are assigned to a Business Information System. These are set into a sequence for proper accomplishment.
   See Database Object Model.

Database Object Model: The Database Object Model includes database objects, database object tables, membership rationale, database object table processes, database object process columns, database object states, database object information systems, database object state & database object information system, database domain & database object, and the database

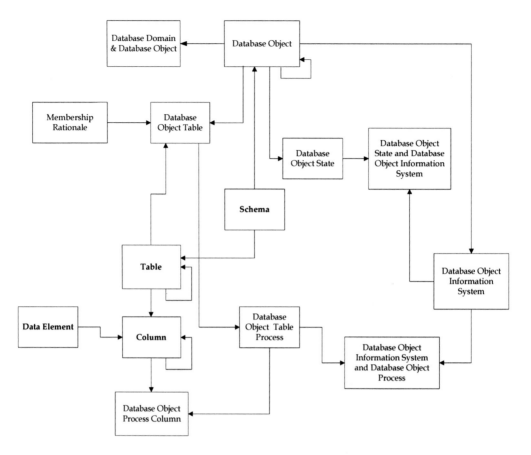

Figure 10. Database Object Model.

object system & database object process. Figure 10 depicts the meta model for defining database object classes.

Database Object Resource Life Cycle Node Assignment: A Database Object Resource Life Cycle Node Assignment represents the association between a Resource Life Cycle node and a database object class. A database object may be assigned to one or more Resource Life Cycle nodes and a Resource Life Cycle node may be related to one or more database objects.
   See Database Object Model.

Database Object State: Database Object States are the value states of one or more database objects that represent the after-state of the successful accomplishment of one or more recognizable business events. Examples of business events are auto accident initiation, involved vehicle entry, involved person entry, and auto accident DUI involvement. Database state changes are initiated through named business events that serve business functions. The business function, auto accident investigation includes the business event, auto-accident-incident initiation, which, in turn, causes the incident initiation database object information system to execute, which, in turn, causes several database processes to cause the auto accident incident to be materialized in the database.
See Database Object Model.

Database Object State and Database Object Information System: A Database Object State and Database Object Information System is the association of one or more Database Object States and Database Object Information Systems. The association exists within a sequence so that the state is properly achieved.
See Database Object Model.

Database Object Table: A Database Object Table is an association of an Implemented Data Model table with a database object. Membership rationale classifies the reason why a table belongs to the database object.
See Database Object Model.

Database Object Table Process: Database Object Table Process is the set of database processes that enforce the integrity of data structure columns, referential integrity between database objects and actions among contained data structure segments, the proper computer-based rules governing data structure segment insertion, modification, and deletion. An example is the proper and complete storage of an auto accident.
See Database Object Model.

Database Object Table Process Column: A Database Object Table Process Column is an association of a specific database object table process and a specific column of a table.

Database Production Status: A Database Production Status represents the classification of the status of the database. Commonly employed values are development, test and production.

Database Recovery: See Backup and Recovery.

Database Update: A Database Update is the process of adding, deleting, or changing data in the database. If the updates affect DBMS columns that are supported by indexes, or other storage structure components, these are normally automatically adjusted by the DBMS.

Database View: See View.

Database View column: See View Column.

DBMS: See Database Management System.

DBMS Column: A DBMS Column, analogous to a column of a table from an Implemented Data Model is intended to be a data-value based partial descriptor of a DBMS table. Not all the DBMS columns of a DBMS table must map to columns from a single table within an Implemented Data Model.

DBMS columns can represent complex facts, that is, arrays, groups, repeating groups, and nested repeating groups. These capabilities are however dependent on the DBMS vendor. Different DBMS vendors have implemented complex facts differently.

Like columns, there are four classes of DBMS columns: content, instance, metadata, and relationships. The first, content, represents the DBMS table's content. For example, if the DBMS table is CustomerAddress, the content columns would be CustomerStreet-1, CustomerStreet-2, CustomerCity, CustomerState, and CustomerZip.

The second, instance, are the set of DBMS columns that have a combined value such that only one row from the DBMS table is found. This set of DBMS columns is commonly called the DBMS table's primary key.

The third, metadata, are the DBMS columns that represent the metadata about the DBMS tables such as who created in an instance of the DBMS table, who updated it, what project caused the row to be added or changed, and finally, what was the date of the add or change.

The fourth, relationships, represent the DBMS columns that, when valued, provide the uniqueness value for a different row in the same DBMS table (recursive relationship) or a different DBMS table (parent DBMS table for a parent-child relationship). In this later situation, the uniqueness column is often called the parent DBMS table's primary key.
See Operational Data Model.

DBMS Column Assigned Column: A DBMS Column Assigned Column represents the association of a DBMS Column to a column.
See Operational Data Model.

DBMS Column Assigned Meta Category Values: A DBMS Column Assigned Meta Category Values represents the assignment of one or more meta category values to a DBMS Column. As of August 2009, meta category values cannot be assigned to DBMS columns.
See Operational Data Model.

DBMS Column Assigned Value Domain: A DBMS Column Assigned Value Domain represents the assignment of a value domain to a DBMS column. An assigned value domain is a value-based constraint on the DBMS column. The assigned value domain cannot be the same as that assigned the data element, attribute, or column. Nor can a value domain be more expansive than that assigned the data element attribute, or column.
See Operational Data Model.

DBMS Column Constraint: A DBMS Column Constraint is the specification of a process that operates on only one DBMS column within the DBMS table to which it is associated that must test true when no updating is occurring. An action that causes a violation to the DBMS column constraint is rejected.
See Operational Data Model.

DBMS Data Type: A DBMS Data Type is a DBMS vendor's classification of the values represented by a column of a row of data. Each DBMS data type imposes a set of rules regarding allowable values and allowed operations on the values. An example is adding an integer value to a date value, but disallowing the adding of two dates.

Depending on how strictly a DBMS conforms to the SQL:1999 or later standard, there can be two broad classes: primitive data types and data structure data types. The first class supports to simple facts. These simple fact data types exist in almost all DBMSs as these SQL data types were established by the middle 1980s. The primitive data type, or simple fact data types, are represented by character, integer, binary, and the like.

Data structure data types enable the definition of complex facts. These were introduced to the SQL language within SQL:1999. These included arrays, repeating groups, and nested repeating groups. Contained within each data structure data type are the primitive data type specifications for the ultimately represented simple facts. For example, Telephone Numbers may be a data structure type: array. The array element may have the primitive data type of character.

See Operational Data Model.

DBMS Data Type Picture: DBMS Data Type Picture is the picture clause associated with a data type so that a complete DDL script can be produced for the Clarion development environment that generates business information systems.

See Operational Data Model.

DBMS Environment: The DBMS Environment entity is intended to carry information that indicates that the business information system is serviced by one or more than one DBMS such as Oracle or Sybase.

See Business Information Systems Model

DBMS Record: A DBMS Record is a DBMS term that represents the values of an index, pointers (owner, next, prior), or other storage structure components. When the DBMS record instance represents the storage of rows, it may contain less than one, one, or more than one row from one or more than one table.

DBMS Schema: A DBMS Schema represents a formally defined collection of DBMS tables and other artifacts within the enterprise. An Operational Data Model is equivalent to a DBMS schema. A DBMS schema is a DBMS structure that encapsulates all its contained DBMS tables and supporting DBMS schema objects such as data types, procedures, constraints, including the interrelationships of the various DBMS schema objects. The string, "DBMS" prefixes each of these component names because, within this data model

generalization level, these components are directly representative of the real and operating databases under the control of a specific DBMS.
See Operational Data Model.

DBMS Subschema: See View.

DBMS Table: A DBMS Table is intended to be a well-defined expression of one policy within a DBMS schema. Ideally, the collection of all the DBMS tables within a DBMS schema should define an overarching policy in which each DBMS table represents a subordinate coherent DBMS table-based policy. A DBMS table may contain DBMS columns that map to columns from multiple Implemented Data Model tables. This enables operational databases to be non-third-normal form while the corresponding Implemented Data Model is a collection of third normal form tables.

A DBMS table is bound to a particular DBMS and is the type specification of a set of rows of data across those DBMS columns. DBMS Tables can include subordinate specifications including constraints, primary and foreign keys, and other table centered features.

Within the scope of the Operational Data Model generalization level, DBMS tables are the type specifications for rows of data because this level is bound to a particular DBMS and is related to any specific business information systems. Every DBMS table should relate back to a specific policy within the domain of the DBMS table's schema. DBMS tables can be subtyped to represent collections of DBMS columns that have a common set and several non-intersecting sets.

See Operational Data Model.

DBMS Table Assigned Assertion: A DBMS Table Assigned Assertion represents one or more Assertions that are assigned to a DBMS Table. Commonly, Assertions are in the form of a Data Integrity Rule.
See Operational Data Model.

DBMS Table Assigned Stored Procedure: A DBMS Table Assigned Stored Procedure represents one or more Stored Procedures that are assigned to a DBMS table. SQL assertions are a form of a Data Integrity Rule.
See Operational Data Model.

DBMS Table Assigned Trigger: A DBMS Table Assigned Trigger represents one or more triggers that are assigned to a DBMS Table.
See Operational Data Model.

DBMS Table Candidate Key: A DBMS Table Candidate Key represents a collection of DBMS columns within a DBMS table that, when their values are collectively employed, result in the retrieval or update of a single row of data for that DBMS table. There may be multiple candidate keys within a DBMS table. DBMS columns of candidate keys are not allowed to overlap each other or the DBMS table's primary key. The set of DBMS table candidate keys not chosen as the DBMS table's primary key are also called alternate keys.
See Operational Data Model.

DBMS Table Candidate Key Assigned DBMS Column: A DBMS Table Candidate Key Assigned DBMS Column represents one or more DBMS Columns assigned to a DBMS Table Candidate Key. The DBMS columns exist within an implemented sequence. Candidate key DBMS columns are not allowed to include any DBMS columns within the DBMS table's primary key.
See Operational Data Model.

DBMS Table Constraint: A DBMS Table Constraint represents a process that operates on only the columns within the table to which it is associated and that must test true when no updating is occurring. An action that causes a violation to the DBMS table constraint is rejected.
See Operational Data Model.

DBMS Table Foreign Key: A DBMS Table Foreign Key is an exact replication of a related DBMS table's primary key. The name of the foreign key should match closely the relationship it represents. The DBMS columns of the foreign key should be able to be deleted entirely from the DBMS table without any loss of policy. The DBMS columns of the foreign key are not allowed to overlap the DBMS columns of the DBMS table's primary key. In addition to the foreign key's DBMS columns, there are additional rules governing inserts, updates, and deletes. In a recursive relationship, the DBMS table of the foreign key is the same as its corresponding primary key table.
See Operational Data Model.

DBMS Table Foreign Key Assigned DBMS Column: A DBMS Table Foreign Key Assigned DBMS Column represents one or more DBMS Columns assigned to a DBMS Table Foreign Key. The DBMS columns exist within an implemented sequence. Foreign key DBMS columns are not allowed to include any DBMS columns within the DBMS table's primary key.
   See Operational Data Model.

DBMS Table Primary Key: DBMS Table Primary Key is the designation of one or more DBMS columns that can be used to locate one row instance. Traditionally, the value set of a primary key is unique across all rows of a DBMS table. The ANSI SQL Data Language Standard also allows non-unique primary keys.
   There can only be one primary key within a DBMS table. DBMS columns of primary key are not allowed to overlap each other or the DBMS table's candidate key.
   See Operational Data Model.

DBMS Table Primary Key Assigned DBMS Column: A DBMS Table Primary Key Assigned DBMS Column represents one or more DBMS Columns assigned to a DBMS Table Primary Key. The DBMS columns exist within an implemented sequence.
   See Operational Data Model.

DBMS Table Secondary Key: DBMS Table Secondary Key represents a collection of DBMS columns within a DBMS table, that when their values are collectively employed, would result in the retrieval or update of one or more rows of data for that DBMS. There can be multiple secondary keys within a DBMS table. DBMS columns of secondary key are allowed to overlap each other or the DBMS table's secondary key.
   See Operational Data Model.

DBMS Table Secondary Key Assigned DBMS Column: A DBMS Table Secondary Key Assigned DBMS Column represents one or more DBMS Columns assigned to a DBMS Table Secondary Key. The DBMS columns exist within an implemented sequence.
   See Operational Data Model.

Deadly Embrace: Deadly Embrace represents the state or condition that prevails when each of two or more business information system processes attempts to exclusively lock rows that are already exclusively locked by different business information system processes. The attempted lock may also be at the DBMS record instance, area instance, file instance, or database instance level.

    A deadly embrace is often resolved by stopping one of the run-units, rolling back all the run-unit's transactions that have already been performed, and attempting a run-unit restart a predetermined number of times before a permanent abort, or attempting a run-unit restart periodically for a predetermined wall-clock time before a permanent abort.

Degree (Of a Relation): The degree of a relation is the quantity of columns in a table.

Delimiter: A Delimiter is a flag that separates and organizes items of data. A delimiter is also called a punctuation symbol, or separator.

Deliverable: A Deliverable is a product that is produced during the accomplishment of a project. A deliverable is an instance of a deliverable template. For example, the data model for Marketing would contain a number of methodology work products such as entity relationship diagrams, object, tables, columns, and so forth.
    See Project Management Model.

Deliverable Template: A Deliverable Template is the prototypical specification of a deliverable that is produced during a project. For example, all the sections, subsections and descriptions of what would be in a Data Model.
    See Project Management Model.

Deliverable Template Type: A Deliverable Template Type is a classification of a set of Deliverable Templates. Examples are Data Models, Process Models, or Information Systems Plans.
    See Project Management Model.

Derived Data: Derived Data represents data that is drawn from the values of other data elements. For example, Total-Order-Cost could be computed from Sum (Line-item-cost + Shipping-cost + Taxes).

Derived Data Element: Derived Data Elements represent the result of some sort of calculation or transformation of either a collection of data elements or compound data elements or a combination of both.
    See Data Element Model.

Derived Data Element Assigned Compound Data Element: A Derived Data Element Assigned Compound Data Element represents one or more Compound Data Elements assigned to a Derived Data Element.
    See Data Element Model.

Derived Data Element Assigned Data Element: A Derived Data Element Assigned Data Element represents one or more Data Elements assigned to a Derived Data Element.
    See Data Element Model.

Determinant: A Determinant represents a column that is used singly or in combination with other columns to uniquely select rows from a table. If only one column is needed for the determinant, it is the entire primary key of the table. If multiple columns are needed, the determinant is a part of a table's primary key.

Device Media Control Language (DMCL): See Physical Schema.

Dictionary (Storage Structure Component): The Dictionary is a component of the DBMS storage structure contains the compiled schema, defined subschemas, and whatever other components that the DBMS vendor deems necessary to provide knowledge about the database's internal or external organization. The dictionary stores the database's names, integrity rules, pictures, etc. This storage structure component may reside in one or more O/S files, or may reside in the DBMS's integrated metadata management system.

Discrete and Release Development Environments: Discrete and Release Development Environments represent two different classes of accomplishing business information system projects. Discrete represents the accomplishment through traditional one-off project management methods such as waterfall or spiral methodologies.

Once the overall set of business information system projects is completed, the organization must transform itself from a one-off project development environment to a multi-project, multi-database, and multi-business information systems environment that generates many changes across a broad database and business information systems topology to maintain an overall level of organization and management across the involved systems. The alternative to waterfall or spiral environment is called a release environment. Both environments are needed.

Distributed Database: A Distributed Database is a database that is physically distributed such that different processors control separate partitions of database data.

Division: Division represents a relational data model operation that partitions a relation, based on the contents of another relation.

Document: A Document is a complex collection of business data that is usually published by some enterprise, e.g., a survey, or report of the U.S. Bureau of Census important to the enterprise. A document is typically decomposed and some aspect of that division is input into the database application. The analysis of a document produces a mapping between the cells of data on the document and the view columns that represent those cells to the database application.

Document Cell: A Document Cell represents a unit of a document of interest to an enterprise database, usually as an input.

DOS: Disk operating system

Dynamic Backout: See Automatic Backout.

Dynamic Relationship: A dynamic relationship is a mechanism that relates a row from a related-from (a.k.a., parent) table to rows of the related-to table (a.k.a., child). Dynamic relationships are represented as column values in the related-to table. That is, there is a column in the related-to table that contains the primary key value of the row of the related-from table. This column can be specially defined to the DBMS and is called a foreign key. When the value of a dynamic relationship column within the related-to table changes, so too does the existing relationship change. The changed value in the related-to table points to a different row in a related-from table. Hence, this is a relationship change.

See ANSI Database Standards. See SQL Data Language Standard. See NDL Data Language Standard. See Data Model. See Relationships. See Static Relationship.

Element: See Data Element.

Embedded Pointer: An Embedded Pointer is a DBMS relationship mechanism that is stored within the row that points to another record. This pointer is usually available only to the DBMS. Embedded pointers are static relationships.

See Data Model. See Relationships. See Static Relationship.

Encode/Decode Tables: Encode/Decode Tables are a set of codes and values employed to explain data that is contained in the database. An example is D.C. meaning District of Columbia.

End-User: An End-User is a person, at any organizational level, whose occupation requires the use of a computer, but does not require knowledge of computers or programming.

Enterprise: An Enterprise is a grouping of organization units that have common collections of data, processes, activities within a business or a company and sometimes beyond corporate affiliations as in the case of data interchanges. An enterprise is therefore not just a synonym for a business or a company. Rather, it is intended to convey a common data, process, or activity view across the organizational units sharing that view.

The enterprise may be a university, a corporation (large or small), and it may be centralized or decentralized. For very small enterprises, many of the enterprise database components may be treated trivially. For large enterprises, these very same components are treated robustly. The database components include architectures (data, database process, etc.), models (specific designs for data, database process, etc.), methodologies (work steps to effect architectures and models), and the repository (specialized database application for storage of all enterprise components).

Enterprise Architecture: An Enterprise Architecture is an architecture that consists of five distinct architecture classes. These are:

- The Enterprise's Architecture class.
- The Database Object Class architecture class.
- The Data Architecture classes.
- The Resource Life Cycle Analysis architecture class.
- The Business Information Systems Plans architecture class.

Each of these is defined in this book.

Enterprise's Architecture Class: An Enterprise's Architecture Class is an architecture for the enterprise itself, the engineering and structure of the enterprise's mission, organizations, functions and database domains are provided such that they can be extended and/or integrated with other more technical architectures such as hardware, business information systems, and business events.

Enterprise Database: Enterprise Database is an organizational operating condition in which there are both defined policy coherence and integrity as well as consistency in policy transformations throughout the enterprise irrespective of functional and organizational style, and irrespective of policy transformation technology (that is, computers, operating systems, programming languages, and database management systems).

Enterprise Resource Planning (ERP): Enterprise Resource Planning (ERP) is an enterprise-wide information strategy often implemented as a very large business information system designed to coordinate all the business resources, information, and activities.

An ERP supports business functions such as Manufacturing, Supply Chain Management, Financials, Projects, Human Resources and Customer Relationship Management.

Ideally, ERP is based on a common database and a modular software design. In reality, ERP vendors seldom have their database and business processes open and easily understood and malleable.

Ideally, a common database can allow every department of a business to store and retrieve information in real-time. In reality, ERP facilities are only able to be employed through highly proprietary database designs and ERP system designs.

Entity: An Entity is a collection of facts that are commonly called attributes. Every entity should relate back to a specific policy within the domain of the entity's subject. Entities can be subtyped to represent collections of attributes that have a common set and several non-intersecting sets. An entity is intended to be a well-defined expression of one policy within a subject area. The collection of all the entities within a subject area should define the complete set of policy for that area. Some entities and even some subject areas may never be represented within Implemented Data Models. Additionally, some attributes within an entity may never be employed. Entities may be subtyped.

See Specified Data Model.

Entity Candidate Key: Entity Candidate Keys represent a collection of attributes within an entity that, when their values are collectively employed, would result in the retrieval or update of a single row of data for that entity if that entity had actually been a table. There may be multiple candidate keys within an entity. The set of candidate keys not chosen as the entity's primary key are also called alternate keys. Attributes of candidate keys are not allowed to overlap each other or the entity's primary key.

See Specified Data Model.

Entity Candidate Key Assigned Attribute: An Entity Candidate Key Assigned Attribute is one or more attributes assigned to an entity candidate key. The attributes exist within a specified sequence. Candidate key attributes are not allowed to include any attributes within the entity's primary key.

See Specified Data Model.

Entity Foreign Key: An Entity Foreign Key is an exact representation of a related entity's primary key. The name of the foreign key should match closely the relationship it represents. The attributes of the foreign key should be able to be deleted entirely from the entity without any loss of policy. The attributes of the foreign key are not allowed to overlap the attributes of the entity's primary key. In addition to the foreign key's attributes there are additional rules governing inserts, updates, and deletes.
    See Specified Data Model.

Entity Foreign Key Assigned Attribute: An Entity Foreign Key Assigned Attribute is one or more attributes assigned to an entity foreign key. The attributes exist within a specified sequence. Foreign key attributes are not allowed to include any attributes within the entity's primary key. An entity foreign key assigned attribute cannot contain any attribute from the entity's primary key.
    See Specified Data Model.

Entity Primary Key: A Primary Key is the designation of one or more attributes that can be used to locate one row instance. Traditionally, the value set of a primary key is unique across all rows of an entity. The ANSI SQL Data Language Standard also allows non-unique primary keys.
    See Specified Data Model.

Entity Primary Key Assigned Attribute: An Entity Primary Key Assigned Attribute represents one or more attributes assigned to an entity primary key. The attributes exist within a specified sequence.
    See Specified Data Model.

Entity Relationship Diagram: An Entity Relationship Diagram is a diagram that illustrates entities, and the relationships among entities.

Environment Type: An Environment Type is an entity that is intended to distinguish whether the business information system is executing on a desktop, server, or mainframe.
    See Business Information System Model

Error Recovery: Error Recovery is a process that corrects or bypasses the effects of a fault to restore a computer system (software or hardware) to a prescribed condition. Error recovery means that abnormal terminations are not allowed to occur--by design.

Exclusive Control: An Exclusive Control is a lock applied to a row that prevents other users from accessing that row while the lock is held. The level of control may be broader, that is, table, area, O/S file, or database.

Extent: A list of unsigned integers that specifies an array.

External Document: An External Document is a document that is retained as a more refined description of some aspect of the database system. This may relate to detailed diagrams, flow charts, detailed explanation of formulas, and the like. An external document may be free form text material, such as a policy or regulation that may be referenced as the basis for the definition of one or more items such as a mission, function, organization, data element, table, column, or data integrity rule.

Fact: A fact is a specification of a pragmatic truth that can, at least in theory, be checked and either confirmed or denied. Within the context of the Whitemarsh Metabase System's data models, that is, Data Element, Specified, Implemented, Operational, and View, fact specifications exist within the context of a data element concept or data element from the Data Element Model, attribute of an entity from the Specified Data Model, column of a table from the Implemented Data Model, DBMS column of a DBMS table from the Operational Data Model, and a view column of a view from the View Data Model. In all of these contexts, facts have names, semantics, and data types. The data type of a fact makes its values either simple or complex.

    A simple data type fact represents a single value such as a person's first name. In this case, the simple fact value often has a data type such as character, number, date, or time. An example is Person First Name. An example value for the fact is George.

    Complex fact data types not only represent a structure of values but also contain a data type such as character, integer, or date for specific fact structure contained facts.

    If all the data values represented by a fact's data type are defined to be the same length, the data component represents fixed length values. If represented values are allowed to be different lengths, the data component represents variable length values.

Some complex fact data types cause values to multiply occur. In this case, the fact might be Telephone Numbers, and as such, the contained values might be for a Home Phone Number, Work Phone Number, or Cell Phone Number. In this case, the fact's data type would be an array. An example is Telephone Numbers. Value examples: 1-717-648-5913, 1-215-428-3982, 1-540-297-1297.

Some even more complex facts can have a group data type. Groups can have multiple contained facts where each can have a different data type but only a single value instance. An example is Address. The contained facts in this case might be House Street Number, Street Name, Street Type, City, State, Postal Code, and Country. A value example is: 5, South Rock, Street, Shamokin, PA, 19172, US.

There can also be groups that repeat. These fact data types are called repeating groups. Such would be the case for the fact, Employee Skills. In this example, there might be Skill Name, Skill Competence Level, and Skill Last Employed Date. A value example is: <Carpentry, Expert, 10/15/2008>, <Electrician, Expert, 10/15/2008>.

Finally, complex facts can have data types that allow nested structures. This final fact data type is called a nested repeating group. For example, there might be the Dependent First Name, Dependent Middle Name, Dependent Last Name, and Dependent Birthdate, Birth City, and Birth State. There might be for each dependent a set of addresses, telephone numbers, and skills. A value example might be: <<<Karen Elizabeth Shannahan, 4/30/1952, Philadelphia, PA, <5, South Rock ,Street, Shamokin, PA , <1-717-648-5913, 1-717-428-3982, 1-540-297-1297>, <soccer, basketball, baseball> > >.

In summary, fact data types are simple or complex. Simple fact data types represent single values such as a Person First Name. Complex fact data types represent structures of values such as Telephone Numbers (i.e., an array), Address (i.e., a group), Employee Skills (i.e., a repeating group), and Dependents with Addresses, Phones, and Skills (i.e., a nested repeating group).

Within Whitemarsh, Data Element Concepts and Data Elements from the Data Element Model are simple facts. Attributes of entities from the Specified Data Model are simple facts as well.

The Implemented Data Model conforms to the capabilities of ANSI SQL. Consequently, the fact specifications of columns of tables can be either simple or complex. Complex facts can be arrays, groups, repeating groups, and nested repeating groups. In ANSI SQL, an array is called an array. A group is called a Row Type. A repeating group is called a multi-set. A nested repeating group would be a multi-set that has a multi-set as one of its contained facts. The data types, single value, array, group, repeating group, or nested repeating group all existed in the very first DBMS of the late 1950s. It was appropriately called ADAM (Advanced Data Management).

An Operational Data Model is bound to specific DBMS. Hence, the bound DBMS can restrict their DBMS column specifications to be either simple or complex.

The View Data Model only supports simple facts. Thus, there are no view column arrays, groups, or repeating groups.

See Database Management Systems. See Database Management Systems History.

Fact Name: A Fact Name represents a shorthand definition of a fact, for example, "Date of birth," "Country of Citizenship," or "Age of Employee (years)." Fact names are present in Data Element Model's Concepts, Conceptual Value Domains, Value Domains, Data Element Concepts, and Data Elements. Fact names exist within the Specified, Implemented, Operational, and View Data models as well as attribute, column, DBMS column, and view column, respectively. Properly named, the hierarchy of names from a data element through a view column should tell an unfolding semantic story. Any wrenching breaks in the story need to be examined and corrected.

Fail Soft: Fail Soft is a type system failure that results in a gradual shut down of database activity in support of a subsequent restart.

Field: See Fact.

Field Length: See Fact.

File: A File is a collection of records known to the operating system under a single name that is accessed by a single O/S access method.

File Block: A File Block is a self-contained set of data/metadata that represents a coherent set of data from within a record of a file. For example, if a file contains personnel data, and if a record is for one employee, a file block might be the education data for the employee.

File Cell: A File Cell is a discrete item of data with well-defined semantics that occupies specific space within a record instance in a file.

FIPS: Federal Information Processing Standards.

Fixed Length Fact: See Fact.

Fixed Length Record: See Table.

Foreign Key: See Key.

Form: A Form is an organized set of business data that is input to the database application. The analysis of the form produces a mapping between the cells of data on the form and the external view columns that represent those cells to the database application.

Form Cell: A Form Cell is a specific unit of data that is to be contained on a form into which data is to be recorded.

Framework: A Framework is a two-dimensional view into a collection of objects. When Frameworks are within Information Technology, the columns are commonly major categories of the objects, and the rows are unfolding evolutions in specification of the column-based objects.
See Knowledge Worker Framework. See Zachman Framework.

Fully Functionally Dependent: Fully Functionally Dependent means that a column's value that can only be identified via the entire primary key.

Function: A Function within the Whitemarsh context is a set of activities performed by persons. The Whitemarsh relationship is that mission-organizations perform functions. Additionally, the same function may be performed by different mission-organization. Thus, there is a many-to-many relationship between mission-organization and function.

See the Mission-Organization-Function-Position-Assignment model. See Mission versus Function.

Functional Decomposition: Functional Decomposition represents a top-down division of activity into lower levels of greater detail that can become defined computer software modules.

Group: See Fact.

H2: H2 is the database languages' committee. Its official name is ANSI INCITS H2 Technical Committee on Database Languages. In July 2009, the name ANSI INCITS H2 Technical Committee on Database Languages was changed to DM32.2.

The strategy for the name change is to align two INCITS committees L8 and H2 with the corresponding two committees within the ISO SC32 WG2 and WG3. WG2 is the committee for metadata, and WG3 is for database languages. WG4 is for SQL applications such as Spatial and Text.

H2 started as X3H2 in 1978. The objective of the committee was to create a database standard from the 1978 CODASYL JOD for network data languages (NDL). That effort continued from 1978 through 1986. During the first two years, the DDL for network structures was developed. At the end of 1980, Phil Shaw, the representative from IBM proffered that a data definition language was unprovable unless it was accompanied by a DML. Len Gallagher of NIST developed a BNF-based NDL DML and presented it to the committee.

The scope of H2's charter was expanded in 1980 to standardize a relational data language (RDL). After two years of development, RDL had progressed so significantly that it was far advanced beyond any SQL DBMS that existed at that time. Since standards are to standardize "existing" practice, it was decided to remove a great deal of the RDL facilities and to create a much smaller standard. It was also renamed from RDL to SQL.

From about 1984, both the NDL and the SQL documents proceeded through the standardization bureaucracy. That included public reviews, responses to comments, and final document voting and formatting. The SQL and the NDL were both submitted to ANSI at the end of 1986.

At the time of ratification, the H2 chair was Don Deutsch (General Electric). The vice chair was Oris Friesen (Honeywell). Michael Gorman (Whitemarsh) was the secretary, and Len Gallagher (NIST) was the International Representative from ANSI to ISO. There were 35 other members of H2 at the time of the NDL and SQL ratification. Don Deutsch and Michael Gorman are the only two 1978 charter members remaining on H2.

The NDL standard was essentially finished and never proceeded to a second edition. SQL on the other hand proceeded to a 1989, 1992, 1999, 2003, and 2008 versions. What is ironic about NDL never going to a second edition is that its essential data model features have been gradually incorporated into ANSI SQL starting with SQL:1999. Tables 5 and 6 present the lineage of ANSI database standards.

ANSI committees are intended to have its membership spread across academia, industry, and government. Since 1978, the vast majority of H2 members have been from the DBMS vendor industry. There has been at most two members of academia, and fewer than a half-dozen members from the U.S. Government. There have been fewer than 10 user organizations that have been members on H2 since 1978. Whitemarsh is one of those users.

The only government agency that maintained membership for an extended period of time was NIST. Its membership lasted from 1978 through 1996. NIST (The National Institute of Standards and Technology) greatly supported database standards from 1978 through to 1996.

Starting in 1996, NIST decided to abandon participation in the development of data management standards. Industry protested greatly both directly to NIST and also to members of Congress. To justify its decision to abandon data management standards participation, NIST commissioned a study that it expected would prove that its participation had no effect on DBMS features similarity across vendors, the ability to port SQL-based applications from one SQL DBMS to another, and on a reduction in U.S. Federal Government procurement costs of DBMSs. The study however dramatically showed the opposite. During the year before the study was commissioned, the NIST's costs to create and administer SQL conformance tests cost about $600K. The benefits to agencies were $35 million in reduced procurement costs. Despite the dramatic proof of NIST's worth to data management standards and in controlling features, compatibility, and database application interoperability, NIST both resigned from H2, and abandoned the SQL conformance testing it was performing on behalf of the various U.S. Federal Government agencies .

See ANSI Database Standards. See SQL Data Language Standard. See Network Data Model.

ANSI/X3H2 Event	Year								
	78	80	82	84	86	88	90	92	94	96
Start of X3H2	X								
NDL-DDL Development	X	X	X	X					
NDL-DML Development		X	X	X					
NDL Processing				X	X				
RDL Development			X	X					
Change RDL To SQL				X					
SQL:1986 Development				X	X				
SQL:1986 Processing				X	X				
SQL Referential Integrity Revision (SQL 1989)				X	X	X			
SQL Embedded Language Std.				X	X	X			
SQL:1992 Development						X	X		
SQL:1992 Processing								X	
	78	80	82	84	86	88	90	92	94	96

Table 5. Lineage of H2 Database Language Standards – 1978 through 1996.

HASH/CALC Logical: HASH/CALC Logical is an access strategy in which the DBMS column's value is used to locate a row that has been physically stored in either primary key order or in an as-entered order. The HASH/CALC algorithm can be employed as an alternative to a hierarchically organized index or a binary tree index.

HASH/CALC Physical: HASH/CALC Physical is an access strategy in which the DBMS column's value is used by a formula to determine the physical location of the data.

When a hash routine is used to determine a physical address, the initially determined address is called the row's home address. If that space is already occupied by a rightful owner of that home address, the new row is stored elsewhere, with a pointer in the existing home record pointing to the new row (now called a synonym). When the home address is occupied by a synonym from another home address, that synonym row is displaced to another location to make room for the address's rightful owner.

ANSI/X3H2 Event	Year								
	96	98	00	02	04	06	08	10	12	14
SQL1999 Development	X	X	X							
SQL1999 Processing				X						
SQL/MM Development	X	X	X	X	X					
SQL/XML Development				X	X					
SQL/XML Processing					X					
SQL: 2003			X	X						
SQL: 2008					X	X	X			
	96	98	00	02	04	06	08	10	12	14

Table 6. Lineage of H2 Database Language Standards – 1996 through 2014.

Heuristics: Heuristics is a method of obtaining a solution through inference or trial-and-error that uses approximate methods while evaluating the progress toward an acceptable goal.

Hierarchical Data Model: A Hierarchical Data Model is a data model consisting of tree-structured tables that are hierarchically related through static relationships. Each table belonging to the hierarchy consists of simple facts. Further, each row may have multiple descendants, but only one owner row.

The row operations allowed on the hierarchy are FIND, GET, STORE, and DELETE. The relationship operations allowed are GET OWNER, GET MEMBER, GET NEXT, ADD TREE, and REMOVE TREE.

Some hierarchical DBMSs allow indexes only at the top (root segment), while others allow indexing of any or all data elements.

Hierarchical Index: A Hierarchical Index is an index that has its unique values organized into a series of levels. On each level are records of index values and the addresses (pointers) of the records of index values of the next lower level. At the lowest level, the index entries point to the rows.

Home Address: See Hash.

Host Language Interface: A Host Language Interface represents the process of incorporating data manipulation verbs into a programming language such as COBOL or Fortran. Included in the interface are the specification of data to be obtained from or placed into the database, and the specification of the mechanism for receiving messages from or sending messages to the DBMS. It is identified to the application programmer for logical and physical file manipulations. The tools are embedded in the host language (e.g., COBOL, C, or C++) and are accessed usually through CALL statements, but sometimes by extensions in the language.

Implemented Data Model: Implemented Data Models are models of databases that are independent of any particular DBMS such as Oracle or DB2. In the Whitemarsh Metabase System, Implemented Data Models can be exported to SQL DDL.

Implemented Data Models, illustrated in Figure 11 contain schema, table, column, SQL data types, primary key, primary key column, foreign key, foreign key column, candidate key, and candidate key column.

The Implemented Data Models obtain their data structures from one or more Specified Data Models, and in turn, provide these database data structures for use in the construction of DBMS specific database data models, that is, Operational Data Models.

Implemented Data Models are defined as tables, columns and relationships within schemas. Tables cannot be related across schemas. All the tables in this data model generalization level should be in at least third normal form to ensure data model clarity and quality design. There is a many-to-many relationship between an Implemented Data Model and an Operational Data Model. The reason is because a given Operational Data Model might be a data warehouse and some of its DBMS tables and columns could be drawn from multiple Implemented Data Models.

There can be relationships among the tables within one schema as well as data types, assigned value domains and other appropriate metadata for complete data models. There can also be assigned semantic modifiers, data

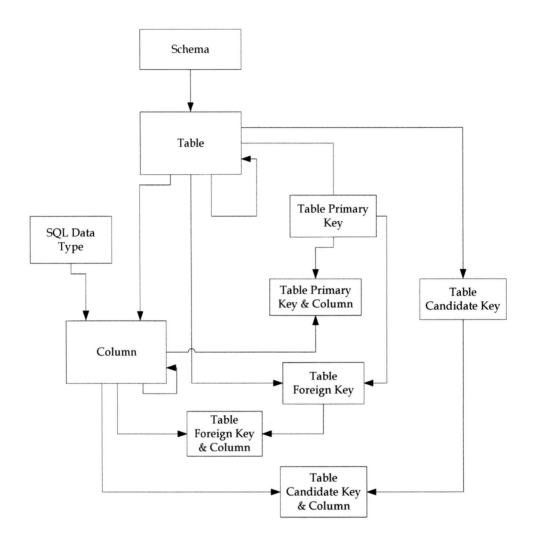

Figure 11. Implemented Data Model.

use modifiers, and value domains assigned in the Implemented Data Model. Thus, as with the Specified Data Model there can be automatic name, definition, and abbreviation construction. Because the Implemented Data Model comes from a metadata management system database, any semantic assignment conflicts between the Specified and Implemented Data Models are immediately discovered and prevented. If the semantics already assigned to attributes of entities within the Specified Data Model are sufficient, these are automatically inherited by columns of tables in the Implemented Data Model.

Each table may be constructed through the deployment of a collection of attributes from a single Specified Data Model entity, or collections of attributes from multiple Specified Data Model entities within one or more subjects. An entity or sub-collection of attributes from one entity can be used to form different data structures in multiple tables. The relationship between the Specified Data Model and the Implemented Data Model is thus, many-to-many, as it exists in real-world data modeling environments.

Tables in the Implemented Data Model can be subtyped. Columns can also be complex to support nested structures of arbitrary depth. The data types assigned to an Implemented Data Model are those allowed by the ANSI SQL standard.

Finally, because the Implemented Data Model is built from a foundation of the data models of concepts from the Specified Data Model, a complete cross reference between the two classes of models is easily reported.

Implemented Data Model Relationship: An Implemented Data Model Relationship is a relationship mechanism that relates one instance of one table to a set of instances of another table. While there are eight classes of relationships, the common ones are the one-to-many, and one-to-one. In the case of one-to-many, the relationship mechanism is the primary key columns of the "related-from" table matching the foreign key columns of the "related-to" table. The term, foreign key, comes from the fact that it's really a "copy" of the "related-from" table's primary key. Relationships should always be named and defined to the extent that the real purpose of the relationship is clear. For recursive relationships, the "related-from" table and the "related-to" table are the same.

Independent Logical File Data Model: An Independent Logical File Data Model (ILF) is a data model consisting of independently defined tables (often called files). Each table can contain simple or complex facts, enabling each of its rows to look like a hierarchy of data. Some ILF DBMSs default to having all the rows from only one file reside on one O/S file, while other ILF DBMSs default to having all rows from all the tables residing in one O/S file. Finally, some ILF DBMSs permit the mapping of a table's instances to O/S files to be defined in a physical schema definition language.

The row operations allowed in the ILF data model are FIND, GET, STORE, DELETE, and MODIFY. Relationship operations usually are limited to JOINs.

See ANSI Database Standards. See Data Models. See Database Management System History.

Index: See Key.

Inferential Relationship: An Inferential Relationship is a type of relationship between two tables, where neither relationship is dependent on the primary key of either table. A typical example is PRODUCT-CONTAINER. The basis of the relationship is the dimensions of the product and that of the container. The relationship states that a product is likely to be able to fit in the container, but does not imply that a given product is actually stored in a given container.
See Data Model.

Information: Information is data evaluated within a specific context that may be applied to solving a particular problem, or used in making a decision.

Information Engineering: Information Engineering is a broad discipline that addresses data requirements, data analysis, data architecture, data modeling, and database design. Included are all the Whitemarsh data model generalization levels, that is, Data Element Models, Specified Data Models, Implemented Data Models, Operational Data Models, and View Data Models.
See Data Model.

Information Need: An Information Need is just what its name implies, a need for information. It should however be formal enough to represent some significant IT assets such as a quarterly financial report, the current state of inventory, an order, and the like. Information needs are created through analysis and are characterized.
Information needs are ultimately allocated to Resource Life Cycle Nodes. That is, a database and/or an information system required by a resource life cycle node to produce an information need that, in turn, fulfills the need of some functional area of an organization that is accomplishing a mission of the enterprise

Information needs are both typed and characterized. While it would not be common, it certainly would be within the scope of an information need to be a data mart that is processed by OLAP (online analysis processing software).

See Information Needs Analysis Model.

Information Need Analysis Model: The information need analysis model is a collection of database tables within the Whitemarsh Metabase System. The data model for the information needs analysis model is presented in Figure 12. The information need analysis model enables the recording of the information (a.k.a. query results or reports) needed by various organizations in their functional accomplishment of missions and what databases and information systems provide this information.

The tables in the information need analysis model includes the information needs, information need types, rankings, mission-organization-function-ranked-information-needs, characteristics, characteristic types, and information need characteristic assignments.

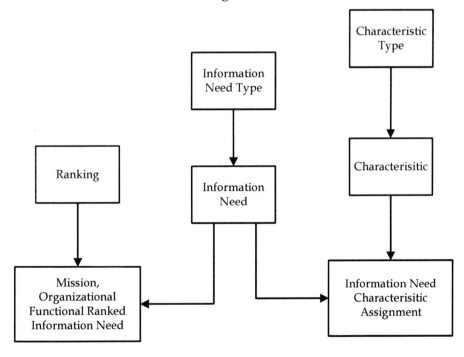

Figure 12. Information Needs Analysis Model.

Data Management's Concepts & Terms

Information Need Characteristic Assignment: An Information Need Characteristic Assignment is the assignment of the characteristic to the information need. For example, if the information need was a Financial Report, it might be quarterly, hard-copy, and summary.
   See Information Needs Analysis Model.

Information Need Type: An Information Need Type is a classification of an information need. This may be according to functional area such as finance, administration, sales, etc., or may be some other information need grouping.
   See Information Needs Analysis Model.

Information Resource Management: See Data Administration.

Insertion: An Insertion is the process whereby a row is added to a database. For Network Data Model DBMSs row insertion often involves the automatic adjustment of next, prior, and other pointers. There are three modes of insertion in the ANSI/NDL Data Language Standard, Automatic, Structural, or Manual. If Automatic, the DBMS automatically connects the row to all sets for which it is defined as a member. For Structural, the row is connected to the owner if and only if the identified field value specified in the member matches the identified field value in the member. If Manual, the row merely becomes a part of the database without being connected to any database set. The membership is established only through the use of the DML verb Connect.

Installation and Maintenance: Installation and Maintenance activities relate to the actual installation of the DBMS at a computer center. These activities begin with an installation survey, software delivery, system generation, test database installation, problem resolution, and on-going DBMS patches and new release installation and testing.

Instance: An Instance is a set of values representing a specific occurrence, for example, a database object class, table, or column.

Integrity: Integrity is a state of database consistency.

Integrity Constraints (DBMS Enforced): Integrity Constraints (DBMS Enforced) are constraints on data values and their relationships.

Internal Schema: See DBMS Schema.

Interrogation: Interrogation is the process of accessing column values from the database through a user schema interface via any one of a number of different interrogation languages.
See also Host Language Interfaces (HLI). See Natural Language.

Inverted Access: Inverted Access is a term that indicates a mode of processing that is the inverse (inverted) to that of traditional data processing. Traditional data processing locates and acquires contexts (rows) and discovers column values. The inverted approach discovers rows based on the values of one or more columns. That is, from value to context, rather than from context to value.
See Database Management System History.

ISO: International Standards Organization.

Job Title: A Job Title is the name assigned to the overall set of activities that are performed. An example is Functional Data Administrator.
See Project Management Model.

Join: A Join is an operation that takes two tables as operandi and produces a new table by concatenating the rows by matching the values of the columns stated to be the basis of the join. While the columns of values must be JOINable (same domain) the column names must not be required to be the same.

Journal File: A Journal File is a computer file that stores rows that can be used to restore a database subsequent to a failure. In some DBMSs, these rows are before and after images of DBMS record instances that result from updates. In other DBMSs these rows contain a highly condensed version of the update.

Justify: Justify is a process that adjusts the value representation in a nonnumeric field to the right or left boundary (i.e., margin) ignoring blanks at the front or back.

Keeplist: A Keeplist is a sequence of database keys maintained by the DBMS for the duration of the session associated with its creating module and referenced by data manipulation language statements.

Key: A Key is a table column or a designated collection of columns that can be employed by a specially constructed "Where clause" of the DBMS to locate one or more rows. In SQL:1986 through SQL:1992, all columns are simple facts and can be part of a key. In SQL:1999 and more recent, only simple fact columns can participate in a key. In general the four types of keys are primary, candidate, foreign, and secondary.

A primary key is the designation of one or more columns that can be used to locate one row. Traditionally, the value set of a primary key is unique across all instances of a row. In the event a DBMS does not provide for the enforcement of uniqueness, there is no semantic difference between primary and secondary keys. The ANSI SQL standard does not require unique primary keys.

A candidate key is the designation of one or more columns that can be used to locate one row. The candidate key is not the primary key, by decision of the data analysts. Candidate keys not chosen as the primary key for a table also known as alternate keys. A candidate key column cannot be a column within that table's primary key.

A foreign key is the designation of one or more columns within one table that is the primary key of another table. If the relationship is recursive, the primary key table and the foreign key table are the same. The purpose of a foreign key is to represent a relationship between two rows and to imply automatic actions whenever data value changes occur on the foreign key's value. A foreign key column cannot be a column within that table's primary key.

A secondary key is the designation of one or more columns within one table whose values are not required to be unique across the set of rows for which it is a key. If the DBMS enables the imposition of uniqueness on a secondary key, there is no semantic difference between a secondary key and a candidate or primary key.

Key Value: The actual contents of a key at a given time.

Knowledge Worker Framework: The Knowledge Worker Framework is an overarching framework within which all the work products key to the development of business information systems are organized and categorized. The Knowledge Worker Framework provides a well-ordered column and row structure, along with work product integration, non-redundancy and inter-cell relationships. This enables a do-once, use many times environment saves time, money and promotes understanding and exchange.

The Knowledge Worker Framework columns are: Mission, Database Object, Business Information System, Business Event, Business Function, and Business Organization. Each of these Knowledge Worker Framework columns is defined within this book. Additionally, the Whitemarsh metadata management system, Metabase System, is engineered to capture the Knowledge Worker Framework implied metadata.

The rows in the Knowledge Worker Framework are the same as from the Zachman Framework, that is, Scope, Business, System, Technology, Deployment, and Operations.

The Knowledge Worker Framework metadata is exchangeable between Knowledgeable Framework instances. That is because the Knowledge Worker Framework is implemented through the Whitemarsh Metabase System. It is thus precise, specialized to databases and business information systems, and exchangeable.

Language: A Language is a set of characters, conventions, and rules that is used for conveying information. The aspects of language are pragmatics, grammar, semantics, and syntax.

Line: A Line is a term used to identify a specific telecommunications link.

List: See Collection Data Type.

List Processing: List Processing implies AND or ORing lists of row identifiers (usually DBKEYs) together. Each list of DBKEYs is most often created as a consequence of a select statement, e.g., Select Employees Where Degree EQ PhD AND Jobcode EQ Engineer. In this example, the two lists are the DBKEYs from the select Degree EQ PhD, and those from Jobcode EQ Engineer. These two lists of DBKEYs are ANDed together to find the set of rows that qualify. In this case, it would only be the employees that possessed both the PhD and also the JobCode of Engineer. In contrast, if the operator was OR instead of AND, the final list would be all employees who had a PhD or who had the JobCode of Engineer.

In short, if the two lists are "OR'ed" all the unique items from both lists are kept on the final lists. If the two lists are "AND'ed" only the items in common from each list are kept on the final list.

When the columns are from tables that are not the same, but are relatable, a normalization process must occur. That is, raise or lower one set of DBKEYs from one level to the other. Static relationship DBMSs that accomplish this, in the case of downward normalization, do so by utilizing the GET MEMBER operation with the pointers from the parent DBKEYs to determine the DBKEYs of the members of the selected OWNERs. Since the two sets of DBKEYS relate to rows from the same table, the lists are able to be ANDed. Upward normalization works the opposite.

List processing DBMSs typically allow other Boolean operations (AND, OR, NOT), relational operations (LT, LE, EQ, NE, GE, GT), and parentheses.

Load (Data): Load is a term that represents the process of taking data that is outside the database and bringing it into the data component of the storage structure. Included in data loading are all other processes necessary to build indexes, relationships (static only) and all other necessary components of the storage structure. A database is loaded when all these activities have been successfully accomplished. The loading process may be accomplished through a single DBMS command or a series of separate job steps.

A database unload is the process of returning data back to a DBMS independent format on some storage media for possible transport to another computer, or DBMS, or for use by another access method.

Lock: A Lock represents the situation that prevails when one run-unit program is granted exclusive access to rows, and all the other run-units must wait until the first program releases the lock. The lock may be, depending on the DBMS, at the row, the DBMS record instance, area instance, O/S file instance, or database instance level. Additionally, the run-unit can be in HLI, or any of the natural languages. Finally, certain DBMS functions may cause a lock, for example, logical database reorganization.

Log File: See Journal File.

Logging: Logging represents the process of writing log records.

Logical Data Model: A Logical Data Model is a data model that is independent of any particular DBMS. Each logical data model has a schema, a collection of tables that are related one to the other via primary and foreign keys. Each column has a data type and may be further constrained by restricted value clauses. Most logical data models exist in Third Normal Form and do not contain nested table and/or nested column data structures that are defined within the ISO/ANSI SQL standard.

See Implemented Data Model for an explanation of Whitemarsh's analogous data model generalization level and for an understanding of the key differences.

Logical File: See Table.

Logical Record Facility: See View.

Logical Reorganization: Logical Reorganization is the DBMS process of making changes to the DBMS schema of the database through the addition, deletion or modification of DBMS columns, DBMS tables or inter-table relationship types (static only) contained within the current DBMS schema. Logical reorganization often automatically invokes physical (database) reorganization, to some extent.

Logical User View: See View.

Management Level: Management Level is a named and defined level of bureaucratic management within an organizational setting. Examples could be executive, senior, mid-level, and first-level.

See Business Information Systems Model.

Many-to-Many Relationship: A Many-to-Many Relationship is a type of relationship whereby an owner table can have one of its rows relate to one or more rows of a second table. The second table would be serving in the role of a member table. At the same time, one of the member rows, now serving in the role of an owner, can relate to one or more member rows of the table that was formerly serving in the role of an owner table.

A typical example for the many-to-many relationship is Department-Buildings. A Department may be located in more than one

Building, while at the same time a Building may have multiple Departments located within it.

Some DBMSs allow many-to-many relationships to be implemented directly by having the pointed-to identifier of the related rows stored in the pointed-from table. The "pointer" column would be an array complex fact. Other DBMSs can enable many-to-many relationships only indirectly. That is, by having a common associative table such as Department-Building in which the primary key of Department and the primary key of the Building are stored as a concatenated primary key.

Member: A Member is a term that represents a row that is owned by another row of the same or different table in a CODASYL, ANSI NDL, or hierarchical data model DBMS. SQL-based DBMSs often employ the term, member, for the foreign key table of a primary-foreign key relationship. Data modeling also employs the term, member, for relationship specifications.

Membership Rationale: Membership Rationale is a classification of the reasons why a table belongs to a database object as evidenced through the database object table.

Message Processing: Message Processing is a process of the DBMS in which information about the status of a command, the database and the DBMS is provided to the run-unit or the process that is currently accessing the DBMS.

Messages: Messages are text statements that are able to be provided to users through various languages.

Meta Category Value Type: Meta Category Value Types are collections of categories in which meta category values reside. For example, the meta category value type, precision, might contain the meta category values: approximate, estimated, and final. A meta category value type enables the same meta category value to have different contextual definitions within different meta category value types.

See Data Element Model.

Meta Category Value Type Classification: Meta Category Value Type Classifications are broad classifications of the meta category value types and in turn, meta category values. There are two: prefix and suffix.

The prefix meta category value type classification causes all assigned meta category values to appear before the common business name of the data component (i.e., data element concept, data element, attribute, or column). Essentially, prefix semantics serve as a collection of meaning "modifiers" that amend the base meaning of the fact.

The suffix meta category value type classification causes all assigned meta category values to appear after the common business name of the data element. Essentially, suffix semantics serve as a collection of "class words" that characterize the intended use or type of value of the fact. Suffix meta category value types typically include: units, and use type.

See Data Element Model.

Meta Category Values: Meta Category Values are words or phrases that have a specific and controlled meaning in the enterprise. Meta Category Values are the individual semantics assigned to data components in support of the complete semantic specification of the data component. Meta category values are collections within meta category value types. Meta category value collections can be hierarchically organized.

A specifically assigned meta category value becomes an explicit part of a data component's name. These words/phrases are either prefixed to the common business name of a data component, or suffixed to its common business name. In the case of the former, these are semantic modifiers, and in the case of the later, they are data use modifiers. An example of semantic modifiers is geography such as United States, New England, Rhode Island, and Providence.

There can be other classes of semantic modifiers including for example, temporal, or precision. Only one semantic modifier of each class can be assigned. Data use modifiers are for example, data type or role. Only one data use modifier of each class can be assigned. Assignments are always checked to ensure that proper semantic nesting is enforced.

See Data Element Model.

Meta Language: A Meta Language is a language used to specify itself, or another language. The specification of the ANSI NDL and the ANSI SQL is in a BNF format meta language.

See Backus Naur Form (BNF).

Metabase System Business Event Process

Accomplish Business Information System Database Object Assignments: This process assigns various business information systems to database objects.

Accomplish Business Information System View Assignment: This process assigns various views to business information systems and categorizes each view to be either an input view or an output view.

Create, Modify or Delete Application Types: This process creates an application type that is employed to distinguish different business information systems.

Create, Modify or Delete Business Event Cycle Structure Types: This process creates various classifications of business event cycles used to identify specific collections of records in Business Event Cycle Structures.

Create, Modify or Delete Business Event Cycle Structures: This process creates specific instances of assemblies of business event cycles.

Create, Modify or Delete Business Information System: This process creates the name and specification of a business information system. Business information systems may be hierarchically organized.

Create, Modify or Delete Business Events: This process creates specific business events and represents their associated business functions and business information systems as well as associating business events within proper business event cycles and business event calendars.

Create, Modify or Delete Business Event Cycle: This process creates specific instances of business event cycles that are gathered into assemblies for use in properly representing business events. Examples include: End of School cycle, Back to School Cycle, Vacation Cycle, and a Holiday Cycle.

Create, Modify or Delete Business Information System Level: This process creates a level-based classification schema for categorizing business information systems. This level is assigned to each business information system.

Create, Modify or Delete Business Information System View Role: This process causes the creation, modification, and/or deletion of a particular input or output role to a business information system view role.

Create, Modify or Delete Calendar Cycle Structures: This process creates specific instances of assemblies of business event calendar cycles.

Create, Modify or Delete Calendar Cycle: This process creates specific instances of business event calendar cycles that are gathered into assemblies for use in properly representing business events.

Create, Modify or Delete Calendar Cycle Structure Types: This process creates various classifications of business event cycles that are used to identify specific collections of records in Business Event Calendar Cycle Structures.

Create, Modify or Delete DBMS Environment Types: This process creates a DBMS Environment type that is employed to distinguish different business information systems.

Create, Modify or Delete Predominant User Type: This process creates a predominant user type that is employed to distinguish different business information systems.

Create, Modify or Delete [Application] Environment Types: This process creates an application environment type that is employed to distinguish different business information systems.

Metabase System Business Term Process

Accomplish Business Term Assignment: This process assigns a business term to one or more contexts.

Accomplish Business Term Interrelationship: This process creates interrelationships among business terms.

Create Business Term from a Candidate Business Term: This process creates an instance of a business term from a candidate business term that is found by the discovery process.

Create, Modify, or Delete Business Term: This process creates an instance of a business term that can be assigned to wherever it is used.

Discover Business Terms: This process "reads" definitions, descriptions, and names that have been constructed in the metadata across all the metadata models and offers candidates for business terms from an existing set of business terms.

Metabase System Concept Process

Accomplish Data Element Concepts to Concept Reassignments: This process causes a change in the existing assignment of one or more data element concepts to one concept.

Accomplish Data Elements to a Compound Data Element Assignments: This process assigns one or more data elements to a compound data element.

Create, Modify or Delete Concept Structure Types: This process creates various classifications of concepts that are used to identify specific collections of records in concept structures.

Create, Modify or Delete Concept Structures: This process creates specific instances of assemblies of concepts.

Create, Modify or Delete Concepts: This process creates an instance of concept

Metabase System Conceptual Value Domain Process

Accomplish Data Element Concepts to Conceptual Value Domain Reassignments: This process causes a change in the existing assignment of one or more data element concepts to one conceptual value domain.

Accomplish Value Domain to Conceptual Value Domain Reassignments: This process enables the reassignment of value domains to a conceptual value domain. Only one value domain is allowed to be assigned. As a value domain is assigned if there are any value domains already assigned to a descendant data element concept, data element, attribute, column, or DBMS column, the assigned value domains are evaluated to ensure that there are no conflicts.

Create, Modify or Delete Conceptual Value Domain Structure Types: This process creates various classifications of conceptual value domains that are used to identify specific collections of records in conceptual value domain structures.

Create, Modify or Delete Conceptual Value Domains: This process creates a conceptual value domain.

Create, Modify or Delete Conceptual Value Domain Structures: This process creates specific instances of assemblies of conceptual value domains.

Accomplish Data Element Classifications to Data Element Assignments: This process assigns one or more data element classifications to a data element.

Metabase System Data Element Classification Process

Create, Modify or Delete Data Element Classification Structure Types: This process creates various classifications of data element classifications that are used to identify specific collections of records in data element classification structures.

Create, Modify or Delete Data Element Classification Structures: This process creates specific instances of assemblies of data element classifications.

Create, Modify or Delete Data Element Classification: This process creates a data element classification.

Metabase System Data Element Process

Accomplish Data Element Classifications to Data Element Assignments: This process assigns one or more data element classifications to a data element.

Accomplish Data Element Concepts to Concept Reassignments: This process causes a change in the existing assignment of one or more data element concepts to one concept.

Accomplish Data Element Concepts to Conceptual Value Domain Reassignments: This process causes a change in the existing assignment of one or more data element concepts to one conceptual value domain.

Accomplish Data Elements to a Compound Data Element Assignments: This process assigns one or more data elements to a compound data element.

Accomplish Data Elements to Business Domain Reassignments: This process causes a change in the existing assignment of one or more data elements to one business domain.

Accomplish Data Elements to Data Element Concept Reassignments: This process causes a change in the existing assignment of one or more data elements to one data element concept.

Accomplish Data Elements to Value Domains Reassignments: This process enables the reassignment of value domains to a data element. Only one value domain is allowed to be assigned. As a value domain is assigned, if there are any value domains already assigned to a parent data element concept, or a descendant, attribute, column, or DBMS column, the assigned value domains are evaluated to ensure that there are no conflicts.

Accomplish Derived Data Elements to Compound Data Element Assignments: This process assigns one or more derived data elements to a compound data element.

Accomplish Derived Data Elements to Data Element Assignments: This process assigns one or more data elements to a derived data element.

Create, Modify or Delete Compound Data Element Structures: This process creates specific instances of assemblies of compound data elements.

Create, Modify or Delete Compound Data Element Structure Types: This process creates various classifications of compound data elements that are used to identify specific collections of records in compound data element structures.

Create, Modify or Delete Compound Data Elements: This process creates a compound data element that serves as the collective for the assigned data elements.

Create, Modify or Delete Data Element Classification: This process creates a data element classification.

Create, Modify or Delete Data Element Classification Structures: This process creates specific instances of assemblies of data element classifications.

Create, Modify or Delete Data Element Classification Structure Types: This process creates various types of data element classification structures that are used to identify specific collections of records in data element classification structures.

Create, Modify or Delete Data Element Concept: This process creates a specific instance of a data element concept.

Create, Modify or Delete Data Element Concept Structures: This process creates specific instances of assemblies of data element concepts.

Create, Modify or Delete Data Element Concept Structure Types: This process creates various classifications of data element concepts that are used to identify specific collections of records in data element concept structures.

Create, Modify or Delete Data Elements: This process creates a data element.

Create, Modify or Delete Derived Data Elements: This process creates a derived data element.

Promote Data Element Concept to Concept: This process promotes a data element concept to be a concept. The existing data element concept is related to the newly created concept.

Promote Data Element to Data Element Concept: This process promotes a data element to be a data element concept. The meta category values and value domains are removed from the data element and allocated to the newly created data element concept. The data element concept is assigned to the "unknown" conceptual value domain and the "unknown" concept.

Reallocate Business Domains: This process causes a change in the existing allocation of one or more business domains to a different business domain.

Remove Data Element Concept Meta Category Value Assignments: This process removes the meta category value assignments from a data element concept.

Metabase System Data Integrity Rule Process

Accomplish Data Integrity Rule Assignment: This process assigns a data integrity rule to one or more contexts.

Accomplish Data Integrity Rule Interrelationship: This process creates interrelationships among data integrity rules.

Create, Modify, or Delete Data Integrity Rule: This process creates an instance of a data integrity that can be assigned to wherever it is used.

Metabase System Database Domain Process

Create, Modify, or Delete Database Domain and Database Object Association: This process creates an association between a database domain and a database object.

Create, Modify, or Delete Database Domain: Select a particular mission leaf and create a database domain corresponding to the "noun-story" that is implied by the mission leaf.

Reallocate Database Domains: This process reallocates a database domain within a database domain hierarchy to a different database domain.

Metabase System Database Object Process

Accomplish Database Object Information Systems to Database Object Table Process Assignment: This process causes an assignment of one or more database object table processes to a database object information system.

Accomplish Database Object Information Systems to Database Object Table Process Reassignment: This process causes a change in the existing assignment of one or more database object table processes to a one database object information system.

Accomplish Database Object State to Database Object Information System Assignments: This process causes an assignment of one or more database object information systems to a database object state.

Accomplish Database Object State to Database Object Information System Reassignment: This process causes a change in the existing assignment of one or more database object information systems to one database object state.

Accomplish Database Object Table Process to Column Reassignment: This process causes a change in the existing assignment of one or more database object table columns to one database object table process.

Accomplish Database Object Table Process to Column Assignment: This process causes an assignment of one or more database object table columns to one database object table process.

Accomplish Database Object to Database Domain Reassignment: This process causes a change in the existing assignment of one or more database objects to one database domain.

Accomplish Database Object to Schema Reassignment: This process causes a change in the existing assignment of one or more database objects to one schema.

Accomplish Database Object to Table Reassignments: This process causes a change in the existing assignment of one or more tables to one database object.

Create, Modify or Delete Database Object Information Systems: This process creates a database object information system within the scope of a database object.

Create, Modify or Delete Database Object Table Assignment: This process creates one or more database object tables, that is, one or more tables assigned to a database object. All the tables that are assigned to be in a database object must be within the same schema as the database object.

Create, Modify or Delete Database Object: This process creates a database object within the scope of a schema.

Create, Modify or Delete Database Object Table Membership Rationale: This process creates a database object table membership process that is employed to identify collections of database object tables within a database object according to their membership rationale.

Create, Modify or Delete Database Object Table Process: This process creates a database object table process within the scope of a database object table.

Create, Modify or Delete Database Object State: This process creates a database object state within the scope of a database object.

Metabase System Environment: The Metabase System environment is a metadata database surrounded by a metadata management system that is able to be used by knowledge workers as they accomplish all phases of their requirements development, business information system generation, and maintenance tasks. The Metabase System environment is a combination of the features from Computer Aided Systems Engineering (CASE) systems, and metadata management systems. A quality Metabase System can be employed by whole teams and organizations. It enables databases and business information systems to be integrated, non-redundant, and based on harmonious semantics across all their project domains. The Metabase System environment contributes to the effort by ensuring that there are minimal redundancy definition and maximal reuse of all Knowledge Worker Framework work products.

Metabase System Function Process

Accomplish Mission-organization and Function Assignments: This process assigns one or more functions to pairs of mission-organizations.

Create, Modify or Delete Functions: This process creates a function.

Reallocate Functions: This process reallocates a function within a function hierarchy to a different function of the same or different function hierarchy.

Metabase System Implemented Data Model Process

Accomplish Assign Columns to Column Reassignments: This process causes a change in the existing assignment of one or more columns to one column.

Accomplish Assign Columns to Data Elements Reassignments: This process causes a change in the existing assignment of one or more columns to one data element.

Accomplish Assign Columns to SQL Data Types Reassignments: This process causes a change in the existing assignment of one or more column's SQL data type to a different SQL data type.

Accomplish Assign Columns to Attribute Reassignments: This process causes a change in the existing assignment of one or more columns to one attribute. If there is a conflict between the data element that is already assigned to the column and the data element assigned to the attribute, the column is assigned to the unknown data element.

Accomplish Columns to Table Reassignments: This process causes a change in the existing assignment of one or more columns to a different table. If the column is part of any type of key, the reassignment is rejected.

Accomplish Tables to Schema Reassignments: This process causes a change in the existing assignment of one or more tables to one Schema.

Accomplish Tables to Tables Reassignments: This process causes a change in the sub/super type relationship among tables within a given schema.

Create Many Columns: This process causes the creation of many columns by tagging one data element and a set of tables. As each column is created, it is assigned to the table and also to the data element upon which its semantics is based. The column is also assigned to the "unknown" attribute.

Create, Modify or Delete Allocation of Columns to the Candidate Key: This process allocates one or more columns to a candidate key.

Create, Modify or Delete Allocation of Columns to the Primary Key: This process allocates one or more columns to a primary key.

Create, Modify or Delete Candidate Key: This process creates a candidate key within a specific table. A sub-table cannot have a candidate key.

Create, Modify or Delete Tables: This process creates, modifies or deletes a table including all its columns, primary keys, and any contained foreign keys.

Create, Modify or Delete Foreign Keys: This process creates a foreign key. The target table is identified, then the source primary key is identified. Then the referential actions and other SQL necessary information are entered. The foreign key name is automatically created and consists of the parent table name, must/may depending on chosen referential actions, an action word, and the child table name.

Create, Modify or Delete Primary Key: This process creates a primary key within a specific table. A sub-table cannot have a primary key.

Create, Modify or Delete Schema: This process creates a schema.

Create One Column: This process causes the creation of one column by tagging one data element and one table. As the column is created, it is assigned to the table and also to the data element upon which its semantics is based.

Create SQL Data Types: This process creates an SQL data type and enables it to be related to a value domain data type.

Export SQL DDL: This process traverses the complete set of tables, columns, and keys for a given schema and formulates a set of SQL DDL that completely represents the schema-based data model.

Import Attribute from Specified Data Model: This process causes the importation of a single attribute of an entity from a subject in the Specified Data Model to be imported into a table of a schema of the Implemented Data Model.

Import Entity Set from Specified Data Model: This process imports a set of entities from the Specified Data Model that are associated with one subject. All associated keys and columns are made. Relationships from the newly created table to the Specified Data Model entities are also created.

Import Entity Tree from Specified Data Model: This process imports a set of interrelated entities from the Specified Data Model. All associated keys and columns are made. Relationships from the newly created table to the Specified Data Model entities are also created.

Import SQL DDL: This process imports a full stream of SQL DDL and creates a full set of tables, columns, and keys for the selected schema.

Maintain Column Meta Category Values: This process enables the allocation of meta category values to a column. Only one meta category value from each meta category value type is allowed to be assigned. As a meta category value is assigned, if there are any meta category values already assigned either to a parent data element, attribute, or data element concept, the assigned meta category values are evaluated to ensure that there are no semantic conflicts.

Maintain Column Value Domains: This process enables the allocation of value domains to a column. Only one value domain is allowed to be assigned. As a value domain is assigned, if there are any value domains already assigned either to a parent attribute, or a data element, or to the data element parent's data element concept, or to a descendant DBMS column, the assigned column value domains are evaluated to ensure that there are no value domain hierarchy conflicts.

Maintain Columns: This process provides update support for a column.

Promote Column to Attribute: This process promotes a column to be an attribute. The meta category values and value domains are removed from the column and are allocated to the newly created attribute.

Promote Column to Data Element: This process promotes a column to be a data element. The meta category values and value domains are removed from the column and are allocated to the newly created data element. The data element is assigned to the "unknown" conceptual value domain and the "unknown" data element concept.

Promote Implemented Data Model Table to Specified Data Model Entity: This process promotes an Implemented Data Model table to be a Specified Data Model entity within an existing subject. Created are all the associated attributes and as appropriate primary keys, and candidate keys. Relationships between the newly create Specified Data Model entity attributes and the Implemented Data Model table columns are automatically created.

Promote Implemented Data Model to Specified Data Model: This process promotes an entire Implemented Data Model to be a Specified Data Model. Created is the subject (from the schema), all entities, attributes and all keys. Relationships between the newly create Specified Data Model entity attributes and the Implemented Data Model table columns are automatically created.

Remove Column Attribute Assignments: This process removes the relationships between a complete set of columns of a table and their corresponding attributes.

Remove Column Data Element Assignments: This process removes the relationships between a complete set of columns of a table and its corresponding data element.

Remove Column Meta Category Values: This process removes meta category value assignments from a column.

Report Column Data Hierarchies: This process reports a column, its associated data element, data element concept, conceptual value domain and concept, as well as its associated DBMS columns. For each appropriate subject, entity, schema, table, DBMS schema, and DBMS table are also shown.

Synchronize Local Columns Definitions: This process enables the synchronization of a set of local definitions associated with a column to each other.

Metabase System Information Needs Analysis Process

Accomplish Mission-Organization-Function Ranked Information Need Assignment: This process assigns one or more information needs to a mission-organization-function. The process then allows the assignment of a particular rank to the mission-organization-function information need.

Create, Modify or Delete Information Need Type: This process creates an instance of an information need type that can be used to classify collections information needs.

Create, Modify or Delete Ranking: This process creates an instance of ranking that can be used to classify collections of mission-organization-function information-needs.

Create, Modify or Delete Information Need: This process creates an instance of an information need within a given information need type.

Create, Modify or Delete Characteristic: This process creates an instance of a characteristic within a given characteristic type.

Create, Modify or Delete Association Between Information Need and Characteristic: This process creates an association between an Information need and a particular Characteristic.

Create, Modify or Delete Characteristic Type: This process creates an instance of a Characteristic Type that can be used to classify collections of characteristics which, in turn, can be used to categorize information needs.

Data Management's Concepts & Terms

Metabase System Information Systems Plan Process

Accomplish Association Between Business Information System and Database Object Information System: This process creates an association between an information system and a database object information system.

Accomplish Association Between Business Information System and Business Event: This process creates an association between an information system and a business event.

Accomplish Association Between Business Information System and Resource Life Cycle Node: This process creates an association between an information system and a resource life cycle node.

Accomplish Association Between Business Information System and View: This process creates an association between an information system and a view.

Create, Modify or Delete Application Types: This process creates a characteristic of an information system, Application Types, that can be used to classify collections of business information systems. Examples are management information systems, operational control systems, etc.

Create, Modify or Delete Business Information System Levels: This process creates a characteristic of an information system, Level, that can be used to classify collections of business information systems. Examples are control, management, and operational.

Create, Modify or Delete Business Information System: This process creates a business information system.

Create, Modify or Delete Construction Methods: This process creates a characteristic of an information system, Construction Method, that can be used to classify collections of business information systems. Examples are custom, code generator, or COTS (commercial off the shelf).

Create, Modify or Delete DBMS Environment: This process creates a characteristic of an information system, DBMS Environment, that can be used to classify collections of business information systems. Examples are Single brand, Multi-brand.

Create, Modify or Delete Environment Type: This process creates a characteristic of an information system, Environment Type, that can be used to classify collections of business information systems. Examples are mainframe, server, or desktop.

Create, Modify or Delete Predominant User Class: This process creates a characteristic of an information system, Predominant User Class, that can be used to classify collections of business information systems. Examples are Executive, middle management, and line management.

Create, Modify or Delete Programming Language: This process creates a characteristic of an information system, Programming Language, that can be used to classify collections of business information systems. Examples are COBOL, Fortran, 4GL, or some other programming language environment.

Create, Modify or Delete Status: This process creates a characteristic of an information system, Status, that can be used to classify collections of business information systems. Examples are development, maintenance, and production.

Metabase System Meta Category Value Process

Create, Modify or Delete Data Element Meta Category Values: This process enables the allocation of meta category values to a data element. Only one meta category value from each meta category value type is allowed to be assigned. As a meta category value is assigned, if there are any meta category values already assigned either to a parent data element concept, or to a descendant attribute or column, the assigned meta category values are evaluated to ensure that there are no semantic conflicts.

Create, Modify or Delete Data Element Concept Meta Category Values: This process enables the allocation of meta category values to a data element concept. Only one meta category value from each meta category value type is allowed to be assigned. As a meta category value is assigned, if there are any meta category values already assigned to a descendant data element, attribute, or column, the assigned meta category values are evaluated to ensure that there are no semantic conflicts.

Create, Modify or Delete Meta Category Value: This process creates a meta category value.

Reallocate Meta Category Value Types: This process causes a change in the existing allocation of one or more meta category value types to a different meta category value type.

Reallocate Meta Category Values: This process causes a change in the existing allocation of one or more meta category values to a different meta category value.

Remove Data Element Concept Meta Category Value Assignments: This process removes the meta category value assignments from a data element concept.

Remove Data Element Meta Category Value Assignments: This process removes the meta category value assignments from a data element.

Metabase System Meta Category Value Process

Create, Modify or Delete Meta Category Value Type: This process creates a meta category value type.

Create, Modify or Delete Meta Category Value Type Class: This process creates a meta category value type class.

Metabase System Mission Process

Create, Modify or Delete Missions: This process creates a mission and as appropriate, a subordinate mission within an existing mission.

Reallocate Missions: This process reallocates a mission within a mission hierarchy to a different mission.

Metabase System Operational Data Model Process

Accomplish DBMS Column to DBMS Table Reassignment: This process reassigns a DBMS column from one DBMS table to another.

Accomplish DBMS Columns to DBMS Data Type Reassignment: This process causes a change in the existing assignment of a DBMS column's data type to a different DBMS data type.

Accomplish DBMS Columns to DBMS Column Reassignment: This process causes a change in the existing assignment of one or more DBMS columns to one DBMS column.

Accomplish DBMS Tables to DBMS Schema Reassignment: This process causes a change in the existing assignment of a DBMS table from one DBMS schema to another DBMS Schema.

Accomplish DBMS Tables to DBMS Table Reassignment: This process causes a change in the sub/super type relationship among DBMS tables within a given DBMS schema. If a DBMS table's primary key is a foreign key in another table, then the DBMS table cannot be reassigned.

Allocate DBMS Columns to the Candidate key: This process assigns one or more columns to a candidate key.

Allocate DBMS Columns to the Primary Key: This process assigns one or more columns to a primary key.

Allocate DBMS Columns to the Secondary Key: This process assigns one or more columns to a secondary key.

Create DBMS Columns: This process creates a DBMS column.

Create, Modify or Delete Candidate Key: This process creates a candidate key.

Create, Modify or Delete Primary Key: This process creates a primary key.

Create, Modify or Delete Secondary Key: This process creates a secondary key.

Create, Modify or Delete Foreign Keys: This process creates a foreign key. The target DBMS table is identified and the source primary key is identified. Then the referential actions and other SQL necessary information are entered. The foreign key name is automatically created and consists of the parent DBMS table name, must/may depending on chosen referential actions, an action word, and the child DBMS table name.

Create, Modify or Delete DBMS Table Candidate Key: This process creates a candidate key.

Create, Modify or Delete DBMS Tables Primary Key: This process creates a primary key.

Export SQL DDL: This process traverses the complete set of DBMS tables, DBMS columns, and keys for a given DBMS schema and formulates a set of SQL DDL that completely represents the DBMS schema-based data model.

Import Column from Implemented Data Model: This process causes the importation of a single column of a table from a schema in the Implemented Data Model to be imported into a DBMS table of a DBMS schema of the Operational Data Model.

Import SQL DDL: This process imports a full stream of SQL DDL and creates a full set of DBMS tables, DBMS columns, and keys for the selected DBMS schema.

Import Table Set from Implemented Data Model: This process imports a set of tables from the Implemented Data Model that are associated with one schema. All associated keys and DBMS columns are made. Relationships from the newly created DBMS table are automatically created back to the Implemented Data Model tables.

Import Table Tree from Implemented Data Model: This process imports a set of interrelated tables from the Implemented Data Model. All associated keys and DBMS columns are made. Relationships from the newly created DBMS tables to the Implemented Data Model tables are also created.

Maintain DBMS Column Value Domains: This process enables the allocation of a value domain to a DBMS column. Only one value domain is allowed to be assigned. As a value domain is assigned, if there are any value domains already assigned either to a parent column, a data element, data element parent data element concept, the assigned value domains are evaluated to ensure that there are no value domain hierarchy conflicts.

Promote DBMS Table Column to Implemented Data Model: This process promotes a DBMS column to be an Implemented Data Model table column. The meta category values and value domains are removed from the DBMS Column and allocated to the newly created column.

Promote DBMS Table to Implemented Data Model: This process promotes a DBMS Table to be an Implemented Data Model table. The meta category values and value domains are removed from the DBMS Table Columns and allocated to the newly created Implemented Data Model Table Columns.

Promote Operational Data Model to Implemented Data Model: This process promotes an entire Operational Data Model to be an Implemented Data Model. Created is the schema (from the DBMS schema), all tables, columns and all keys. Relationships between the newly created Implemented Data Model table columns and the Operational Data Model table columns are automatically created.

Remove DBMS Table Column to Column Assignments: This process removes the relationships between a complete set of DBMS columns of a DBMS table and their corresponding columns.

Report DBMS Column Data Hierarchies: This process presents a DBMS column, its associated column, attributes, data elements, data element concepts and concepts. For each, the appropriate subject, entity, schema, table, DBMS schema, and DBMS table are also shown.

Synchronize Local DBMS Columns Definitions: This process enables the synchronization of a set of local definitions associated with a set of DBMS columns to each other.

Metabase System Organization Process

Accomplish Mission and Organization Assignments: This process assigns one or more organizations to a mission.

Create, Modify or Delete Organizations: This process creates an organization and as appropriate, a subordinate organization within an existing organization.

Reallocate Organizations: This process reallocates an organization within an organization hierarchy to a different organization.

Metabase System Position and Person Process

Create Mission-Organization-Function and Position: This process creates one or more associations between a position and a set of mission-organization-functions.

Create, Modify, or Delete Position-Person Association: This process creates an association between a person and a position.

Create, Modify or Delete Person: This process creates a person.

Create, Modify or Delete Management Level: This process creates a management level.

Create, Modify or Delete Position: This process creates a position. This process also allows the allocation of a particular management level to that position.

Metabase System Resource Life Cycle Process

Accomplish Resource Life Cycle Node Business Information Systems Assignments: This process assigns one or more business information systems to a resource life cycle node.

Accomplish Resource Life Cycle Node Mission Assignments: This process assigns one or more missions to a resource life cycle node.

Accomplish Resource Life Cycle Node Information Need Assignments: This process assigns one or more information needs to a resource life cycle node.

Accomplish Resource Life Cycle Node Database Object Assignments: This process assigns one or more database objects to a resource life cycle node.

Create, Modify or Delete Resource Type: This process creates a resource type that, in turn, is used to classify collections of resources.

Create, Modify or Delete Resource: This process creates a resource within the context of a resource type. Resources may be hierarchical.

Create, Modify or Delete Resource Life Cycle Node: This process creates a resource life cycle node within the context of a resource.

Create, Modify or Delete Resource Life Cycle Node Structure: This process creates a relationship between two resource life cycle nodes from two different resources.

Create, Modify or Delete Resource Life Cycle Node Structure Type: This process creates various classifications of resource life cycle structures that are used to identify specific collections of records in resource life cycle structures.

Metabase System Specified Data Model Process

Accomplish Attributes to Data Element Reassignments: This process causes a change in the existing assignment of one or more entity attributes to a data element.

Data Management's Concepts & Terms

Accomplish Attributes to Entity Reassignments: This process causes a change in the existing assignment of one or more entity attributes to a different entity.

Accomplish Entities to Entity Reassignments: This process causes a change in the sub/super type relationship among entities within a given subject.

Accomplish Entity to Subject Reassignments: This process causes a change in the existing assignment of an entity to a given subject.

Accomplish Subject to Subject Reassignments: This process causes a change in the hierarchical relationship among subjects.

Allocate Attributes to the Primary Key: This process causes the allocation of one or more attributes to a primary key. No candidate key attribute can be assigned to a primary key. A sub-entity cannot have a primary key.

Allocate Attributes to the Candidate Key: This process causes the allocation of one or more attributes to a candidate key. No primary key attribute can be assigned to a candidate key.

Create Many Attributes: This process causes the creation of many attributes by tagging one data element and a set of entities. As each attribute is created, it is assigned to the entity and also to the data element upon which its semantics is based.

Create, Modify or Delete Foreign Keys: This process creates a foreign key. The target entity is identified and the source primary key is identified. The referential actions and other SQL necessary information are then entered. The foreign key name is automatically created and consists of the parent entity name, must/may depending on chosen referential actions, an action word, and the child entity name.

Create, Modify or Delete Candidate Key Definition: This process creates a candidate key within a specific entity. A sub-entity cannot have a candidate key.

Create, Modify or Delete Subjects: This process creates a subject. When the subject is a sub-entity, the parent subject is identified.

Create, Modify or Delete Entities: This process creates an entity. When the entity is a sub-entity, the parent entity is identified.

Create, Modify or Delete Primary Key Definition: This process creates a primary key within a specific entity. A sub-entity cannot have a primary key.

Create One Attribute: This process causes the creation of one attribute by tagging one data element and one entity. As the attribute is created, it is assigned to the entity and also to the data element upon which its semantics is based.

Export SQL DDL: This process traverses the complete set of entities, attributes, and keys for a given subject and formulates a set of SQL DDL that completely represents the subject-based data model. Since there are no data types in the Specified Data Model CHAR 1 data types are created by default.

Import SQL DDL: This process imports a full stream of SQL DDL and creates a full set of entities, attributes, and keys for the selected subject.

Maintain Attribute Meta Category Values: This process enables the allocation of meta category values to an attribute. Only one meta category value from each meta category value type is allowed to be assigned. As a meta category value is assigned, if there are any meta category values already assigned either to a parent data element, data element parent data element concept, or to a descendant column, the assigned meta category values are evaluated to ensure that there are no semantic conflicts.

Maintain Attributes: This process enables an update to all the attributes of an entity attribute.

Maintain Value Domains: This process enables the creation of value domains that are assigned to data element concepts, data elements, attributes, columns, and DBMS columns.

Promote Attribute to Data Element: This process promotes an attribute to be a data element. The meta category values and value domains are removed from the attribute and allocated to the newly created data element. The data element is assigned to the "unknown" conceptual value domain and the "unknown" data element concept.

Remove Attribute Data Element Assignment: This process removes the assignment between one or more attributes and corresponding data elements.

Remove Attribute Meta Category Value Assignments: This process removes the meta category values that are currently assigned to attributes.

Report Data Hierarchies: This process displays the completely interlinked set of attributes within entities their assigned columns in tables, DBMS columns within DBMS tables, and their parent data element and data element concept.

Synchronize Local Attribute Definitions: This process enables the synchronization of a set of local definitions associated with an attribute to each other.

Metabase System: The Whitemarsh Metabase System is a metadata management system. It is not generalized. Rather, it is specialized to meet the majority of the metadata needs of the Knowledge Worker Framework. The Metabase System is SQL-engine based with an explicit SQL schema in support of ODBC-based reporting through report writers like Crystal Reports. The functional modules and corresponding Metabase System models of Metabase System are:

- Business Information Systems
- Data Elements
- Database Objects
- Implemented Data Models
- Information Needs Analysis
- Mission-Organization-Function-Position-Assignment
- Operational Data Models
- Resource Life Cycle Analysis
- Specified Data Models
- View Data Models

Because the Metabase System operates through ODBC it can be hosted on an SQL DBMS.

The Whitemarsh Metabase System allows for the definition of metadata-based data model schemas, the instantiation of metadata databases, and the export of specification metadata that is employed by code generators such as Clarion and DBMSs to create operational database information systems.

Metabase System Value Domain Process

Accomplish Data Elements to Value Domains Reassignments: This process enables the reassignment of value domains to a data element. Only one value domain is allowed to be assigned. As a value domain is assigned, if there are any value domains already assigned to a parent data element concept, or a descendant, attribute, column, or DBMS column, the assigned value domains are evaluated to ensure that there are no conflicts.

Accomplish Value Domain to Conceptual Value Domain Reassignments: This process enables the reassignment of value domains to a conceptual value domain. Only one value domain is allowed to be assigned. As a value domain is assigned if there are any value domains already assigned to a descendant data element concept, data element, attribute, column, or DBMS column, the assigned value domains are evaluated to ensure that there are no conflicts.

Accomplish Value Domain Value to Value Domain Reassignments: This process causes a change in the existing assignment of one or more value domain values to one value domain.

Create, Modify or Delete Value Domain Value Structures: This process creates specific instances of assemblies of value domain value structures.

Create, Modify or Delete Value Domain Values: This process creates one or more value domain values for any given value domain.

Create, Modify or Delete Value Domain Value Data Types: This process creates data types that control value domain values. Value domain data types have descendent SQL data types and DBMS data types.

Create, Modify or Delete Value Domain Structures: This process creates specific instances of assemblies of value domain structures.

Create, Modify or Delete Value Domain Structure Types: This process creates various classifications of value domain structures that are used to identify specific collections of records in value domain structures.

Create, Modify or Delete Value Domain Value Structure Types: This process creates various classifications of value domain value structures that are used to identify specific collections of records in value domain value structures.

Create, Modify or Delete Value Domains: This process creates one or more value domains for a particular conceptual value domain.

Metabase System View Data Model Process

Accomplish DBMS Columns to View Column Assignments: This process assigns one or more DBMS columns to a view column.

Accomplish View Column to Compound Data Element Assignments: This process assigns one or more view columns to a compound data element.

Accomplish View Column to Derived Data Element Assignments: This process assigns one or more business information systems to a resource life cycle node.

Create, Modify or Delete View Columns: This process creates view columns within a view.

Create, Modify or Delete View Column Structure Type: This process creates various classifications of view column structures that are used to identify specific collections of records in view column structures.

Create, Modify or Delete View Column Structure Process: This process provides the ability to describe the process in a sort of pseudo code in support of the transformation process between one or more view columns of one view transformed to one or more view columns in another view.

Create, Modify or Delete View Column Structure: This process creates a relationship between two view columns in different views.

Create, Modify or Delete Views: This process creates a view.

Generate View Columns: This process creates view columns for an entire table.

Generate Views: This process creates views for every table in a DBMS Schema.

Metadata: Metadata is a generic term that identifies all classes of specifications across the enterprise. Thus, all data and process specifications are metadata. All requirements are metadata. A metadata database is a database in which metadata is stored. In this book, the table of contents and the index are metadata. All the defined terms and concepts are content.

A metadata management system is a software system that captures, stores, reports, and manages metadata. The Whitemarsh system that manages the metadata databases is the Metabase System. Whitemarsh has employed the term, Metabase System, in this context since 1982. Sophisticated metadata management systems, like the Metabase System, are multi-user and support the capture and reporting of metadata in a non-redundant, integrated manner across the enterprise.

Metadata Management System: A Metadata Management System is a DBMS based information system that manages metadata in a database-centric environment.

There are three types of metadata management systems: passive, semi-active, and active. A passive metadata management system is one that is loaded with data made available to it through specialized data loading programs.

A semi-active metadata management system is one that obtains its data automatically whenever DBMS schemas, views, or DML programs are compiled.

An active metadata management system not only obtains its data at compile time, it is also automatically accessed by executing run-units for data editing and validation functions, security and privacy, valid use of subschemas, and the like.

A modern metadata management system contains all the data necessary to describe and control the corporate data structures, rules, policies, databases, programs, systems, subsystems, and the like. The modern metadata management system contains sufficient metadata-based data models for it to serve as the information model of the enterprise and also as a common data semantics resource for database and business information system development.

Metadata Management System Database
A Metadata Management System Database is a database that contains the metadata specifications from across all the different enterprise architectures. The database is such that it supports complete non-redundancy and integration in support of re-use. An enterprise can have multiple metadata repository databases for different areas of its business. That is, there can be one for customer management, another for manufacturing, and different ones for inventory, and marketing. In such cases, the metadata specifications contained in these metadata repository databases are isolated one from another. In short, stove-pipes of metadata.
   See Metabase System.

Metric: A Metric is the identified quantity of staff hours required to perform a particular activity in support of a named methodology work product.

Mission Assigned Business Term: A Mission Assigned Business Term represents one or more business terms assigned to a mission.
   See Mission-Organization-Function-Position-Assignment Model

Mission Assigned Database Domain: A Mission Assigned Database Domain represents one or more database domains assigned to a mission.
   See Mission-Organization-Function-Position-Assignment Model

Mission: Missions are hierarchically organized textual descriptions that define the very essence of the enterprise. Missions represent the ultimate goals and objectives of enterprise accomplishment through the different business functions and organizations related to the missions. An enterprise is incomplete if one of its missions is not defined. Not all enterprises accomplish their missions simultaneously or in their ideal state. Missions are accomplished over time and are subject to revisions.
   For a large enterprise, the mission descriptions are from 25 to 35 pages of text in addition to hierarchical diagrams. The missions do not detail what the business is doing, or who is doing it, or how it is done. These are the purview of mission-related organizational and functional analyses.
   See Mission-Organization-Function-Position-Assignment Model

Mission-Organization Assigned Business Function: A Mission-Organization Assigned Business Function represents one or more business functions assigned to a mission-organization.
   See Mission-Organization-Function-Position-Assignment Model

Mission-Organization
A Mission-Organization is the association of an organization with a mission. There can be multiple organizations associated with a mission, and an organization can be associated with multiple missions. The description contained within the Mission-Organization may be more refined than the description contained in either the mission or the organization.
   See Mission-Organization-Function-Position-Assignment Model

Mission-Organization-Function: A Mission-Organization-Function is the association of a mission-organization with a function. A mission-organization can be associated with multiple functions and a function can be associated with multiple mission-organizations. One or more mission-organization-functions may be associated with a business information system. When they are, business events are created. This process is accomplished within the Business Information Systems module.
   See Mission-Organization-Function-Position-Assignment Model

Mission-Organization-Function Position Assignment: The mission-organization-function position assignment represents the assignment of a position to a mission-organization-function.
   See Mission-Organization-Function-Position-Assignment Model

Mission-Organization-Function Position Role: A Mission-Organization-Function-Position Role represents the assignment of a particular role that a position occupies with respect to a particular function within an organization as it accomplishes a mission. Once a position is assigned, its role can be detailed.
   See Mission-Organization-Function-Position-Assignment Model

Mission-Organization-Function-Position-Assignment Model: The Mission-Organization-Function-Position-Assignment Model is depicted in Figure 13 and contains, mission, organizations, function, database domains, management levels, mission-organizations, mission-organization-functions,

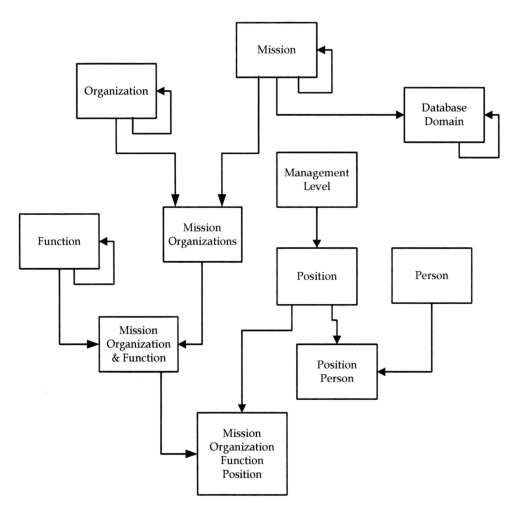

Figure 13. Mission-organization-function Position Assignment Model.

position, persons, position-person, and mission organization function position.

Mission-Organization-Functional Ranked Information Need: A Mission-Organization-Functional Ranked Information Need represents a ranked information need for a specific mission-organization-function. Once the functional areas of an organization accomplishing a mission of the enterprise have been created within the Metabase System module, Mission-Organization-Function-Position-Assignment (MOFPA), and after the

Information Needs have been created, selected sets of information needs are assigned to the Mission-Organization-Function. Once assigned, their rank is defaulted to unknown. This needs to be changed by reviewing each mission-organization-function ranked information need and adjusting its rank.

See Information Needs Analysis Model.

Mission Resource: Mission Resources are the association of a resource with a mission. Each mission may be related with one or more resources and each resource may be related to one or more missions.

See Mission-Organization-Function-Position-Assignment Model

Mission versus Function: Missions and Functions different. Missions are hierarchically organized descriptions of the characteristics of the enterprise idealized end results. Mission descriptions are noun-based sentences. In contrast, functions are descriptions of how to accomplish an end result. Functions are "human-activity" based and are verb-based sentences.

Missions are apolitical. They are devoid of who, how, and technology. There should only be ONE mission description for a given mission. There should be only one mission description for an enterprise. In contrast, function hierarchies are commonly affected by performing organizations and styles of activities. There can be a number of equivalent activity descriptions for a given function.

Databases and business information systems are based on missions. In contrast, "Human" activities and organizations are based on business functions.

When a business fundamentally changes its missions, it is essentially re-engineered. In contrast, when a business optimizes its activities only its existing functions are re-engineered. Its missions remain the same.

Finally, Missions are strategic and long range, In contrast, functions are tactical to operational, medium to short range, and are organizationally sensitive

Module: The Module is a self-contained component of a program that retrieves, updates, or processes data. A module may reside in multiple programs.

Data Management's Concepts & Terms

Multi-User Mode: See Concurrent Operations.

Multiple Database Processing: Multiple Database Processing is a facility offered through the DBMS to allow an application run-unit (Host Language Interface or natural language) access to more than one database. Access to each different database may be through different views. With the advent of Window's ODBC or JDBC, an application program sends SQL commands to ODBC/JDBC, which, in turn, communicates with the DBMS. The DBMS, in turn, interacts with the database. Because of either ODBC or JDBC, application run-units are almost always able to be capable of multiple database processing.

See also physical database.

Multiset: See Collection Data Type.

Multithread: See Concurrent Operations.

Multivalued Dependency: A Multivalued Dependency is a one to many (1 to M) or many to one (M to 1) association among data elements.

Natural Language: A Natural Language is a language that is almost always invented by a DBMS vendor to provide access to the database. The program that results from a natural language normally cannot be used on any other DBMS vendor's system.

The typical three types of natural languages are procedure-oriented, query-update, and report writer. Not all DBMSs have all three. Some have only one, which may be either the procedure oriented language, or a combination of the query-update and report writer languages.

A procedure oriented language is a natural language that typically allows looping, branching, computation, print formatting, data record, selection, retrieval, storage, and modification. This language is sometimes called a fourth generation language (4GL). The ANSI/SQL Persistent Stored Module (PSM) language is a procedure oriented language without either a presentation layer or a data access layer.

A query-update language is a natural language that selects, retrieves, and either updates, or formats and prints (outputs) the data in one language statement or "sentence." This does not mean, however, that these statements are all simple and short. Some SQL statements can be well more than 50 lines long. Some SQL statements are hundreds of lines. The reason some SQL statements are hundreds of lines long versus five to ten lines each is because SQL is a single-result paradigm language. The alternative to this is the creation of temp tables, one after each statement.

A report writer typically contains verbs to select, sort, and specially format data into reports. Special formatting controls usually include control breaks, subtotals, totals, headers, footers, column titles, page numbering and the like.

The four different natural languages execution modes are HLI (Host Language Interface), direct, interpretive, and compiler.

HLI implies that the natural language expression is actually data to an HLI program, which determines the actions to be performed and accomplishes the activity, as if the natural language run-unit had been written as an HLI program.

Direct execution natural language implies that the query expression itself is "data" to a computer program that interprets this "data" and directly executes its implied commands against the database through subroutine calls, etc.

Interpretive natural languages take each statement of the natural language run-unit, decodes it and executes it. If a loop is required to acquire successive records of data, the natural language instruction is reinterpreted, line by line, during each cycle of the loop.

Compilers executing natural languages translate the natural language statements into another language which is compiled into a run-unit that is executed. When the run-unit is to be reexecuted without source code changes, the compile step does not have to be re-accomplished. Clarion operates in this manner.

With the advent of ODBC and JDBC, some vendors have created natural languages that can interact with multiple DBMSs. Clarion is a 4GL that accomplished this. It accesses SQL DBMS through ODBC or JDBC.

Navigate: Navigate represents a process of a set of DML commands explicitly executed by a run-unit to obtain one row after another within a set of rows through commands like GET OWNER, GET NEXT, or GET MEMBER.

Generally, the navigation logic for a static relationship DBMS is expressed explicitly in the run-unit DML. With the advent of views, the DML logic has been moved to an intermediary processing interface between the run-unit and the DBMS (which accesses the database).

For dynamic relationship DBMSs, the relationship operations of PROJECT, JOIN, etc. are navigation commands. These too may be explicitly stated in queries, or executed through the view intermediary.

Whether the DBMS is using indexes or embedded pointers is immaterial to the notion of navigation.

NDL Data Language Standard: The NDL Data Language Standard is a language that supports the network data model standardized by ANSI-INCITS H2 Database Languages Committee. NDL tables can have single- or multi-dimensional columns. The row operations are FIND, GET, STORE, DELETE, and MODIFY. The relationship operations are CONNECT, DISCONNECT, GET OWNER, GET MEMBER, and GET NEXT. The combination operations supported are RECONNECT (DISCONNECT and CONNECT), and INSERT (STORE and CONNECT).

The ANSI network data language (NDL) specifies table structures, relationships, and the operations on the structures. The specification provides the syntax and semantics of the schema and subschema. NDL specifies only the semantics of the operations, as the syntax of data processing languages is the function of other ANSI committees.

The relationships supported through the NDL's DDL are owner-member, owner-multiple member, singular single member, singular multiple member, and recursive. The facilities of the NDL are set out in Figure 6.

See ANSI Database Standards. See CODASYL Model. See CODASYL Set.

Network: A Network is a set of relationships among owner table rows and member tables rows such that a single member row may be related to more than one row from different owner tables.

Network Data Model: The network data model is characterized by having static based relationships among tables such that a given table, identified as a member table, can be related to more than one table identified as owner tables.

See the NDL Data Language Standard.

Nested Repeating Group: See Fact.

Next Key (Next Pointer): A Next Key (Next Pointer) is the DBKEY of the row that is the logical successor of the current row.

Non Procedural Language: A Non Procedural Language is a high level language requiring very little syntax and few data format declarations suitable for non data processing users to learn and become productive in a very short time.

See also Natural languages.

Normal Forms: Normal Forms provide strategies that determine a table's level of risk to semantic uniqueness and/or update anomalies. There are five normal forms that proceed from the highest risk (1st Normal Form) to the lowest risk (5th Normal Form).

Figures 14 through 18 show the process for transforming a non-first normal form data structure to a fifth normal form. The first figure, Figure 14 provides a data structure for a student that contains the student's SSN, Birthdate, Major, Dean, and a set of courses the student is taking.

Student SSN
Birthdate
Major
Dean
Courses (RG)
    Course-Section-Number
    Teacher-Id
    Grade

Figure 14. Pre-Normal Form.

Student SSN
Course-Section-Number
Birthdate
Major
Dean
Teacher-Id
Grade

Figure 15. First Normal Form.

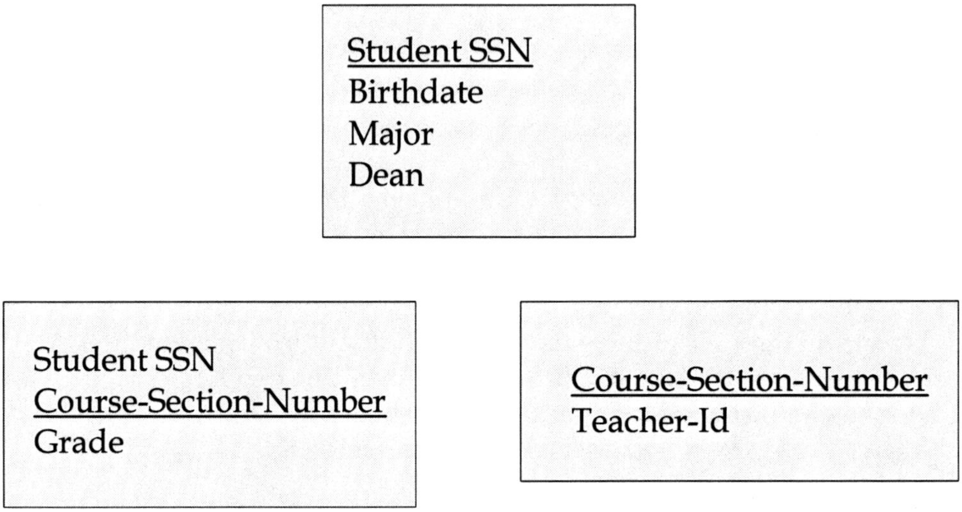

```
┌─────────────────┐
│ Student SSN     │
│ Birthdate       │
│ Major           │
│ Dean            │
└─────────────────┘
```

```
┌──────────────────────────┐     ┌──────────────────────────┐
│ Student SSN              │     │ Course-Section-Number    │
│ Course-Section-Number    │     │ Teacher-Id               │
│ Grade                    │     │                          │
└──────────────────────────┘     └──────────────────────────┘
```

Figure 16. Second Normal Form.

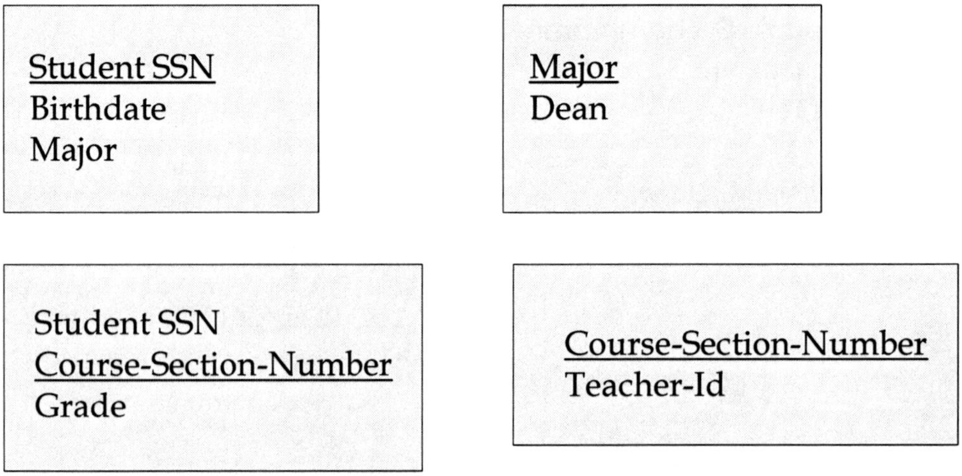

```
┌─────────────────┐     ┌─────────────────┐
│ Student SSN     │     │ Major           │
│ Birthdate       │     │ Dean            │
│ Major           │     │                 │
└─────────────────┘     └─────────────────┘
```

```
┌──────────────────────────┐     ┌──────────────────────────┐
│ Student SSN              │     │ Course-Section-Number    │
│ Course-Section-Number    │     │ Teacher-Id               │
│ Grade                    │     │                          │
└──────────────────────────┘     └──────────────────────────┘
```

Figure 17. Third Normal Form.

```
┌─────────────────────┐   ┌─────────────────────┐   ┌─────────────────────┐
│ Student SSN         │   │ Student SSN         │   │ Major               │
│ Birthdate           │   │ Major               │   │ Dean                │
└─────────────────────┘   └─────────────────────┘   └─────────────────────┘

┌─────────────────────────┐           ┌─────────────────────────┐
│ Student SSN             │           │ Course-Section-Number   │
│ Course-Section-Number   │           │ Teacher-Id              │
│ Grade                   │           └─────────────────────────┘
└─────────────────────────┘
```

Figure 18. Fourth Normal Form.

The first data structure problem is that there are multiple instances of courses for each student. For a college graduate that could be about 50 courses. Thus, in Figure 14, Courses is a repeating group complex fact. In this form, there is no key-based way to select a particular course. The student's SSN would have to be employed to access the rows, and then programming logic would have to traverse all 50 course rows to find a particular course to discover the grade or the teacher.

The ultimate objective of a completely normalized data structure is to use a key to select the exactly desired row. Thus, this pre-normal form fails that criteria.

The first normal form represents data that has been organized into a single two-dimension flat table. Figure 15 illustrates a first normal form data structure. In this data structure, the Students's four columns from Figure 14 have been "moved" down into the Courses repeating group. When this is done, the primary key is a combined value from the columns, Student SSN, and Course Section Number.

In the non-normal form, there is one row for each student. In this first normal form, the quantity of student rows equals the count of all courses taken by the student. There would be about 50 rows for each student. There is therefore, 50 occurrences of the Student's Birthdate, Major and Dean. The problem with the data in this form is that for each student there is now 50 birthdates, 50 majors, and 50 deans because the granularity of the row is now at the Student-SSN + Course Section Number level. If the student's birthdate is wrong, it can only be fixed by updating 50 rows.

While the update test is different, the result is the same. Fifty rows have to be accessed to accomplish a complete update. Again, the test of single-key-based update fails.

The second normal form represents data in first normal form and also that has all its non-primary key columns functionally dependent on the entire primary key. Figure 16 illustrates a second normal form data structure. In this normal form there are now three different tables, Student, Student Course, and Teacher.

The reason the first normal form table was divided into three tables was to enable the unique selection of one and only one student with the SSN, and one and only one teacher with the Course Section Number, and finally, the selection of one and only one Grade via the primary key of Student Number and Course Section Number. In this structure there is one student row, and for the student's grades there would be 50 rows. There would be only one Course Section Number row for each course per semester that has the Teacher's Id. A student is able to be selected with one key value and the birthdate can be changed with one update. Hence the update test passes. But the student table is still not in third normal form.

Third normal form represents data that is in second normal form and that additionally has no dependencies between any non-key columns and any other non-key columns. Figure 17 illustrates third normal form. The key difference between the second and third normal forms is that in the second normal form Student table from the Figure 17, two of the columns, Major and Dean have a relationship, one with the other. In normal forms that represent a "non-key" dependency. To make that table into third normal form, the table has to be divided into a pure student table and a major table.

In the Figure 17, Third Normal Form, there is one only student row, only as many Major rows as there are majors, and the same quantity of rows for the other two tables as in Third Normal Form.

Fourth normal form represents data that is in third normal form and that additionally has its primary key related to all columns in the row such that it contains no more than one nontrivial multivalued dependency on the primary key. Table Student-SSN in Figure 17 has two columns, Birth-Date and Major. Both these columns depend on the Student-SSN in that knowing the Student-SSN you know the student's birthdate and you know the Student's Major.

The reason this table is not in fourth normal form is because the Student's birth-date and Major have nothing to do with each other. Consequently, each has to be moved to its own table, one for the Student's major and the other for the Student's Birthdate. This is shown in Figure 18. The quantity of rows in the Student Major table is the same as the Student SSN table as is in the Student SSN Third Normal Form example. The other tables contain the same quantity of rows as in the Third Normal Form example.

Fifth normal form represents data that is in fourth normal form and that additionally has the characteristic that if its primary key is a concatenated key, none of the columns of the concatenated key can be derived from another column of the concatenated key. Figure 18 is also in fifth normal form. The only multi-part primary key is the Student-SSN & Course-Section-Number key. Both these key parts have nothing to do with each other. They are clearly independent. Hence neither is derived from the other.

Most data modeling efforts are only to the Third Normal Form. This is both sufficient and adequate for database projects. As with most situations, there are tradeoffs between non-normal forms and the Third Normal Form. Third Normal Form is best for updating and non-normal form is best for reporting.

Normalize: Normalize is the process of conforming to or reducing to a norm or a standard, such that all members of the group are commutative. Commutative means that the members of the group are able to be combined in such a manner that the result is independent of the order in which the elements are combined. For example, the fractions, 1/3 plus 1/4 are not commutative. However, 4/12 plus 3/12 is commutative with the result being 7/12.

The process of combining proper fractions is the process of finding the "lowest common denominator." It is therefore a process of normalization. Once the common denominator is found, the fractions can be combined.

As another example, if the total salary of all departments is desired, and if the managers' salary were stored in the department rows, and the employees' salary were stored in the employee's rows, the DBMS could not simply select the department managers, the employees, and combine the salaries. That's because the DBMS does not "know" which department manages which employees. Consequently, the managers must be "normalized" down to the level of the employees before the appropriate manager's salary can be combined with the manager's employees.

Unfortunately, the term "normalization" has taken on a special meaning for the relational data model. That is because the relational data model only allows simple rows, that is, tables of simple (single value) columns. In relational terminology, the process of removing multi-valued items, or repeating groups, that is, of adhering to a standard, is called the process of "normalization." Records that are "flat" are said to be in a "normal form." The gradations of normal quality range from one to five.

Notwithstanding the relational use of the term normalization, the process is useful for other data models. That is, each data aggregate within a data element of a complex row should conform to at least the third normal form.

See Normal Forms.

Normalized Data: Normalized Data is that data that has been placed into a structure that conforms to at least the third normal form.

Null: Null is the name assigned to an absence of value within a column. In this case, the value can only be "unknown."

ODBC: See Open Database Connectivity.

O/S File: An O/S File is a collection of record instances known to the operating system under a single name, and that are accessed by a single O/S access method.

OLAP: Online Analytical Processing, or OLAP, is an approach to quickly provide answers to analytical queries that are multi-dimensional in nature. OLAP is part of the broader category, business intelligence, which also encompasses relational reporting and data mining. Statistics packages such as SPSS are an example of OLAP. When users ask for a full set of descriptive statistics from a data sample, the statistics are produced in one OLAP operation and is presented to the user.

OLTP: Online transaction processing, or OLTP, refers to a class of systems that facilitate and manage transaction-oriented applications, typically for data entry and retrieval transaction processing. An order/entry system is an example of an OLTP system.

One-to-One Relationship: A One-to-One Relationship is a type of relationship between two rows from two different tables. There is one owner row, and only one member row. Further, the DBMS enforces that there cannot be more than one member row. A typical example might be Product-Factory. The one-to-one relationship would enforce that one and only one Factory manufactures the particular Product. In SQL, this would be accomplished by putting the product Number in the Factory table and requiring a Unique Key property on the column, Factory.Product.

One-to-Many Relationship: See Owner-single-member Relationship.

Open Database Connectivity (ODBC): An Open Database Connectivity (ODBC) is a database access driver that enables an application system to invoke calls to a generic SQL engine. These calls are reinterpreted by the ODBC driver to be the call to a specific SQL engine. Thus, any data manipulation language agent through ODBC can access any SQL engine. The ODBC is thus a universal translator. ODBC is a set of SQL engine call specifications that was originally published by Microsoft. The ANSI SQL/CLI (call level interface) is the ANSI standard for ODBC.

Operational Data Model: Operational Data Models are models of databases that conform to the requirements of a particular DBMS such as Oracle or DB2. Additionally, the database's design must conform to the expected processing requirements of the particular set of database applications supported by the particular database. Operational data models are somewhat equivalent to the term, Physical Database. The meta model for the Operational Data Model is set out in Figure 19.

Operational Data Model designs vary because of many factors such as transaction volume, the host operating system, and the computer hardware size and throughput capabilities. Regardless, DBMS tables and/or DBMS columns of an Operational Data Model database should all relate back to tables and/or columns of an Implemented Data Model.

Operational Data Models are defined as DBMS tables, DBMS columns and relationships within DBMS schemas. "DBMS" is employed here to signify that these data model components are tied to a specific DBMS. There are many-to-many relationships between an Operational Data Model DBMS columns and View Data Model view columns.

The Operational Data Model is similar to the Implemented Data Model in its characteristics. The triple for the Operational Data Model is DBMS Schema, DBMS table, and DBMS column.

A key difference in the Operational Data Model from the Implemented Data Model is that it represents the data structures that result in SQL DDL streams that feed the DBMS to actually make the databases. In the

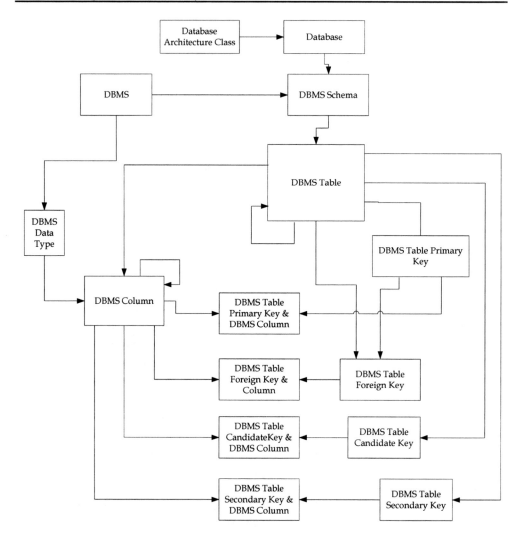

Figure 19. Operational Data Model.

Whitemarsh Metabase System, the Operational Data Model can export SQL DDL.

There may be multiple Operational Data Models for a given Implemented Data Model. Each Operational Data Model may contain a different subset of an Implemented Data Model's tables and columns, or in some cases, all its tables and columns. It may also be the case that a complete set of a table's columns are transformed into differently named columns. For example, there might have been an Implemented Data Model table for telephone numbers that, in the Operational Data Model, are transformed into TelephoneNumber-1 through TelephoneNumber-5. This is a kind of Operational Data Model denormalization may be created to improve performance.

There may also have been multiple Implemented Data Models for a given Operational Data Model. This commonly occurs in data warehouse data model designs where the Operational Data Model for the data warehouse is sourced from multiple Implemented Data Models.

The Operational Data Model can contain subtyped DBMS tables, and substructures in DBMS Columns. It can also have an assigned value domain and the data types reflect that of the containing DBMS.

Operational Data Model Relationship: An Operational Data Model Relationship is a relationship mechanism that relates one instance of one DBMS table to a set of instances of another DBMS table. While there are eight classes of relationships, the most common are the one-to-many, and one-to-one. In the case of one-to-many, the relationship mechanism is the primary key DBMS columns of the "related-from" DBMS table matching the foreign key DBMS columns of the "related-to" table. The term, foreign key, comes from the fact that it's really a "copy" of the "related-from" DBMS table's primary key. Relationships should always be named and defined to the extent that the real purpose of the relationship is clear. For recursive relationships, the "related-from" table and the "related-to" table are the same.

Order: Order represents the placement of rows into an arrangement specified by such rules as numeric or alphabetic order. Order is also a synonym for sort.

Ordered: Ordered is a term to represent a sequence of rows depending on the value of user-specified column-based collating sequence.

Organization: An Organization is a unit within an enterprise. It is hierarchical so any quantity of organizational levels can be represented.

Outer Join: An Outer Join is a relational operation that joins a tuple from one table to a tuple from another table when the columns, which are the basis for the join, are NULL. There are two outer joins, left and right for when only one side of the join column is NULL.

Data Management's Concepts & Terms

Overflow: Overflow represents a technique that stores and subsequently selects or modifies rows that are not able to be located in the normal location the access strategy initially seeks to find them in.

Owner: An Owner is a term that represents a row that has semantic ownership of one or more dependent rows of a CODASYL, ANSI NDL, or hierarchical data model owner-member relationship. SQL-based DBMSs often employ the term owner for the primary key based table of a primary to foreign key relationship. Data modeling also employs the term, owner, for relationship specifications. An owner row may itself be a member row in another relationship instance.

Owner Key (Owner Pointer): The DBKEY of the owner row.

Owner-multiple Member: An Owner-multiple Member relationship is a type of relationship in which there is one owner table, and more than one member table. There may be one or more member rows of each type for each owner instance. A typical example for the relationship is Employees, where Company is the owner, and Part-Time-Employees, Full-Time-Employees, and Retired-Employees are the members. Owner-multi-member relationships are unique to the CODASYL and ANSI NDL Data Language Standards.
   See Data Model. See Relationships.

Owner-Single Member Relationship: An Owner-Single Member Relationship is a type of relationship in which there is one owner table, and one member table. There may be one or more member rows for each owner row. In a typical example for the relationship Company Calendar, the Year is the Owner, and Month is the member.
   See Data Model. See Relationships.

Packed Decimal: Packed Decimal is a representation of numeric values that compresses each character representation in such a way that the original value can be recovered.

Padding: Padding is a technique used to fill a data element value instance, row, or DBMS record instance, with dummy data, usually zeros or spaces.

Page: See DBMS Record.

Parameter: A Parameter is a column or an array of columns that specifies, supplies or receives the value(s) of the corresponding argument in the invocation or return of a procedure.

Password: A Password is a character string that enables a user to have full or limited access to a system or to a set of data.
   See Security Schema.

Person: A Person is someone who can be assigned within the scope of the Mission-Organization-Function-Position Assignment Metabase System module.

Phone: A Phone number is the number that some can be reached via the telephone. It commonly includes country code, area code, exchange, number, and possibly extension.
   See Project Management Model.

Phone Type: A Phone Type is the classification for the phone number. An example is Cell, Office, or Home.
   See Project Management Model.

Physical Attribute: See Data Type.

Physical Data Model: A Physical Data Model is different from a Logical Data Model in only one respect. It is bound to the particular characteristics of the DBMS under which it is to operate.
   Physical data model columns, depending on the DBMS's capabilities, can be complex facts and subtyped DBMS tables. Physical data models can possess sophisticated column, table, and schema defined processes defined in the DBMS stored procedure language. These are commonly known as stored procedures and execute either before or after a process occurs.
   A physical data model is generally similar to the Whitemarsh Operational Data Model with this difference. In the Whitemarsh Metabase System, the relationship between an Implemented Data Model and an Operational Data Model can be many-to-many. Traditionally, there is only a one-to-many relationship between a logical data model and a physical data model. That is because the physical data model is just a binding of all, or a subset, or a

recasting of the corresponding set of tables and columns from a single logical data model. The physical data model's domain is either the same or a subset of the logical data model. The Whitemarsh Operational Data Model, in contrast, can have a many-to-many relationship with its corresponding Implemented Data Models. That is needed to represent multiple data model subsets from different Implemented Data Models as is common within data warehouse databases.

See Operational Data Model.

Physical Database: A Physical Database is defined as that physical occurrence of all storage structure components that result from the definition of all the tables within a single database schema. Included in these resultant components are the database's storage structure, the DBMSs access strategy for storing and retrieving rows, and the processes for data loading, update, and database maintenance.

A single database could be as little as a single O/S computer file, or a large quantity of O/S computer files. The number of files and the organization of each file is immaterial.

In most DBMSs, a database is able to be removed from an on-line status to an off-line status by a backup command. That space is immediately available for use by a different database. Further, if the backed-up database is desired to be placed on-line again, it may be restored onto different on-line storage space and accessed by the DBMS just as before without having to again go through the process of data loading.

Two or more databases are two or more physical occurrences of the components just described.

Physical Record: See DBMS Record.

Physical Reorganization: Physical Reorganization is the DBMS process of making physical changes to the organization of the database. Included, for example, would be the reorganization of logical database rows into a different physical order; the "repacking" of rows within DBMS record instances to eliminate empty space, etc.

Physical reorganization is commonly subdivided into changes to the following physical database components: Dictionary, Indexes, Relationships, and Data.

Dictionary reorganization, that is, the database's schema is almost always automatically accomplished during logical reorganization.

Index reorganization is a DBMS vendor process that optimizes the physical organization of the index pages within the physical database.

Relationship reorganization is similar to the index reorganization given that there is a physical database storage structure component for relationships that is separate and apart from data.

Data reorganization is the DBMS process that centers on the optimization of rows within the DBMS records. This data reorganization can be very specialized to meet certain processing needs.

Physical Schema: The Physical Schema is a linguistic expression of the syntax and semantics of a physical data model.

Included in the physical schema is information about the database's storage structure allocation to storage devices, the physical organization of rows, the allocation of rows across O/S files or areas, DBMS record blocking factors and the like. The physical database schema is communicated through a data storage definition language (DSDL).

Pointer: A Pointer is a DBMS created addressing mechanism, typically a DBKEY, which interrelate rows within a relationship. Cursors are almost always populated by DBKeys.

See Owner, Next, and Prior keys.

Populate: See Load.

Position: A Position is a named and defined collection of work tasks that can be performed by one or more persons. Positions are often assigned to one or more organizations.

See Mission Organization Function Position Assignment model.

Precedence Vector: A Precedence Vector is a relationship between two nodes of different Resource Life Cycle that indicates that the target Resource Life Cycle Node is enabled in some significant way by the source Resource Life Cycle Node.

See Resource Life Cycle model.

Precision: Precision is a measure of the ability to distinguish between nearly equal values.

Predominant User: The Predominant User entity is intended to distinguish among the types of users of the business information system. The example contained in the Reference data segregates users by the gross business level they represent.

See Business Information System model.

Primary Key: See Key.

Prior Key (Prior Pointer): The DBKEY of the row that is the logical precedent of the current row.

Privacy: See Security and Privacy.

Privacy Key: See Security and Privacy.

Privacy Lock: See Security and Privacy.

Procedural Language: A Procedural Language is a software language such as COBOL or Fortran that enables looping, branching, prompting, data reads and writes, and the like.

Procedure Oriented Language: See Natural Languages.

Process Driven Methodology: A Process Driven Methodology is one wherein the data is defined almost exclusively to suit the needs of the process within which the data is encased. A process driven methodology is centered on business processes such as Obtain Customer, Build Product, Manage Project. Each of these processes is decomposed into more detailed levels of processes. At the point where the process cannot be further divided, the next step is to determine what, if any data is needed to support the process. Most commonly at that point, all the data names are conformed to the localized containing processes.

For example, if the process is to Create Invoice Detail records, a data name might be Invoice Detail Product Number, Invoice Detail Product Unit Cost, and Invoice Detail Product Quantity. The most common outcome of a process driven effort is a vast increase in the quantity of process-oriented fact names. This leads to suboptimal database designs, ones that are process-centric. In addition to process-driven names, the data is often semantically compromised by localized data types, localized value domains, and localized processing rules. All this leads to a massive increase in the quantity of small databases that are unable to be integrated in a manner appropriate or meaningful for enterprise-wide database.

When enterprise-wide database is demanded, the forest of stove-pipe databases are interconnected with massive quantities of extract-transform-load (ETL) processes. The is very expensive, the results suboptimal, and the forest of stove pipes remain.

Program: A Program is an occurrence of computer code contained in the program's modules to accomplish a specific objective. The program's language may be natural, O/S command language, or compiler (e.g., Fortran, or COBOL). Each program should be described in a metadata management system and in the program itself. Programs almost always are additionally described in external documentation to the extent that neither the metadata management system nor the program listings are sufficient. A program typically contains one or more modules which interact with data from one or more views. For the purposes of this book, the languages in which a program is written may be either host or natural.

Project: A Project is a named set of activities that are to accomplish a specific component of an enterprise database. A project has a schedule and produces a named set of work products.

See Project Management Model.

Project Management Model: The Project Management Model is the metadata model that reflects the Whitemarsh approach to project management. The metadata model for this approach is depicted in Figure 20. The meta entities in the project management model include: Assigned Task, Base Line, Base Line Staff, Base Line Work Environment Factor, Contract, Contract & Organization, Contract Resource, Contract Role, Deliverable, Deliverable Template, Deliverable Template Type, Job Title, Organization, Phone, Phone Type, Project, Project Template, Project Template & Deliverable Template, Project Template & Task Template, Project Template Type, Resource, Resource Life Cycle Node, Skill, Skill Level, Skill Level Type, Staff, Staff Skill Level, State, Status Type, Task, Task & Work Environment Factor, Task Template, Work, Work Environment Factor, Work Environment Factor Type, and Work Environment Multiplier Type.

The Whitemarsh approach concentrates on the management of "nouns" while other project management approaches focus on the management of

Data Management's Concepts & Terms

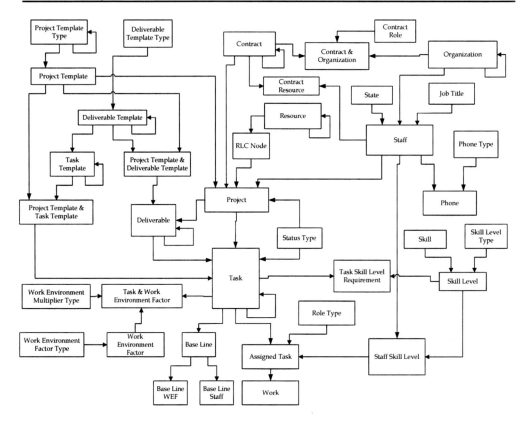

Figure 20. Project Management Model

"verbs." Clearly, since there is no one sacred, perfect way to produce a deliverable (i.e., the nouns), if the focus of project management is to identify and control the "methods" (i.e., the verbs) by which deliverables are produced, then, to have enterprise-wide project management and/or to have enterprise-wide metrics, the enterprise must first carve the processes into stone through which work is done. Not only is this impossible, it is also highly undesirable. It is impossible because it is inconceivable that there is only one way to accomplish any product. It is undesirable because it is insulting to project staffs to presume to control their every technique, process and step. Not only can't it be done, no one will tolerate it being done.

Whitemarsh project management manages "nouns" by collecting the quantities of resources expended to produce deliverables. Whitemarsh project estimates are therefore based on the staff hours required to produce deliverables rather than to accomplish tasks.

This technique enables different styles of project management to be employed or be set one against the other by comparing the resources expended to produce deliverables. There might be one project template for mainframe development, another for micros, and finally a methodology for web-based systems even though all the deliverables might be essentially the same.

Alternatively, there might be multiple project templates that produce the same set of deliverables to serve the needs of different styles or techniques as might be the case for the data-driven and process driven approaches.

The Whitemarsh project management approach enables enterprise-wide project reporting in terms of the cost and effort to produce deliverables versus the accomplishment of activities. As work techniques improve, either through the increased skill of staff, or through the adoption of different techniques, the efforts remain comparable because it is the quantity of resources expended to produce the deliverables that are compared rather than the activities, which can no longer be compared because the activities that produce the deliverables are now different.

Project Template: A Project Template is a model specification of a class of project. Associated with that model project specification is a set of task templates, and deliverable templates. A project template, once chosen, governs individual projects. For example, project templates could define efforts for business model development, information systems plans, or an individual report.

See Project Management Model.

Project Template & Deliverable Template: A Project Template & Deliverable Template is the association of a project template with a deliverable template. Ultimately this enables the specification of a set of deliverables for a given project to be modeled from a deliverable tuned according to a specific project template. For example, an enterprise data model (project template) operational data model specification (the deliverable template).

See Project Management Model.

Project Template & Task Template: A Project Template & Task Template is the association of a project template with a task template. Ultimately this enables the specification of a set of tasks for a given project to be modeled from a task tuned according to a specific task template. For example, the

enterprise data model (project template) development of an operational data model specification (the task template).
See Project Management Model.

Project Template Type: A Project Template Type is a classification of a set of project templates. Examples are Information Technology, Business Process Analysis, Market Analysis, Manufacturing Plant Engineering.
See Project Management Model.

Projection: Projection is a relational data model operation that takes one relation as an operand and returns a second relation that consists of only the selected columns, with duplicate rows eliminated.

Property Class: Property Class is an inferred collection of policy-homogeneous facts that are defined independently of database objects, but are referenced by a database object for inclusion. Examples of property classes are Critical Dates, and Bibliographic Information. The Employee table would likely include the property class, Bibliographic Information. The database objects for Contract, Orders, and Shipping Ticket would likely include the Critical Dates property class.
When a give property class is cited within multiple database objects, the inferred set of facts may be different. An example is the inferred facts for the property class, Critical Dates, would be different for Contract from those for Purchase Order.

Pure Alphabetic: Pure Alphabetic is a character string representation in which there are only letters.

Pure Numeric: Pure Numeric is a representation in which only numbers are expressed.

Qualification: Qualification represents a selection of a subset of stored data.

Quality Assurance: Quality Assurance represents the policy, procedures, and systematic actions established in an organization for the purpose of providing and maintaining some degree of confidence in the data integrity and accuracy throughout the life cycle of the data, which includes input, update, manipulation, and output.

Query Update Language: See Natural Languages.

Queue: A Queue is a telecommunications term indicating a temporary storage area for various items like data streams, messages, and the like.

RAM: Random access memory.

Random Access: See HASH/CALC Physical.

Ranking: Ranking represents the ordering of a collection of Mission-Organization-Function Ranked Information Needs. The collection represents the set of information needs determined important for a functional area of an organization that is accomplishing a mission of the enterprise. At the outset, all the ranks are defaulted to Unknown. That is, the ranking is unknown. That needs to be changed by first creating a set of rankings such as bottom 50%, mid 40%, and top 10%. This set of rankings is employed to characterize the Mission-Organization-Function Ranked-Information-Needs.
    See Information Needs Analysis model.

Record: See Row.

Record Check: See Table.

Record-Element: See Column.

Record Layout: A Record Layout represents a description of the arrangement and structure of columns in a table.

Record Length: A Record Length is a measure of the length (size) of a row, usually expressed in units of character, words, or bytes.
    See Table.

Record Type: See Table.

Recovery: Backup is described earlier. Recovery is the converse to backup. Recovery is a process through which the backup of the database is copied from backup media onto mass storage to make it immediately usable by DBMS run-units. Normally, a recovery is instigated through a DBMS command or utility.

Recovery is the process of either repairing damage caused to the database by a DBMS or computer failure, or a process of removing a specific update that was posted to the database by a run-unit.

The two broad classes of recovery are database and transaction. Database recovery affects all current users of the database through after image recovery or before image recovery. Transaction rollback only affects the updates posted by a single user.

A quiet point is a state in which no update transactions are being processed against the database. The quiet point in a database is a state of internal database consistency that is employed in an after-image recovery, a before-image recovery, or a transaction rollback.

After-image recovery is the process of restoring a backup of the database and applying the after-images of database records (that result from updates) to the restored backup until the most recent quiet point. This type of recovery is also called forward recovery because it moves an "old" copy of the database "forward in time."

Before-image recovery is the process of replacing current database records with their before-images until a quiet point is reached. This type of recovery is also called backward recovery because it moves the most "current" version of the database "back in time."

Transaction rollback is the process of removing the update transactions that have been made against the database on behalf of one user. Transaction rollback is typically started by the initiator of the transaction. The actual transaction rollback process is similar to before-image recovery, except that only one user's transactions are removed from the database rather than all the user's transactions.

See Savepoint

Recovery File: See Journal File.

Recursive Relationship: A Recursive Relationship is a type of relationship in which the owner table and the member table are the same. For each instance of a recursive relationship, there is one owner row, and one or more member rows. A typical example for the relationship is Programs, where a Program may be composed of (Sub)programs, which in turn are composed of other (Sub)programs. The depth and breadth are unknown.

See Data Model.

Referential Integrity: See Data Integrity Rule.

Relation: A Relation is a table in which column entries are the same type and the rows (i.e., tuples) represent value instances of the columns.

Relational Algebra: Relational Algebra represents the specification of the operations that manipulate relations. The basic operations of the relational algebra approach can be characterized in three ways.

First, algebraic operators refer to a fixed number of relations; selection and projection are unary operators, i.e., they operate on one relation. Binary operators are union, intersection, difference, join, and division as they operate on two relations.

Second, algebraic operators apply simple selection criteria in which the selection operator applies a criterion that refers to constants and attribute values of individual tuples in one relation only. The join operator applies a selection criterion that refers to two attribute values of individual tuples in two relations. The division operator tests sets of attribute values in two relations for set inclusion. This class of selection criteria can be defined formally by the expressions of the propositional logic.

Third, algebraic operators provide target transformations for tuple restructuring. Projection and division operators choose distinguished attribute values to form derived relations.

Relational Calculus: Relational Calculus represents a language that states the desired results of a relational database manipulation using first-order predicate calculus.

Relational Database: A Relational Database is a collection of relation values (rows) of assorted degrees (tables), each of which satisfies the properties defined by a relation scheme.

Relational Data Model: A Relational Data Model is a data model providing for the expression of relationships among table columns as formal, mathematical relations. Informally, a relation appears as a table of data representing all occurrences of the relationship among the columns of the relation. A row of the table is called a tuple.

The row operations are STORE, DELETE, and MODIFY. The relationship operations are JOIN, PROJECT, DIVIDE, etc.

Relational View: See View.

Relationships: A Relationship represents a semantic affinity between two rows of the same or different tables. Either the DBMS already "knows" about the relationship, or the user is able to discover a hypothesized relationship's existence. In the "DBMS knows" case, the DBMS provides verbs to process the relationship instances that already exist among the rows. These relationships are called static because the basis for the relationship has been embedded in the business data rows or is stored in a separate physical database storage structure relationship data rows component that enables relationships to be processed without accessing actual business data rows. Such embedding is commonly represented by a pointer.

A static relationship DBMS requires formally defined relationships. These formal definitions are needed so that the DBMS can "know" to create the pointers that interrelate rows. Static relationships typically have a name and a set of rules that govern the operations that process rows through the relationship. For example, ordering rules would govern the order of row access for both retrieval and update.

There can be static relationship rules, for example, that prohibit duplicate rows within the relationship of Employee and Jobs, that is, Employee-Job, even though duplicates for employee-job record instances might be allowed under some other relationship in the database. This is in contrast to a duplicates clause that prohibits duplicate employees. There could also be rules that govern participation of rows in the relationship on the basis of column values in one or more record types.

If a static relationship occurs between two or more rows, there is a relationship instance. A relationship instance is the occurrence of the mechanism of relationship, not the rows that participate in the relationship instance. To say that the rows are the relationship as in "the relationship is a set of rows" has the same analogous logical consequence of having two people be their "marriage" relationship, and when the relationship is dissolved, so too are the people.

In dynamic relationship DBMS, the DBMS allows the user to specify common column values such as Department-Id as the basis of the relationship within the queries. On the basis of this query specified relationship, the "user discovers" related rows. The "from" value is in the relationship-source-table and is most commonly the table's primary key such as Department-Id. The "to" value is in the relationship-target-table and is most commonly one of the table's foreign keys such as the target Employee table's Department-Id.

Discoverable are the rows from the Department table and the Employee table that participate in that relationship. In this case, the Department table is related to zero, one, or more rows in the Employee Table.

The DBMS, again through special (but very different) verbs, determines whether any rows belong to a user hypothesized relationship. These relationships are called dynamic because they are dynamically discovered during the execution of the interrogation.

A dynamic relationship DBMS, in contrast, to a static relationship DBMS does not formally define the relationships between/among tables. Relationships for a dynamic relationship DBMS are defined either in the view that may be employed by multiple run-units, or in the run-unit itself.

A critical semantic flaw exists with discoverable/dynamic relationships. There is nothing to prevent the hypothesis of a relationship between a Teacher's degree (e.g., Degree = "MA") and a Student's birth state (e.g., Birth State = "MA"). Likely, this example has no semantic value. In a static relationship based DBMS, such relationship silliness can be prevented through data model design activities. Not so in a dynamic relationship based DBMS. In short, all is not free. Quality design is always a prerequisite to quality databases across the enterprise.

Relationships can also be information bearing or business-value-based. An information bearing relationship is one in which the rules for membership are wholly contained in the run-unit that inserts and disconnects rows to/from the relationship. A value-based relationship is one in which the rules for membership are required to be manifest as a column's value belonging to the MEMBER record. The "information" that might be derived is that the "best" employee is positioned to be the first while the worst employee is positioned to be the last. To achieve "positioning" with a value based relationship, there would have to be a column for Employee Rank were "1" is the best employee and the highest number is the "worst" employee. Under information bearing relationship schemes, static relationships are better than value-based relationships because it's the "position" of the row within the relationship that conveys the information, not the value of the Employee Rank column. In the value based relationship scheme there would have be a constant updating of the Employee Rank column values across all the rows.

SQL:1999's array data type provides the ability to have an information bearing relationship. That's because the position of the value in the array is persistent. However, SQL:1999, unlike a CODASYL set, does not have the ability to perform a an "Insert Before" array position. Thus, in SQL:1999, the values of the array elements would all have to be retrieved, properly reordered according to employees rank and re-stored.

Most static relationship DBMSs can have both static and dynamic relationships, while dynamic relationship DBMSs only have dynamic relationships. This is true for SQL DBMSs that conform to SQL:1986 through SQL:1992. SQL:1999 and beyond DBMSs can also have static relationships.

Notwithstanding, the eight types or kinds of relationships that are able to be defined (static) or created through DML commands (dynamic) are:

- Owner Member,
- Owner Multiple Member,
- Singular (Singular Member),
- Singular (Multiple Member),
- Recursive,
- Many-to-many,
- Inferential,
- One to One.

Each is defined in this book.

See ANSI Database Standards. See SQL Data Language Standard. See NDL Data Language Standard. See Data Model. See Relationships. See Static Relationship. See CODASYL Model. See CODASYL Set. See Referential Integrity within Data Integrity Rule. See Dynamic Relationship.

Relative Addressing: Relative Addressing represents a method of row selection from within DBMS rows that is based on the location of the row relative to the starting address of the first DBMS record instance. If a data record's address is 75, and if the blocking factor is 10, the row would be the fifth data row within the eighth DBMS record instance.

Reorganization: Reorganization represents two types of database reorganization: Logical and Physical. Both apply exclusively within DBMS environments. See Logical Reorganization and Physical Reorganization.

Repeating Group: See Fact.

Report: A Report is a formatted output from an interrogation. The structure and the format of a report contain a heading, description, calculations, and view column references.

Report Writer: See Natural Languages.

Representation: A Representation is a number or symbol used to express a particular concept or meaning. It may be in the form of a name, abbreviation, code, or numeric value.

Resource: A Resource is an enduring asset of value to the enterprise. Included for example are facilities, assets, staffs, money, even abstract concepts like reputation. If a resource is missing, the enterprise is incomplete.
    See Resource Life Cycle Analysis Model.
    See Project Management Model.

Resource Life Cycle: A Resource Life Cycle is the linear identification of the major states that must exist within life of the resource. The life cycle of a resource represents the resource's "cradle to grave" set of state changes.

Resource Life Cycle Analysis: A Resource Life Cycle Analysis is a set of enterprise resources, each set within a life cycle of major state transformations of those resources. These Resource Life Cycles can be interconnected, and used as a lattice work to attach the enterprise's inventory of database and business information systems, which in turn, greatly assists in the formation of Business Information Systems Plans.
    The fundamentals of Resource Life Cycle Analysis were first published by Ron Ross, a well known "data" consultant in his 1992 monograph, Resource Life Cycle Analysis A Business Modeling Technique for IS Planning. Resource Life Cycle Analysis (RLCA) uses a form of business modeling to perform information strategic planning.
    See Resource Life Cycle Analysis Model.

Resource Life Cycle Analysis Model: The Resource Life Cycle Analysis model, depicted in Figure 21, is a collection of tables from the Whitemarsh Metabase System. This model includes Resources (e.g., facilities, materiel and staff), how are they sequenced, interrelated, and how are they supported through databases and information systems.

Data Management's Concepts & Terms

The tables within the resource life cycle model include resource life cycle, resource life cycle node, resource life cycle structure, and resource life cycle structure type, resource, resource type, resource life cycle node database object assignment.

Resource life cycles have relationships across the life cycle nodes, and also between nodes from different resource life cycles. These inter-resource life cycle relationships are called precedence vectors. The name is derived from the fact that the business information system and database objects that are assigned to the source resource life cycle node should exist and be operating prior to the target resource life cycle node's assigned business information systems and database objects. Taken all together, the resource life cycles and the precedence vectors form a lattice work onto which business information systems and database objects can be allocated. Because these resource life cycles exist in a creation-order sequence within a given resource life cycle and between resource life cycles, the ability to construct an enterprise information

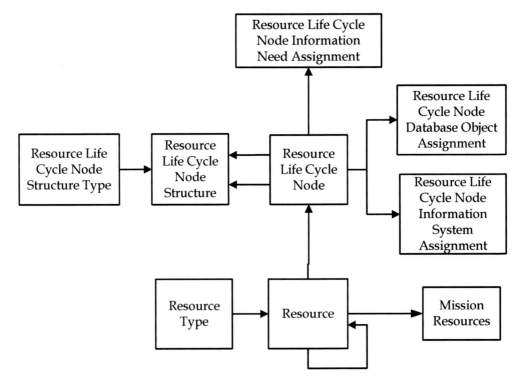

Figure 21. Resource Life Cycle Model.

systems plan is straight forward and able to be justified on the basis of business engineering.

Resource Life Cycle Analysis Node: A Resource Life Cycle Node is a life cycle state within the overall life cycle of the resource. If the resource is Employee, the life cycle may be the following: Employee Requisition, Employee Candidate, Employee New Hire, Assigned Employee, Reviewed Employee, and Separated Employee. It is common for business information systems and database objects to be allocated to specific resource life cycle nodes.
See Resource Life Cycle Analysis Model. See Project Management Model.

Resource Life Cycle Characteristics: Resource Life Cycle Characteristics represent a set of quality characterizations of a resource life cycle. A resource exists within the enterprise if and only if it exhibits the following characteristics: Basic, Centralized, Complex, Enduring, Shareable, Structured, and Valuable.
See Resource Life Cycle Analysis Model.

Resource Life Cycle Characteristic: Basic: The Resource Life Cycle Characteristic: Basic means that the resource must exist for the enterprise to exist.

Resource Life Cycle Characteristic: Centralized: The Resource Life Cycle Characteristic: Centralized means that the resource can be controlled and monitored centrally, even if distributed in creation or use.

Resource Life Cycle Characteristic: Complex: The Resource Life Cycle Characteristic: Complex means that the resource requires development and management.

Resource Life Cycle Characteristic: Enduring: The Resource Life Cycle Characteristic: Enduring means that the resource exists beyond business cycles.

Resource Life Cycle Characteristic: Shareable: The Resource Life Cycle Characteristic: Shareable means that the resource is shared by different functions of the enterprise.

Resource Life Cycle Characteristic: Structured: The Resource Life Cycle Characteristic: Structured means that the resource can be described and organized.

Resource Life Cycle Characteristic: Valuable: The Resource Life Cycle Characteristic: Valuable means that the resource must be protected, exploited, and/or leveraged by the enterprise.

Resource Life Cycle Node Business Information Systems Assignment: A Resource Life Cycle Node Business Information Systems Assignment is an association between a resource life cycle node and a business information system. A business information system may be assigned to one or more resource life cycle nodes and a resource life cycle node may be related to one or more business information systems.
See Resource Life Cycle Analysis Model.

Resource Life Cycle Node Database Object Assignment: A Resource Life Cycle Node Database Object Assignment is an association between a resource life cycle node and a database object. A database object may be assigned to one or more resource life cycle nodes and a resource life cycle node may be related to one or more database objects.
See Resource Life Cycle Analysis Model.

Resource Life Cycle Node Information Need Assignment: A Resource Life Cycle Node Information Need Assignment is the association of one resource life cycle node and an information need. A resource life cycle node may be related to one or more information needs and an information need may be related to one or more resource life cycle nodes.
See Resource Life Cycle Analysis Model.

Resource Life Cycle Node Matrix: The Resource Life Cycle Node matrix is the set of all resources, their life cycles and the precedence vectors among the nodes. Properly drawn the resource Life cycle node matrix resembles a PERT chart.
See Resource Life Cycle Analysis Model.

Resource Life Cycle Node Structure: The Resource Life Cycle Node Structure is the association of one resource life cycle node and another. The association represents a relationship between the two resources for some purpose.
See Resource Life Cycle Analysis Model.

Resource Life Cycle Node Structure Type: A Resource Life Cycle Node Structure Type represents a classification of a set of resource life cycle node structures. An example might be "enablement" and the associated resource life cycle node structure would mean that a "receivable" resource life cycle node from the "receivables" resource "enables" a "paid invoice" resource life cycle node from the "invoice" resource.
See Resource Life Cycle Analysis Model.

Resource Type: A Resource Type represents a collection of resources. Examples are finance resources, or property resources.
See Resource Life Cycle Analysis Model.

Restore: See Backup and Recovery.

Retention: Retention is a subclause of the Network Data Language (NDL) Standard's Set clause. The retention subclause specifies whether the table's membership in the database is FIXED, MANDATORY, or OPTIONAL. If the retention option for the table is FIXED, a member row must remain a member of some set instance from that set type until it is deleted from the database. If the retention option for the table is MANDATORY, a row must remain a member of that specific set instance or some other instance of the set until the row is erased from the database. If the retention option for the table is OPTIONAL, a row can be disconnected from a named set instance, and still belong to the database even though the row belongs to no other set instance.

Retrieval: Retrieval represents the process of obtaining stored data from a database. The process includes the operations of identifying, locating, and transferring the data.

Ring Structure: A Ring Structure is a set of relationships among rows such that the last next pointer points back to the first row of the ring.

RJE: RJE means remote job entry, which means that computer jobs done in batch are submitted for execution from remote locations.

Robust: Robust is a property that enables a system to continue error-free processing despite some failures.

Role: A Role is a named function that is performed by one or more users. An example is accounting clerk.

Rollback: See Backup. See Recovery.

Role Type: A Role Type is a classification of an assigned task within a project. An example might be Manager, Evaluator, Presenter, or Contributor.
   See Project Management Model.

ROM: Read Only Memory is a form of computer memory that is not erased when the computer loses power.

Root Segment: See Hierarchical Data Model.

Row: A row is a horizontal set of data values from a table, one from each column. A row is a tuple. The columns of a row form a relation. Rows are typically the smallest unit of data that can be stored into and erased from a table. In SQL:1986 through SQL:1992, all columns were simple facts. That is, atomic and non-derived. Starting with SQL:1999 and beyond, columns can be complex facts.
   See Table. See Fact. See the SQL Data Language Standard.

Run-Unit: A Run-Unit is the instance of a computer program that accesses a database, normally through a view. The language of the run-unit is immaterial.
   A run-unit command is a request for DBMS services that is transmitted to the DBMS by the run-unit.
   A multiple database run-unit is one that is able to access multiple databases during a single executing session of an instance of the run-unit. A multiple database run-unit must, therefore, be able to access multiple views, each from a different database.
   An HLI run-unit is a host language program, typically COBOL, with the incorporated DBMS verbs that access the database.

A natural language run-unit is an instance of a set of natural language commands that access the database to effect data selection, reporting, or update.

Save: See Backup.

Savepoint: A savepoint is a method of creating intermediate states within an overall database transaction. It is most common to use savepoints for very large or long running transactions. Suppose there is a database transaction that records updates to 1,000 Employees by giving them each a 10% raise, and at the same time adjusting the total department salary for the affected Departments of the Employees. Suppose further that there was an error at the 999th Employee. One way to recover to a state of integrity is to rollback all 999 updates to the Employees and to the various Departments in which the total Department Salary was updated.

A savepoint is a strategy whereby there can be intermediate roll-back positions. In the example, it might be every Department, regardless of the quantity of Employees within that Department. In this example, if the average quantity of Employees per Department was 100, there could be 10 save points. At the end of all the Employee and Departments there could be a final commit. If at any point along the way, only the current Department and its Employee set would have to be rolled back.

In SQL, savepoints were introduced in the ANSI SQL standard prior to SQL:1999 by the Oracle Corporation.

See Backup. See Recovery

Scale: Scale represents the negative power by which a number is multiplied taking into account its base. For example, the value of 104 base 10, scale 2 is 1.04.

Schema: A Schema is a database structure that encapsulates all its contained tables and other classes of schema objects such as data types, procedures, constraints, including the interrelationships of the various schema objects.

Schema Assigned Database Object: A Schema Assigned Database Object represents one or more database objects assigned to a schema.

See Database Object Model.

Secondary Key: See Key.

Security and Privacy: Security and Privacy represents those sets of DBMS and/or application facilities that are defined and enforced to prevent inadvertent and/or unauthorized access to the contents of the database(s) under the control of the DBMS. In general, there are protections for columns, rows and database operations. The security and privacy are specified in a security schema.

For security controlled by the DBMS, the database security specifications are represented through a linguistic expression of syntax and semantics over the interface between the user and the database in order to allow or restrict user access or manipulation of specific rows and/or columns and/or other database operations that may have already been more globally allowed.

Column security is accomplished in some SQL-based DBMSs directly through a special SQL security syntax. If columns are not allowed for specific users, the user cannot perceive that the columns even exist through the interface. Some other early DBMSs implemented security and privacy through clauses contained in the schema.

More modern DBMSs create security and privacy through a separately defined and compiled set of security syntax that is part of the overall database definition process. This security schema is analogous to but different from views.

Row security can only be created through views. If multiple users access data through the same window, but need to access different collections of rows, an additional filter, based on column values in the row, would have to be active in order to discern one row collection from the other. This kind of screening can be placed into view definitions through the use of parameter-based WHERE clauses in views.

Database-operations-security enables certain database processes to be inaccessible such as reading and/or writing.

For application-based security, there can be application level security. This can be accomplished by a special set of security facilities included in each application that provide column, row, and operations security. The complete specification of this type of security is stored in the application's special security database and is managed by the application administered.

Segment: A Segment is a name for a discrete portion of a complex table, usually relating to a repeating group occurrence. For example, if an Employee table has a repeating group, Dependents, each occurrence of the repeating group is a segment.

Selection: Selection represents the identification of a subset of stored data meeting specified criteria.
   See WHERE clause.

Semantics: Semantics represent a meaning attributed to a syntactical form in a language. Semantics are the relationships of characters or groups of characters to their meanings, independent of the manner of their interpretation and use. Semantics apply to almost everything in database including schemas, tables, columns, and relationships. Within tables, semantics govern the meaning of the table's name. An example is Employee Compensation.
   Within columns, the column's name consists of its common business name, for example, Salary, and then the meaning modifiers associated with the name such as Estimated, North American, and Annual. There are also the data use semantic modifiers such as Dollars and Amount. Each of the column's name parts has meaning, and collectively there is also a collective meaning. In the case of the cited column, the name would be Estimated North American Annual Salary Dollars Amount.
   Relationships are semantic expressions of affinity between tables, and once valued between the rows from the tables. An example would be the relationship between an Employee and Skills. Within SQL, relationships are physically materialized by replicating the Employee-Id value from the Employee primary key as a foreign key value as Skill Employee Id. Relationships should also have names In this case the most likely name is Employee Skill. Relationships can also have rules that govern the allowed affinity such as no Skill row can exist without an "owner" employee.

Sequential Search: Sequential Search represents the data record access according to the order represented by a key field.

Serial Search: A Serial Search represents access according to the physical storage order of the records.

Data Management's Concepts & Terms

Serial Storage: Serial Storage is a row storage strategy in which rows are ordered in sequence (sorted) according to the values of one or more key columns in each row, and in which the rows are physically stored adjacent to one another according to this sequence.

Serializability: Serializability is a property in which the effects of a group of transactions are invisible to other groups of actions that are concurrently executing. The effect is that all the transactions in the group are perceived to have executed serially. Further, as each group of transactions successfully completes (that is, after a COMMIT), the effects of the group can be rolled back as a unit.

Set: See Collection Data Type.

Simple Fact: See Fact.

Simple Row: A Simple Row is a tuple that consists only of simple-fact column values.

Simple Table A Simple Table is a set of columns in which all the column data types are simple.

Single Thread: See Concurrent Operations.

Single User Mode: See Concurrent Operations.

Singular, Multiple Member Relationship: A Singular, Multiple Member Relationship is a type of relationship in which there is no owner table, and one or more member record types. There may be one or more member rows of each of the members for each relationship instance. A typical example for the relationship is again High-Achievers, where Part-Time-Employees, Full-time-employees, and Retired-Employees are the members.
    See Data Model. See Relationships.

Singular Set: A Singular Set is a type of relationship among rows in which there is no owner table. If there is only one table identified within the Singular Set, the relationship is a Singular, Single Member Relationship. If there are multiple tables identified within the Singular Set, the relationship is a Singular, Multiple Member Relationship.

See ANSI Database Standards. See SQL Data Language Standard. See NDL Data Language Standard. See Relationships. See Static Relationship. See CODASYL Model. See CODASYL Set.

Singular, Single Member Relationship: A Singular, Single Member Relationship is a type of relationship in which there is no owner table, and only one member record type. There may be one or more member rows of the member for each relationship instance. A typical example for the relationship is High-Achievers, where Full-Time-Employees is the member, and the rows that belong are those determined to be high achievers.
See Data Model. See Relationships.

Skill: A Skill is the name accorded to a set of work accomplishment techniques possessed by a staff member who would be assigned to a particular project task. An example would be Data Modeler.
See Project Management Model.

Skill Level: A Skill level is an assessment that is assigned to a particular task. The assignment is expressed as a number, nn.mm. It represents a number that is employed to multiply a raw staff hours by to arrive at a quantity that is affected by the represented skill level. For example, if the norm hours were 40 and the skill level was 1.25, the expected amount of time required to accomplish the task would be 50. If the value was 0.74, the expected amount of time required to accomplish the task would be 30.
See Project Management Model.

Skill Level Type: A Skill Level Type is a broad classification of a collection of skills of different kinds. Commonly it is expressed as Expert, Journeyman, Apprentice or Novice. Each such classification is assigned a multiplier value that is employed in conjunction with a Skill to arrive at a skill level.
See Project Management Model.

Snapshot: See Backup and Recovery.

Specified Data Model: A Specified Data Model is a data model of concepts that is independent of use within specific databases. Specified Data Models of concepts are defined through entities, attributes and relationships within specific subjects. There is a many-to-many relationship between the Specified

Data Model and the Implemented Data Model. The meta model for the Specified Data Model is presented in Figure 22.

In Specified Data Models, entities can have subtypes to any depth. An example might be for education which might have a common set of attributes for all classes of education, and subtypes for each different education class such as high school, college, or trade school.

Attributes represent the deployment of data elements within entities. Because of this one-to-many relationship between data element and attribute, users can see which attributes employ a data element's semantics regardless of the entity or subject.

Attributes can also be assigned various meaning modifier semantics and data use semantics. This enables automatic name construction for attributes. Automatic definitions and abbreviations are also enabled because there is a persistent relationship between the assigned semantic and the attribute. This too enables finding and reporting attributes regardless of entity and subject on the basis of either a semantic or data use modifier.

There can also be relationships among the entities within one subject, and there can be relationships between entities across subjects. If this were just a data model in a conceptual form, there could not be relationships across different subject-based data models. Each conceptual data model would be a stove-pipe that could only be transformed into a logical stove pipe data model and thereafter into a physical stove pipe data model.

Again, Specified Data Models are not conceptual forms of a data model. Rather, they are well-developed data models in their own right. Each entity within a Specified Data Model should be in third normal form. Specified Data Models are persistent. Their form remains as defined. Its structures, that is,

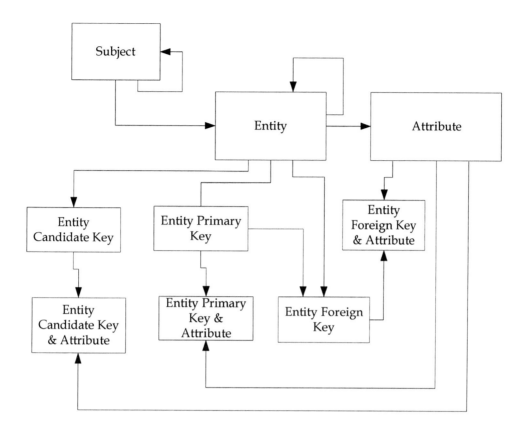

Figure 22. Specified Data Model.

the data models of the concepts, are available as templates for the construction of one or more Implemented Data Models.

Specified Data Model Relationship: A Specified Data Model Relationship is a relationship mechanism that relates one instance of one entity to a set of instances of another entity. While there are eight classes of relationships, the most common are the one-to-many, and one-to-one. In the case of one-to-many, the relationship mechanism is the primary key attributes of the "related-from" entity matching the foreign key attributes of the "related-to" entity. The term, foreign key, comes from the fact that it's really a "copy" of the "related-from" entity's primary key. Relationships should always be named and defined to the extent that the real purpose of the relationship is clear. In the Specified Data Model relationships can be between entities in multiple subjects. For recursive relationships, the "related-from" table and the "related-to" table are the same.

SQL Data Language Standard: The SQL Data Language Standard is a data language for data models that contain data structures, relationships and operations. The SQL language defines tables of columns of data and allows access to the data represented by tables. The facts within the SQL Data Language Standard can be both simple and complex. The SQL Data Language Standard relationships are almost all value-based via primary and foreign keys. Starting with SQL:1999, some of the relationships can be via system generated pointers. The SQL Data Language Standard operations are row-based and relationships-based.

Starting in 1999, the SQL Data Language Standard became unique to the language. The SQL Data Language Standard, by SQL:2003, became a melding of the data structures from the Network, Hierarchical, Independent Logical File, and Relational Data Models.

The SQL language, originally known as the Structured Query Language, was developed to support the relational data model. The language was created by IBM in the early 1970s. The SQL language consists of the following main components:

- Database and data record structure definition including relationship integrity specification, and views.

- Data record operations for insert, update and delete, and relationship operations that accomplish JOIN, PROJECT, DIVIDE, INTERSECTION, and DIFFERENCE.

- Data record selection operations from a single data record or through nested subqueries to then select shared data value related data records.

- Privacy definition and control

- Concurrent update and retrieval data control

- Transaction processing

Because the SQL language is commonly employed through traditional programming languages like COBOL, SQL contains record-at-a-time processing commands, that is, cursor operations, that operate against selected sets of records.

The SQL language was first standardized in 1986. The basis for forming the standard was to standardize only those facilities that the vendor-members of the H2 committee could agree upon. Simply, the goal of the standard was to fix a base-line of established practice. From 1986 through to the next standard, 1989, other features were standardized including referential integrity. Referential integrity is an old concept and has been in CODASYL network database management systems since the late 1960s.

By the time the SQL language became standardized by ANSI in 1986, several vendors, such as IBM (DB/2), Oracle, Sybase, and Informix had become very popular. These DBMSs gained market share against non-SQL DBMSs such as Cullinet's IDMS, IBM's IMS, Information Builder's Focus, and Software Ag's Adabas. The non-SQL DBMS vendors were then under significant pressure to either develop SQL language interfaces to their systems or completely transform their DBMSs to the relational data model. In the next 10 years, these vendors created SQL interfaces. By the end of the 1980s, it had become very clear that database designers, programmers, and end users could employ the SQL language to accomplish their activities without having a DBMS that was built on a strictly relational database engine.

The next SQL standard was brought out in 1992. This was a major upgrade to the SQL language. The extensions were mainly in integrity constraints, multiple-language support, transaction processing, full referential integrity, and the like. The fundamental components of the underlying data structures and relationship processing remained the same. That is, tables that contain only single-valued fields.

Starting in 1992, the H2 committee began the development of dramatic extensions to the SQL:1992 standard. The greatest change in the standard is that it no longer adheres to the 1970 relational data model. The second biggest change is that the SQL:1999 language now consists of individual parts that comprise a foundation and then a series of independently specified packages.

Data Management's Concepts & Terms

SQL/1986	SQL/1989	SQL/1992
Basic features, that is	SQL/1986 plus	SQL/1989 plus
Tables Columns Views Basic relational operations Some integrity constraints Language bindings to COBOL, Fortran, C, etc.	Partial Referential Integrity	Assertions Bit data type CASE Character Sets Connection Management DATETIME Domains Dynamic SQL Enhanced constraints Full Referential Integrity Get Diagnostics Grouped operations Information Schema Multiple module support National character sets Natural joins (inner & outer) Row & Table constraints Schema manipulation Subqueries in check clauses Table constraints Temporary tables Transaction Management Union and intersect

Table 7. Comparative 1986 through 1992 SQL Data Language Standard Features.

Provided here, in outline form, are the contents of the SQL:1999 standard.

- Tables that have been enhanced to support new built-in data types (boolean, enumerated, extensions to character sets, translations, and collations)

- BLOB and CLOB data types

- Abstract Data Types (user defined data type with behavior, an encapsulated internal structure, and access characteristics of public, protected, or private)
    ♦ strong typing

- subtypes and inheritance
- encapsulation
- virtual attributes
- substitutability
- polymorphic routines
- dynamic binding
- compile time type checking
- value ADTs

- Array

- Row Types (table person (SSN, name(first, middle, last), address(street, city, state, zip(four, five)))))

- User Defined Functions

- Predicate extensions (for all, for some, similar to, cursor extensions, null values, assertions, view updatability, joins)

- Triggers
  - Different triggering events, update, delete, and insert
  - Optional condition
  - Activation time: before and after
  - Multiple statement action
  - Several triggers per table
  - User-defined ordering
  - Condition and multiple statement action per each row or per statement

- Roles (enhancements to security), & Savepoints

- Recursion

As can be seen from the list of capabilities presented, SQL:1999 is no longer a simple language for defining, accessing and managing tables consisting only of single valued columns of data. With respect to the basic data model capabilities, the SQL:1999 language more closely supports the independent logical file data model from the 1960s. It is therefore true to say that SQL:1999 is more of an implementation of the independent logical file data model (e.g.,

Adabas, Inquire, Datacom/DB, and Sybase) than of the 1970 relational data model.

SQL:1999 has, however, gone way beyond the capabilities of the independent logical file data model by incorporating facilities such as user-defined types, embedded programming language, and libraries of SQL:1999 defined routines for areas like full text management and spatial data. To say that these SQL:1999 extensions are mere "extended interpretations" of the relational data model is like saying that an intercontinental ballistic missile is merely an "extended interpretation" of a spear.

SQL:1999's impact on network and hierarchical data model DBMSs is significant. Network data model DBMSs have traditionally allowed complex data record structures with arrays, groups, repeating groups and nested repeating groups. A very unique characteristic of the SQL:1999 data model is that it now allows arrays. Elements of an array are able to be outward references to other data. Since the order of the elements in an SQL:1999 array is maintained by the SQL:1999 DBMS, the array, with its outward references, is essentially a CODASYL set. This is a dramatic departure from the relational data model.

The only remaining and viable network DBMSs are IDMS by Computer Associates and Oracle DBMS (formerly the VAX DBMS). Both have had an SQL language interface for about 20 years. How Computer Associates plans to take advantage of the existing IDMS facilities with SQL:1999 is not known. A significant customer of Oracle's DBMS (formerly Vax DBMS from DEC) is Intel who uses the Consilium manufacturing package to manage computer chip manufacturing. How the Oracle Corporation plans to take advantage of the existing VAX DBMS facilities with SQL:1999 is also not known

The only two hierarchical DBMSs, System 2000 and IBM's IMS will likely not be impacted at all. System 2000 is no longer being advanced by SAS, and IBM has a full implementation of DB/2 on many different operating systems.

SQL:1999's impact on independent logical file DBMSs, for example, Adabas, Focus, and Datacom/DB is significant. These DBMSs already support many of the SQL:1999 data model facilities. It would seem that these DBMSs could rapidly conform to the SQL:1999 standard. If these vendors embrace the SQL:1999 model, these DBMSs could claim conformance to the SQL:1999 standard.

Simply stated, the SQL:1999 language defines a unique data model. It contains:

- The ability to model CODASYL sets,

- Many of the natural data clustering features of the hierarchical data model,

- Explicit many-to-many and inferential relationships like the independent logical file data model, and finally,

- The unique ability to directly model recursive relationships.

It therefore can only be said that the SQL:1999 data model is unique unto itself. Clearly, it is not the relational data model, CODASYL network, hierarchical, or independent logical file data models. Simply, SQL:1999 is a data model unto itself.

SQL:1999 and beyond support s both simple and complex facts as Table 8 illustrates:

Column Data Type	Definition	SQL 1999
Single Value	Each component represents a single value such as Birthdate with the value 11/11/1987	✔
Array	Each component represents multiple values such as Nicknames with values "Buddy, Guy, Mac"	✔-Note 1
Groups	Each component has subcomponents to represent single-set of values such as Address with Street-1, Street-2, City, State, Zip	✔-Note 2
Repeating Groups	Each component has subcomponents to represent multi-sets of values such as Dependents that contains subcomponents, Dependent Name, Dependent Birth date, Dependent SSN.	✔-Note 3
Nested Repeating Groups	Employee (Dependents (Hobbies))	✔-Note 4

Table 8. SQL:1999 support of Simple and Complex Facts.

Notes:

1	Arrays as a data type for a column
2	ROW data structure of a column
3	ROW data structure for a column wherein each Row structure field has the data type, ARRAY
4	ROW data structure for a column with contained ARRAYs where each ARRAY element is a ROW data structure with contained ARRAYs where each ARRAY element, etc.

SQL:1999 also supports all the eight different types of relationships as illustrated in Table 9.

Name	Example	SQL 1999
One-to-many	Employee to dependents	✔-Note 1
Owner-multiple-member	Territory contains salesmen and customers	✔-Note 2
Singular-one-member	Top performing employees	✔-Note 1
Singular-multiple-member	Top performing current, former, part-time, and retired employees	✔-Note 3
Recursive	Organization contains organization	✔-Note 4
Many-to-many	Automobiles and owners	✔-Note 5
One-to-one	Table and its primary key	✔-Note 6
Inferential	Many houses each with a location, and then buyer with desired location	✔-Note 7

Table 9. SQL:1999 Relationships.

Notes:

1	Traditional relational data model (SQL:1986, 1989, & 1992)
2	Implemented as a ROW(TerritoryId, Salesman REF (SalesmanId), Cust_Id (integer) ARRAY[500]),
3	Developed using Subtables where Employees are partitioned off into their common columns (employee) and their unique columns (current, former, part-time, and retired)
4	Recursion operations built into the language (WITH RECURSION)
5	Cross joins from within elements of ARRAYS contained as data types of column in different tables
6	Effectively as tables and subtables. Most directly with UNIQUE Fkey
7	A single valued non-primary key Location within House and same for Buyer

See Data Model. See ANSI Database Standards. See ANSI SQL.

SQL Data Type: An SQL Data Type is a classification of the values represented by a column of a row of data. The SQL data types represent both simple and complex facts. Each SQL data type imposes a set of rules regarding allowable values and allowed operations on the values. An acceptable example is the adding an integer value to a date value. An unacceptable example is the adding together the values from two dates.

There are two broad classes: primitive data types and data structure data types. The first class conforms to simple facts. The second class conforms to complex facts. The primitive data type, or simple fact data types, are represented by character, integer, binary, and the like.

Data structure data types enable the definition of complex facts. These were introduced to the SQL language within SQL:1999. These included arrays, repeating groups, and nested repeating groups. Contained within each data structure data type are the primitive data type specifications for the ultimately represented simple facts. For example, Telephone Numbers may be a data structure type: array. The array element may have the primitive data type of character.

See Fact. See Data Model. See ANSI Database Standards. See ANSI SQL. See SQL Data Language Standard. See NDL Data Language Standard

Data Management's Concepts & Terms

Staff: Staff represents all the different persons who can be assigned to a project. In the case of a project's staff it represents the project's lead person. In the case of Staff Skill Level, it represents the name of a person who is able to perform a certain skill at a given skill level.
See Project Management Model.

Staff Skill Level: A Staff Skill Level represents a given person possessing a give skill and the ability to perform that skill at a certain level. An example is George McNeil who is a Data Modeler at the Expert level with a 0.75 work performance rating.
See Project Management Model.

State: A state is the name of the U.S. State of the staff member. An example is Pennsylvania.
See Project Management Model.

Static Relationship: A static relationship is a mechanism that relates rows of one table to a row of a different table. Static relationships are represented as DBMS-constructed address-pointers that are stored in the related-from table. The method of changing a relationship between the related-from table row to a different related-to table row requires obtaining the DBMS-constructed row-address from the new related-to table row and replacing the existing related-to address-pointer that exists in the related-from table row.

The Network and Hierarchical data models consist entirely of static relationships. The Independent Logical File data model has static relationships within the data structure of each independent file, but dynamic relationships between independent files. The SQL:1986, :1989, :1992 data model standard for SQL only has dynamic relationships. Starting with SQ:1999 some of the relationships can be static.
See Data Model. See Relationships. See Dyanaic Relationships.

Status Type: A Status Type is a classification of a status that can be assigned to either a project as whole, or to a task as a whole within a project. An example, is Complete, Planned, or Underway.
See Project Management Model.

Storage Structure: A Storage Structure is the physical organization of a database. That is, its complete set of dictionary, indexes, relationships, and data. These data are organized into DBMS record instances. The storage structure is specified through the physical schema.

Stored Procedure: A Stored Procedure is a process that is executed by the DBMS upon request by an end user program.

Subject: A Subject is an area of interest from within the enterprise that is to be represented through structures of data values. Examples can include address structures, person name structures, contracts, purchase orders, and the like. Subjects can be hierarchical. Commonly, subjects are related to policies accomplished by knowledge workers that require "proof of execution." Subjects are not databases, however. Nor are subjects the concepts from within the Data Element Model.
   See Specified Data Model. See Data Element Model.

Subschema (External Schema or User Schema): See View.

Subschema Data Definition Language: See View.

Subschema Record Type: See View.

System: A System is a collection of programs that accomplish a well defined class of actions. The system typically has a flow among programs with a job control language or driver program to govern this flow. A system may be decomposed into subsystems.

System Control: System Control is a collection of facilities and functions within a DBMS environment that relates to audit trails, message processing, backup and recovery, concurrent operations, multiple database processing, reorganization, security and privacy, application optimization, and installation and maintenance. Each of these terms is defined in this book.

Systems Analysis: The combined activity of data analysis and process analysis in support of building business systems.

Table: A Table is intended to be a well-defined expression of one policy within a schema. Ideally, the collection of all the tables within a schema area should define a coherent collection policy.

A table is a policy homogeneous collection of assigned table columns that are drawn from the semantics of data elements, or alternatively, from attributes.

Tables have precise specifications including constraints, primary and foreign keys, and other table centered features. Within the scope of the Implemented Data Model generalization level for data architectures, these table specifications do not represent actual rows of data because this level is not bound to a particular DBMS and is not related to any specific business information systems. These tables, and the entire Implemented Data Model are intended to be one of the five specific data model generalization layers.

Tables can be subtyped to represent collections of columns that have a common set and several non-intersecting sets. Starting with SQL:1999, columns represent both simple and complex facts.

Among a table's columns there are columns that support a table's primary key column, none, one, or more candidate keys, none, one or more foreign keys, and none, one, or more non key columns.

When the columns belonging to the table are in third normal form, the facts are all simple and the rows are called simple rows. If arrays, groups, repeating groups, and nested repeating groups are assigned, the table is not in third normal form, the facts are complex, and the table is called complex. While the ANSI SQL Data Language Standard supports complex tables, the relational data model does not.

Hence, ANSI SQL:1999 and more recent SQL standards are not relational. That means that if you have created an Implemented or Operational Data Model design that has complex tables, or complex columns, DBMSs such as Oracle or SQL Server, DB2 may not be able to compile those SQL Schemas.

It is unfortunate that all SQL DBMS systems have not implemented complex tables and/or complex-fact columns. Some DBMSs have implemented some aspects of SQL:1999 and later standards but they have not done so in a standard's conforming manner consistent with each other. If your database design does not have either complex tables and/or complex columns you are effectively employing entry-level SQL:1992.

This lack of implementation of the ANSI SQL standard makes databases less efficient. Whole tables are created for Telephone Numbers, or other types of arrays, groups, repeating groups and nested repeating groups, all in the name of fealty to the "relational religion." Not only is this unnecessary, it is expensive and non-productive in terms of design, implementation, and maintenance both for database architectures and application programs. DBMS vendors have invented whole collections of difficult to understand, complex to implement, and tedious to maintain "relational-deconstructor" processes and techniques that produce disk-based database storage structures that create the very efficiencies that were thwarted by the all too simple relational data model of 1970.

A table check clause is a collection of data integrity rules that must test "true" before a row is allowed into the database. Typical table check clauses require that all the columns within a table must be valued, or that duplicate rows are not allowed.

Although unlikely, some tables and even some schemas may never be represented within Operational Data Models. Additionally, some columns within a table may never be employed. A table may contain columns that map to attributes from multiple entities. Tables can be sub-typed.

See Implemented Data Model. See SQL Data Language Standard. See NDL Data Language Standard. See ANSI Database Standards. See Fact.

Table Candidate Key: A Table Candidate Key represents a collection of columns within a table that, when their values are collectively employed, result in the retrieval or update of a single row of data for that table. There may be multiple candidate keys within a table. Columns of candidate keys are not allowed to overlap each other or the table's primary key. The set of candidate keys not chosen as the primary key are called alternate keys.

See Implemented Data Model.

Table Candidate Key Assigned Column: A Table Candidate Key Assigned Column represents one or more Columns assigned to a Table Candidate Key. The columns exist within an implemented sequence. Candidate key columns are not allowed to include any columns within the table's primary key.

See Implemented Data Model.

Table Foreign Key: A Table Foreign Key is an exact replication of a related table's primary key. The name of the foreign key should match closely the relationship it represents. The columns of the foreign key should be able to be deleted entirely from the table without any loss of policy. The columns of the foreign key are not allowed to overlap the columns of the table's primary key. In addition to the foreign key's columns, there are additional rules governing

Data Management's Concepts & Terms

inserts, updates, and deletes. In a recursive relationship, the table of the foreign key is the same as its corresponding primary key table.
  See Implemented Data Model.

Table Foreign Key Assigned Column: A Table Foreign Key Assigned Column represents one or more Columns assigned to a Table Foreign Key. The columns exist within an implemented sequence. Foreign key columns are not allowed to include any columns within the table's primary key.
  See Implemented Data Model.

Table Look up: A Table Look Up is a table of codes and values employed to explain data that is contained in the database. An example is D.C. which means District of Columbia.

Table Primary Key: Table Primary Key is the designation of one or more columns that can be used to locate one row instance. Traditionally, the value set of a primary key is unique across all rows of a table. The ANSI SQL Data Language Standard also allows non-unique primary keys.
  There can only be one primary key within a table. Columns of primary key are not allowed to overlap each other or the table's candidate key.
  See Implemented Data Model.

Table Primary Key Assigned Column: A Table Primary Key Assigned Column represents one or more Columns assigned to a Table Primary Key. The columns exist within an implemented sequence.
  See Implemented Data Model.

Task: A task is a collection of activities that are performed during the execution of a project. An example is Data Model Development, or User Acceptance Testing.
  See Project Management Model.

Task & Work Environment Factor: A Task & Work Environment Factor is an association of a Task with a Work Environment Factor. In this assignment, the work environment factor includes not only the assigned factor itself but also the multiplier for that factor. There can be multiple Task & Work Environment Factors that together provide an overall multiplier for arriving at the total staff hours for the particular task. Examples might be Customer Management Data Model Development with infrequent client review,

Customer Management Data Model Development with inadequate data modeling tools, Customer Management Data Model Development with no metadata management support. If each had a multiplier factor of 1.25, the combined work factor is (1.25 x 1.25 x 1.25) 1.95. That would mean that a normative staff hour estimate of 200 hours would be proposed as 390 staff hours.

See Project Management Model.

Task Skill Level Requirement: A Task Skill Level Requirement is the association of a skill requirement for a particular task. An example is a Data Modeler at the Expert level.

See Project Management Model.

Task Template: A Task Template is a template for a given task. The template contains the set of tasks that are considered as best practice. The objective of the task template is to enable the creation of project level tasks that are the minimum essential tasks to achieve success. An example is the set of tasks for building an enterprise data model. Once a project template is chosen for a project, the project template's deliverable and task templates automatically populate the deliverable and task tables.

See Project Management Model.

Teleprocessing Task: A Teleprocessing Task is a small unit of work accomplished by the teleprocessing monitor system whenever needed.

Temporary View Table: A Temporary View Table is a set of data derived by an expression of relational operators applied to a collection of base tables. See View.

Time Charges: Time Charges represent the quantity of hours along with the quantity of work products that were performed during a particular work period.

Top-Down versus Bottom-up Modeling: Top-Down versus Bottom-up Modeling is a comparison of two different approaches to modeling. Data models across the five levels of data model generalizations, that is, Data Element Models, Specified Data Models, Implemented Data Models, Operational Data Models, and View Data Models, can be built either top-down or bottom-up. It makes no sense to presume that data modeling can only be accomplished top-down. If that were the case, all organizations with existing database inventories (which means close to 100% of all organizations) would have to blow up all their Operational Data Model inventories and start over to re-engineer their entire data model environment.

Since "top-down-only" is a non-starter suggestion, there has to be a process of importing existing data models at the Operational Data Model level, inductively arriving at "union" data models on a functional grouping basis at the Implemented Data Model level, and then, by induction once more, distilling out all the data models of the concepts and creating the Specified Data Model level.

While starting top-down might appear to be simpler and quicker, actually it actually takes longer. That is because proceeding from theory to reality always involves many iterations of evolving the theory until it reflects reality. By starting at reality and moving up generalization levels to theory, the process is faster, and certainly has immediate payout.

The top-down approach requires the creation and exposition of all enterprise-wide data elements first, then all Specified Data Models, then all Implemented Data Models, and then through some unknown magic process, mapping the Implemented Data Models to the existing Operational Data Models. Simply put, it takes too long, costs too much, produces too little, and always results in significant culture clashes.

By starting bottom-up, a collection of data models in a given functional area can be identified and loaded into the Metabase System through an SQL DDL import. An examination of these models will likely produce one that is the "least worst" or the "most comprehensive." That model is promoted up to the Implemented Data Model level. Then, the remaining models in the functional area are mapped, or they result in additional tables or more columns. Either way, there quickly evolves a "union" model across the entire functional area. That, in turn, enables immediate "where-used" reporting.

If value domains are available, they can be entered into the Data Element Model and mapped to the appropriate columns of the Operational Data Model. If there are two different value domains for DBMS columns that are, in turn, mapped to the same Implemented Data Model column, there's a data interoperability mismatch at the operational level. Knowing just that produces immediate value.

This bottom-up approach can proceed to discovering columns that are used multiple times (i.e., same meaning but with different names) and making them data elements. Finally, there can be quick discoveries of commonly used concepts about which little data models can be constructed.

This bottom-up approach is a bit messy, but is clearly faster, and never suffers from the "when will this ever be done and be of value" syndrom. The information technology graveyard is full of top-down enterprise data models. No more are needed, ever.

See Data Driven. See Process Driven. See Data Element Model. See Specified Data Model. See Implemented Data Model. See Operational Data Model. See View Data Model.

Topology: A Topology, with respect to data management represents a collection of artifacts across a named domain. There would thus be the named collection of attributes in an entity, columns in a table, data elements within a data element concept, etc.

Transaction: A Transaction is a command, message, or input record that explicitly or implicitly calls for processing action (e.g., updating a record). A transaction is atomic with respect to recovery and concurrency.

Transaction Backout: See Backup and Recovery.

Transaction Processing Monitor: A Transaction Processing Monitor is a software package that interfaces with the on-line end-user. It receives and transmits messages that are subsequently processed by DBMS and standard access programs.

Transitive Dependency: Transitive Dependency represents a semantic relationship between one or more nonkey columns and one or more other nonkey columns.

Tree Structure: See Hierarchical Data Model.

Trigger: A Trigger is a process that automatically executes either before or after an insert, delete, or modify operation takes place.

Truncate: Truncate represents the deletion of characters from a character string, usually from the end of the string.

Data Management's Concepts & Terms

Tuple: A row from a table.

Unload: See Load.

Unordered: Unordered means that there is no repeatable sequence among the members of a collection.

Update (Data): Data Update is the process of changing data values within existing rows, adding new rows to the database, deleting rows from the database, or changing the relationships that relate rows.

Static and dynamic relationship DBMSs change data values in a similar manner. A row is selected, retrieved, changed, and written to the database.

Adding or deleting rows via a dynamic-relationship-based DBMS involves merely adding or deleting rows to or from the appropriate data storage component. Adding or deleting rows to a static-relationship-based DBMS involves the additional step of modifying the relationships that bind the rows together.

Changing the relationships that bind rows together differs significantly between static and dynamic relationship DBMSs. In a static relationship DBMS, the relationship modification process involves four steps.

- The row must be found.

- The row must be disconnected from the relationship that binds it to other rows.

- The new relationship context in which the row is to be stored must be found.

- The row is connected into that relationship.

The process of changing a dynamic relationship, in contrast, is the mere process of changing the column's value that is used within the run-unit to identify the collection of rows that participate in the static relationship.

Data updates that change columns that are indexed, or that change row membership, automatically invoke DBMS processes that adjust the indexes, or the pointers from "neighboring" rows.

User: A User is the name most commonly applied to a person who causes the execution of a job unit.

User Interface: A User Interface represents a system boundary at which the user issues computer language commands.

User Schema (Subschema): See View.

User View: See Vew.

Valid, Invalid, and Range Value Tables: See Data Element Model.

Value Domain Data Type: Value Domain Data Types is a classification of the values represented by a set of data values. The common data types are character, integer, binary, and the like. Each data type imposes a set of rules regarding allowable values and allowed operations on the values. While adding an integer value to a date value would be allowed, adding two dates would not.
   See Data Element Model.

Value Domain Structure: A Value Domain Structure represents a collection of data element concepts that are related and are in turn represented by a collective data element concept.

Value Domain Structure Type: A Value Domain Structure Type represents a classification of a set data element concepts.
   See Data Element Model.

Value Domain Value: Value Domain Values represent the actual values that are defined within the context of a value domain. These include valid, invalid, and range values, and are assigned as constraints to data elements, columns, or DBMS columns. The enumeration may be valid only, invalid only, discrete only, range only, discrete and range, or finally collections of valid and invalid values. In any of the combination cases, the metadata management system must contain a processor to identify conflicts.
   See Data Element Model.

Data Management's Concepts & Terms

Value Domain Value Structure: Value Domain Value Structures represent the mapping between values of different value domains.
See Data Element Model.

Value Domain Value Structure Type: A Value Domain Value Structure Types represents a classification of a set of value domain value structures. For example, Gender Value Mappings, Male Gender Value Mappings and Female Gender Value Mappings, then the actual male gender values that are mapped and the female gender values that are mapped.
See Data Element Model.

Value Domains: Value Domains are the included, excluded, discrete or range sets of values that are allowed within the overall context of the value meanings specified within conceptual value domains. Value domains are used by either data elements or subsets are employed by attributes of entities, columns of tables, or DBMS columns of DBMS tables. Value domains, along with their value domain values and relationships among value domain values, are identified, defined, described, and if appropriate, enumerated. Value domains are also associated with their parent conceptual value domains. Value domains are able to be assigned to data elements, attributes of entities of Specified Data Model subjects, columns of tables of Implemented Data Models schemas, and DBMS columns of DBMS tables of Operational Data Model schemas.
See Data Element Model.

Variable Length Data Element: See Data Element.

Variable Length Record: See Data Record.

Vector: See Data Element.

View: A View is the interface between the Operational Data Model and the Business Information System. Views are defined within the scope of the Operational Data Model for a specific database within a specific DBMS. Retrieval views can contain complex selection logic and also multi-table normalization logic that enable application programs not to have to know the database's structure or to navigate the database. Update views can also contain constraint clauses that check the quality of the data prior to it being sent to the DBMS that in turn updated the database. Some update views are restricted to one table.

The view represents a logical partitioning of the database for an individual's access. In short, a view is the user's window into the database. A view instance is created as a consequence of the execution of the view's components.

To handle the requirements of different programming languages that must "know" about views, a view definition language typically has view column, row, and view column rename clauses.

The view might also have conversion specifications to allow for translation of schema data types to program language data types.

A view may contain the specification of relationships, that is, nested selects and joins, that is to be "executed" whenever the run-unit requests rows through the view.

Whenever a view is derived from other views, it must contain the specification of the navigation logic (access path) necessary to transport the database's rows from the different tables to the view records in the correct sequence for the run-unit. The run-unit perceives a view record instance to be a simple record, and uses commands of FIND, GET, DELETE, STORE, or MODIFY.

See View Data Model.

View Column: A View Column is a column defined within the domain of a view. A view column is a "data" component of a view. A view column can be mapped to one or more compound data elements, or one to or more derived data elements, or to one or more DBMS columns. A view column also forms the basis for the interrelationship among views. Some view columns are the result of a computation that "goes on" inside the view involving multiple DBMS columns. A view column may have a different name, but must contain the same semantics as a DBMS column.

See View Data Model.

View Column Assigned Compound Data Element: A View Column Assigned Compound Data Element represents one or more Compound Data Elements assigned to a View Column. The view columns exist within a specified sequence.

See View Data Model.

View Column Assigned DBMS Column: A View Column Assigned DBMS Column represents one or more DBMS Columns that are assigned to a View Column. This enables a given view to be specified in the Metabase System such that it is applicable to multiple DBMSs and multiple databases. An executing view, of course, is applicable to only one DBMS and one database. The view columns exist within a specified sequence.
   See View Data Model.

View Column Assigned Derived Data Element: A View Column Assigned Derived Data Element represents one or more View Columns assigned to a Derived Data Element. The view columns exist within a specified sequence.
   See View Data Model.

View Column Structure: View Column Structure is the relationship between two view columns of different views that are governed by a specific view column structure process.
   See View Data Model.

View Column Structure Process: A View Column Structure Process is the pseudo code that defines the relationship among all the view columns that are referenced in a set of view column structure records.
   See View Data Model.

View Column Structure Type: A View Column Structure Type represents a classification of a set of view column structures.
   See View Data Model.

View Data Model: View Data Models are the Business Information System and Operational Data Model intersection mechanisms. View data models, depicted in Figure 23, contain the following components: View, View Column, View Column & Compound Data Element, View Column & Derived Data Element, View Column & DBMS Column, View Column Structure, View Column Structure Process, and View Column Structure Type

   View data models consist of views and view columns. They are also related to the business information systems that are the sources or targets of the database data. Views are specifically tied to specific DBMSs and view columns from a source view may be mapped to the view columns of a target view. Finally, view columns may be computed or derived.

View data models give applications a flat "record set" for processing. Included in views can be rename clauses and on-the-fly calculations. View columns not only map to DBMS columns but also, as appropriate, to compound data elements and derived data elements.

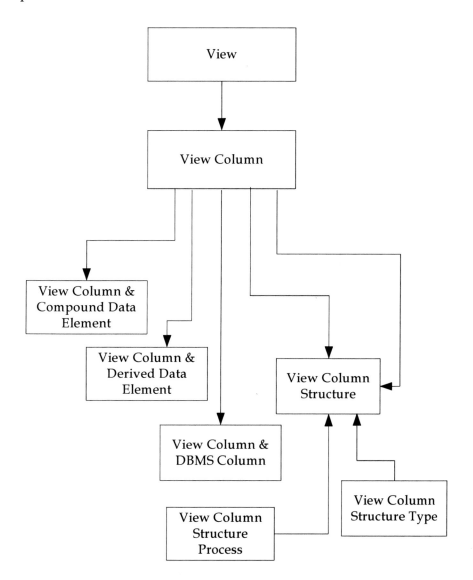

Figure 23. View Data Model.

Virtual Data Element: A Virtual Data Element is a data element whose value(s) is not stored in the database but is derived from stored data by means of user-defined operations.

Virtual Relation: See View.

Volatility: Volatility is a measure of the quantity of row adds and deletes over a period of time, as well as over the total number of database rows.

Warehouse Database: See Data Architecture.

Where Clause: A WHERE Clause consists of one or more WHERE expressions. If there is more than one WHERE expression, they are connected with boolean operators. WHERE clauses are included in at least data record check clauses, views, natural languages, and the host language interfaces.

Where Expression: A WHERE Expression is a set of syntactic units employed by the DBMS to determine whether certain criteria are satisfied. A WHERE expression is simple if it contains no subordinate select expressions.

    An early SQL standard BNF representation of the components of a WHERE expression consists of:

<complex where expression>:: = {<where expression> [boolean operator] }.

<where expression>::= [<left parenthesis>] [statistical operator] <data element name> <operator> <value> [<right parenthesis>]

<operator>::= <unary operator> | <binary operator> | <ternary operator> | <arithmetic operator>

<unary operator>::= <EXISTS> | <FAILS>

<binary operator>::= <GT> | <GE> | <EQ> | <NE> | <LE> | <LT>

<boolean operator>::= <AND> | <OR> | <NOT>

<ternary operators>::= <SPANS> | <RANGES>

<parenthetical operator>::= <left parenthesis> (nesting).

Data Management's Concepts & Terms

```
<arithmetic operator>::= <+> | <-> | <*> | </>

<statistical operator>::= <min> | <max> | <sum> | <count> | <avg> | < sigma>
```

Sophisticated DBMSs allow WHERE expressions that involve any variety of columns to be placed in the same WHERE clause.

Work: Work is the recording of actual hours and a characterization of the accomplishment for those hours against a given assigned task. For example, in the creation of a Customer Data Model, the work might be to clearly identify all the common data elements that act as semantic templates for Customer Data Model table columns.
   See Project Management Model.

Work Environment Factor: A Work Environment Factor is a characterization of an effect on a set of task work that either makes it go faster or slows it down. Each work environment factor is described in terms of its effect on the effort. An example might be adequate data modeling tool support, or no data modeling tool support.
   See Project Management Model.

Work Environment Factor Type: A Work Environment Factor Type is a characterization of the kind of work environment factors. An example might data modeling work environment factors and would encompass client reviews, availability of functional experts, or multi-user work tools.
   See Project Management Model.

Work Environment Multiplier Type: A Work Environment Multiplier Type is a characterization of the kind of effect that a given work environment factor might have on an effort. Examples might be No Effect, Accelerates, or Slows Down. Each effect is characterized by a multiplier value such as 0.75 for a 25% increase in speed or 1.50 for a 50% time penalty.
   See Project Management Model.

Data Management's Concepts & Terms

Work Environment Factor: A Work Factor is a work effort multiplier that most often raises the nominal quantity of staff hours required to produce a methodology work product. The work factors address staff skill assessments, familiarity and prior experience, tools and equipment, work environment, and customer reviews.
　　See Project Management Model.

X3H2: See H2. See ANSI Database Standards. See ANSI SQL. See ANSI NDL.

Zachman Framework: The Zachman Framework is a two-dimensional framework for enterprise Information Systems Development. The Zachman Framework, named after John Zachman, first appeared in the late 1980s. In the last 20 or so years it has been renamed a number of times to meet the needs different uses even through its contents have essentially remained the same.
　　The columns of the Zachman Framework of the late 1980s match the six interrogatives, who, what, when, where, why, and how. Consequently, the Zachman Framework is much less precise but more generalized than the Knowledge Worker Framework.
　　There are many implementations of the Zachman Framework, each different in significant ways.
　　A new Zachman Framework was introduced in 2007/2008 is even more generalized and less precise. Choosing the Zachman Framework implies a choice of one framework for all reasons regardless of precision, specialization, and exchangeability.
　　See Knowledge Worker Framework

INDEX

4GL 1, 56, 113, 130, 131
Abnormal Termination 1
Abstract Data Type 1, 21
Access Control 1
Access Languages 56
Access Method 1, 79, 94, 138
Access Path 2, 189
Access Strategy 2, 9, 54, 56, 57, 59, 83, 142, 144
Action Type 2
After Image Recovery 2, 152
Aggregate 2, 30, 138
Alias 2
American National Standards Institute 2
ANSI . xxx, 1-6, 20, 21, 26, 27, 30, 43, 45, 49, 52, 55, 56, 59, 60, 69, 73, 76, 78, 79,
    81-84, 87, 88, 90, 92, 95-97, 130, 132, 139, 142, 156, 163, 167, 171, 177, 180-
    182, 194
ANSI Database Standards ... 3-5, 52, 56, 60, 73, 82, 88, 132, 156, 167, 177, 181,
    194
ANSI NDL 6, 30, 96, 97, 142, 194
ANSI SQL . xxx, 1, 6, 30, 45, 49, 56, 59, 69, 76, 78, 79, 82, 87, 92, 95, 97, 139, 163,
    177, 180, 182, 194
ANSI/X3/SPARC 3-6, 26, 27
Application Database 6
Application Optimization 6, 57, 179
Application Type 6, 14, 98
Architecture 4, 14, 26, 29-31, 33-35, 53, 74, 88, 192
Archival Database 6, 9
Area .. 3, 6, 7, 10, 30, 34, 35, 53, 55, 70, 75, 77, 88, 90, 94, 126, 128, 143, 145, 151,
    159, 174, 179, 180, 184
Array 7, 51, 66, 77-79, 96, 143, 155, 156, 173-177
Assertion 7, 9, 19, 42, 43, 67
Assigned Task 7, 147, 162, 193
Atomic 7, 162, 185
Attribute . 7, 8, 22, 23, 36, 65, 75-77, 79, 97, 101, 102, 107-110, 113, 114, 120-123,
    143, 153, 168
Attribute Assigned Meta Category Values 8
Attribute Assigned Value Domain 8
Attribute Name 8
Audit Trails 57, 60, 179

195

Authorization Identifier	8
Automatic Backout	8, 72
Automatic Restart	8
B-tree	9
Backout	8, 72, 185
Backup	2, 6, 9, 10, 56, 64, 144, 151, 152, 161-163, 167, 179, 185
Backup and Recovery	2, 9, 10, 56, 64, 161, 167, 179, 185
Backus Naur Form	9, 97
Backward Recovery	9, 152
Base Line	9, 10, 147
Base Line Staff	10, 147
Base Line Work Environment Factor	10, 147
Base Relation	10
Before Image Recovery	10, 152
Benchmark	6, 10
Benchmark Test	10
Binding	48, 143, 173
Blocking Factor	10, 156
BNF	9, 81, 97, 192
Boolean	94, 172, 192
Buffer	10, 11
Buffer Flush	11
Buffers	10, 23
Business Calendar	11
Business Calendar Cycle	11
Business Cycle	11
Business Domains	11, 37, 104
Business Event	11, 12, 14, 17, 63, 93, 98, 99, 112
Business Event Assigned Business Information System	11
Business Event Cycle	12, 98
Business Event Cycle Structure	12, 98
Business Event Cycle Structure Type	12
Business Event Model	12
Business Function	11-13, 16, 63, 93, 127
Business Function Assigned Business Event	12
Business Function Assigned Document	13
Business Function Assigned Form	13
Business Functions	12, 13, 16, 63, 75, 98, 126, 127, 129

Index

Business Information System 11-16, 36, 41, 61, 66, 70, 72, 74, 76, 93, 98, 99, 106, 112, 126, 127, 146, 158, 160, 188, 190
Business Information System and View 14, 112
Business Information System Generators 14, 15
Business Information System Model 14, 76, 146
Business Information System Plan 15, 16
Business Information System Plan Characteristic: Maintainable 15
Business Information System Plan Characteristic: Quality 15
Business Information System Plan Characteristic: Reproducible 16
Business Information System Plan Characteristic: Timely 16
Business Information System Plan Characteristic: Useable 16
Business Information System Resource Life Cycle Node Assignment 14
Business Information Systems ... 11-18, 31, 34, 36, 58, 61, 66, 67, 72, 74, 93, 95, 98, 99, 106, 112, 113, 119, 122, 124, 127, 129, 157-160, 180, 190
Business Information Systems Assignment 160
Business Organizations 16
Business Process 16, 150
Business Rule 17
Business Term 17, 99, 100, 126
CALC 1, 17, 71, 83, 151, 153, 157, 191
Calendar Cycle 11, 17, 99
Calendar Cycle Structure 17, 99
Calendar Cycle Structure Type 17
Call Level Interface 1, 139
Candidate Key 17, 68, 69, 75, 85, 92, 108, 115, 116, 120, 181, 182
Cardinality 17
Case .. 18, 21, 32, 42, 44, 45, 54, 73, 77, 78, 87, 93, 94, 97, 106, 138, 140, 141, 149, 154, 155, 165, 169, 172, 178, 184
Central Version 18
Chair 81
Character 8, 18, 19, 21, 66, 77, 142, 143, 150, 151, 172, 177, 185, 187
Character Fill 18
Characteristic .. 6, 7, 14-16, 18, 19, 30, 38, 42, 45, 47, 48, 58, 59, 89, 90, 111-113, 129, 137, 139, 143, 159, 160, 172, 174
Characteristic Type 18, 111
Check Clause 19, 181
Checkpoint 19
Clarion 2, 18-20, 66, 122, 131
COBOL 1-3, 5, 20, 56, 58, 59, 85, 113, 146, 147, 162, 170, 172

CODASYL 3-6, 20, 21, 52, 81, 96, 132, 142, 155, 156, 167, 171, 174, 175
CODASYL Model 20, 21, 132, 156, 167
CODASYL Set 21, 132, 155, 156, 167, 174
CODASYL Systems Committee 3
Code Generator 19, 112
Collating Sequence 21, 141
Collection Data Type 1, 21, 93, 130, 166
Column .... xxix, xxx, 2, 8, 22, 23, 33, 36, 42, 43, 46, 52, 53, 59, 63-65, 68, 69, 71, 73, 77, 79, 80, 85, 90-93, 95-97, 101, 102, 105, 107-111, 113-117, 121, 123, 124, 131, 137-139, 141, 143, 151, 153-155, 157, 162, 164-166, 175-177, 180-182, 184, 189, 190
Column Assigned Data Integrity Rule 23
Column Assigned Meta Category Values 23, 65
Column Assigned Value Domain 23, 65
Command 8, 9, 23, 27, 28, 94, 96, 144, 147, 151, 162, 185
Commit 23, 163, 166
Communications Link 23, 93
Complex Fact 1, 23, 77, 78, 96, 135
Complex Row 24, 138
Complex Table 24, 165
Compound Data Element 24, 71, 100, 102, 103, 124, 189, 190
Compound Data Element Assigned Data Element 24
Compound Data Element Structure 24, 102
Compound Data Element Structure Type 24
Compression 24
Computer Program 15, 24, 41, 58, 131, 162
Concatenate 24
Concatenated Key 25, 137
Concept Structure 25, 39, 100, 103
Concept Structure Type 25, 39
Concepts ..... i, xxix, xxx, 1, 25-27, 31, 37-39, 78, 79, 87, 100, 102, 103, 117, 121, 125, 157, 167, 169, 179, 184, 187
Conceptual Data Model 25, 26, 50, 168
Conceptual Schema 26, 27
Conceptual Value Domain Structure 27, 101
Conceptual Value Domain Structure Type 27
Conceptual Value Domains 27, 37, 39, 79, 101, 188
Concurrency 185
Concurrent Operations 18, 27, 56, 57, 130, 166, 179

Index

Consistency 8, 27, 28, 74, 90, 152
Contention 28
Contract 28, 29, 31, 57, 147, 150
Contract & Organization 28, 147
Contract Resource 29, 147
Contract Role 29, 147
Cursor 29, 30, 171, 173
Data Administration 30, 52, 90
Data Administrator 29, 30, 91
Data Aggregate 30, 138
Data Analysis 30, 88, 179
Data Architecture 14, 29-31, 33-35, 53, 74, 88, 192
Data Architecture Class 14, 30, 33-35
Data Architecture Reference Model 30, 31
Data Definition 5, 35, 44, 48, 56, 57, 81, 179
Data Definition Language 5, 35, 44, 56, 57, 81, 179
Data Dictionary 20, 36
Data Dictionary/directory 36
Data Dictionary/directory System 36
Data Driven 36, 185
Data Driven Methodology 36
Data Element .. xxix, xxx, 7, 8, 11, 17, 22-27, 30-32, 34, 36-41, 51, 65, 71, 73, 77-79, 88, 96, 97, 100-104, 107-110, 113, 114, 117, 119-124, 138, 142, 168, 179, 183-185, 187-190, 192
Data Element Assigned Data Element Classification 37
Data Element Assigned Data Integrity Rule 37
Data Element Assigned Derived Data Element 38
Data Element Assigned Meta Category Value 38
Data Element Classification Structure 38, 101, 103
Data Element Classification Structure Type 38
Data Element Classifications 37, 38, 101, 103
Data Element Concept Assigned Data Integrity Rule 39
Data Element Concept Assigned Meta Category Value 39
Data Element Concept Structure 39, 103
Data Element Concept Structure Type 39
Data Element Concepts 27, 37-39, 78, 79, 100, 102, 103, 117, 121, 187
Data Element Length 39
Data Element Model .. 11, 17, 22, 24-27, 30-32, 34, 37-41, 71, 77, 78, 96, 97, 179, 184, 185, 187, 188

Data Element Name 192
Data Elements .. 11, 19, 24-26, 31, 32, 34, 36-40, 54, 71, 78, 79, 84, 100, 102, 103,
              107, 117, 121-123, 130, 168, 180, 184, 185, 187-189, 191, 193
Data File 35, 41, 53
Data Flow 30, 41, 53
Data Flow Diagram 41
Data Independence 41, 59
Data Integrity 17, 19, 23, 37, 39, 41-43, 54, 67, 77, 104, 150, 153, 156, 181
Data Integrity Rule 17, 19, 23, 37, 39, 42, 43, 67, 77, 104, 153, 156
Data Integrity Rules 37, 39, 41-43, 104, 181
Data Interoperability 184
Data Item 43
Data Loading 56, 94, 125, 144
Data Manipulation Language 4, 5, 43, 44, 46, 92, 139
Data Model .. xxix, xxx, 4-8, 19-23, 25-27, 29-35, 37, 39, 44-53, 56, 59, 60, 63-70,
           72, 73, 75-79, 82, 84-90, 95, 96, 107, 109, 110, 115-117, 119, 121, 122, 124,
           132, 137, 139-145, 147, 149, 150, 152, 153, 155, 156, 162, 166-171, 173-175,
                                              177-185, 188-191, 193
Data Resource Management 52
Data Security 53
Data Semantics 34, 126
Data Storage Description Language 53
Data Storage Structure 53
Data Store 53
Data Structure 26, 39, 44, 53, 61, 63, 66, 133, 135, 136, 176-178
Data Type 1, 21, 44, 52, 53, 65, 66, 77, 78, 93, 95, 97, 107, 108, 115, 130, 143,
                                          155, 166, 172, 175-177, 187
Data View 53
Data Volatility 53
Data Warehouse 31, 33-35, 53, 85, 141, 144
Database ... 2-6, 8-15, 17, 19-21, 23, 26-28, 30, 31, 34-36, 39-44, 52-64, 70, 72-75,
           77, 79-86, 88-96, 98, 104-106, 112, 119, 122, 125-127, 130-132, 137-139,
           144-147, 150-154, 156-165, 167, 170, 171, 177, 179-182, 184, 186, 188-190,
                                                       192, 194
Database Administrator 54
Database Design 34, 58, 88, 180
Database Domain 54, 61, 104, 105, 126
Database Domain Assigned Database Object 54
Database Key 54

Index

Database Maintenance 56, 144
Database Management 4, 6, 13, 17, 44, 54-57, 60, 64, 74, 79, 88, 91, 171
Database Management System 13, 17, 54, 55, 64, 88, 91
Database Management Systems History 79
Database Nature 60
Database Object . 14, 15, 36, 54, 60-63, 74, 90, 93, 96, 98, 104-106, 112, 119, 150, 158, 160, 163
Database Object Assigned Property Class 60
Database Object Class 61, 62, 74, 90
Database Object Data Structure 61
Database Object Information System 14, 61, 63, 105, 106, 112
Database Object Information System Assignment 14
Database Object Model 60-63, 163
Database Object Process 61, 62, 105
Database Object Resource Life Cycle Node Assignment 62
Database Object State 61, 63, 105, 106
Database Object State and Database Object Information System 63
Database Object Table 61, 63, 96, 105, 106
Database Object Table Process 61, 63, 105, 106
Database Object Table Process Column 63
Database Process 74
Database Production Status 64
Database Recovery 64, 152
Database Update 64
Database View 64
Database View Column 64
DBA 54
DBKEY 54, 132, 142, 145, 146
DBMS ... 1-4, 6, 8-11, 13, 14, 17-19, 25-37, 41, 43, 44, 46-49, 53-60, 64-71, 73, 77, 79, 81-83, 85, 90-92, 94-96, 99, 101, 102, 109, 110, 112, 115-118, 121-125, 130-132, 137-139, 141-145, 151, 152, 154-156, 162, 164, 171, 174, 178-181, 184-192
DBMS Column ... 33, 36, 64, 65, 68, 69, 77, 79, 101, 102, 109, 115, 117, 123, 139, 189, 190
DBMS Column Assigned Column 65
DBMS Column Assigned Meta Category Values 65
DBMS Column Assigned Value Domain 65
DBMS Column Constraint 65
DBMS Data Type 65, 66, 115

Data Management's Concepts and Terms

DBMS Data Type Picture 66
DBMS Environment 14, 27, 66, 99, 112, 179
DBMS Record 10, 11, 28, 66, 70, 91, 94, 142-145, 156, 179
DBMS Schema 41, 66, 67, 91, 95, 110, 115-117, 125, 139
DBMS Subschema 67
DBMS Table 25, 29, 32-34, 36, 64, 65, 67-69, 77, 110, 115-117, 139, 141
DBMS Table Assigned Assertion 67
DBMS Table Assigned Stored Procedure 67
DBMS Table Assigned Trigger 68
DBMS Table Candidate Key 68, 116
DBMS Table Candidate Key Assigned DBMS Column 68
DBMS Table Constraint 68
DBMS Table Foreign Key 68, 69
DBMS Table Foreign Key Assigned DBMS Column 69
DBMS Table Primary Key 69
DBMS Table Primary Key Assigned DBMS Column 69
DBMS Table Secondary Key 69
DBMS Table Secondary Key Assigned DBMS Column 69
DBTG 20
DD/DS 36
DDL 5, 35, 44, 45, 48, 56, 66, 81, 83, 85, 109, 116, 121, 132, 139, 140, 184
Deadly Embrace 70
Degree (Of a Relation) 70
Delimiter 70
Deliverable 70, 147-149, 183
Deliverable Template 70, 147, 149
Deliverable Template Type 70, 147
Derived Data 38, 42, 71, 102, 103, 124, 189-191
Derived Data Element 38, 71, 102, 103, 124, 190
Derived Data Element Assigned Compound Data Element 71
Derived Data Element Assigned Data Element 71
Determinant 71
Device Media Control Language 71
Dictionary (Storage Structure Component) 71
Discrete and Release Development Environments 72
Distributed Database 72
Division 72, 81, 153
DMCL 53, 71
DML 5, 43-46, 48, 56, 81, 83, 90, 125, 131, 156

Document 13, 15, 36, 72, 77, 81, 147
Document Cell 36, 72
Domain .. 8, 9, 11, 23, 26, 27, 37, 38, 40, 54, 61, 65, 67, 75, 91, 100-102, 104, 105,
             108-110, 117, 121, 123, 124, 126, 141, 144, 185, 187-189
DOS 72
DSDL 53, 56, 145
Dynamic Backout 72
Dynamic Relationship 59, 60, 73, 131, 154-156, 186
Editor 20
Element . xxix, xxx, 7, 8, 11, 17, 22-27, 30-32, 34, 36-41, 51, 58, 65, 66, 71, 73, 77-
      79, 88, 96, 97, 100-104, 107-110, 113, 114, 117, 119-124, 138, 142, 151, 168,
                         176, 177, 179, 183-185, 187-190, 192
Embedded Pointer 73
Encode/decode Tables 73
End-user 73, 185
Enterprise .. 11, 15-17, 26, 30, 34-36, 40, 54, 66, 72-74, 88, 97, 125, 126, 128, 129,
                  141, 147-151, 155, 157-160, 179, 183-185, 194
Enterprise Architecture 34, 74
Enterprise Database 72, 74, 147
Enterprise Resource Planning (Erp) 74
Entity 7, 22, 25, 31, 32, 34, 36, 66, 70, 75-77, 87, 109, 110, 117, 119-121, 146,
                                168, 169, 185
Entity Candidate Key 75
Entity Candidate Key Assigned Attribute 75
Entity Foreign Key 76
Entity Foreign Key Assigned Attribute 76
Entity Primary Key 76
Entity Primary Key Assigned Attribute 76
Entity Relationship Diagram 76
Environment Type 14, 76, 99, 113
Error Recovery 77
Exclusive Control 77
Extent 26, 77, 87, 95, 141, 147, 169
External Document 77, 147
External Schema 179
External View 80
Fact . xxix, 1, 2, 7, 23, 26, 30, 34-36, 40, 43, 44, 51-53, 57, 66, 77-81, 87, 92, 96, 97,
                132, 135, 141, 146, 156, 158, 162, 166, 169, 177, 180, 181
Fact Name 79

Fail Soft 79
Field .... xxix, 4, 24, 36, 79, 90, 91, 165, 176
Field Length 79
Fifth Normal Form 133, 137
File ... xxix, 4, 6, 19, 29, 35, 36, 41, 43, 48-50, 53, 57-59, 70, 77, 79, 80, 85, 87, 91,
   94, 95, 138, 144, 152, 170, 173-175, 178
File Block 80
File Cell 80
FIPS 80
First Normal Form 133, 135, 136
Fixed Length Fact 80
Fixed Length Record 80
Foreign Key 43, 61, 68, 69, 73, 76, 80, 85, 87, 92, 96, 108, 115, 116, 120, 141,
   142, 165, 169, 181, 182
Form . 4, 5, 8, 9, 13, 14, 20, 25, 26, 35, 36, 39, 66, 67, 77, 80, 81, 85, 87, 88, 94, 95,
   97, 130, 131, 133-138, 153-155, 157, 158, 162, 165, 168, 172, 180
Form Cell 36, 80
Fortran 1-3, 5, 20, 56, 58, 85, 113, 146, 147, 172
Fourth Generation Language 1, 130
Fourth Normal Form 135-137
Framework 4, 20, 80, 93, 106, 122, 194
Fully Functionally Dependent 80
Function 11-13, 16, 19, 29, 54, 55, 63, 74, 77, 80, 81, 88-91, 93, 107, 111, 118,
   122, 126-129, 132, 136, 143, 145, 151, 162, 184, 193
Functional Decomposition 81
Glossary .... xxix, 34
Group 1, 3-5, 20, 30, 44, 51, 78, 79, 81, 132, 135, 137, 156, 165, 166
H2 .... 3, 5, 21, 81-84, 132, 171, 194
Hash/CALC Logical 83
Hash/CALC Physical 83, 151
Heuristics 84
Hierarchical Data Model 29, 60, 84, 96, 142, 162, 174, 175, 185
Hierarchical Index 85
Hierarchy 36, 41, 45, 79, 84, 87, 104, 107, 109, 115, 117, 118
Home Address 83-85
Host Language Interface 57, 85, 130, 131
Implemented Data Model .. xxx, 19, 22, 23, 26, 30, 32-34, 37, 52, 63, 64, 67, 77,
   78, 85-87, 95, 107, 109, 110, 116, 117, 139-141, 143, 168, 180-182, 184, 185
Implemented Data Model Relationship 87

Independent Logical File .... xxix, 4, 6, 29, 43, 48-50, 59, 87, 170, 173-175, 178
Independent Logical File Data Model 49, 87, 173-175, 178
Index .... xxix, 66, 83, 85, 88, 125, 145, 195
Inferential Relationship 88
Information .. i-3, 9-18, 20, 26, 31, 34, 36, 41, 44, 52, 53, 58, 61, 63, 66, 67, 70, 72, 74-76, 80, 88-90, 93, 95, 96, 98, 99, 105, 106, 108, 111-113, 116, 119, 120, 122, 124-129, 145, 146, 149-151, 155, 157-160, 171, 172, 180, 185, 188, 190, 194
Information Engineering 44, 52, 88
Information Need 18, 88-90, 111, 119, 128, 129, 160
Information Need Analysis Model 89
Information Need Characteristic Assignment 90
Information Need Type 18, 90, 111
Information Needs 15, 88-90, 111, 119, 122, 129, 151, 160
Information Resource Management 90
Information System .. 11-16, 36, 41, 61, 63, 66, 70, 72, 74, 76, 88, 93, 98, 99, 105, 106, 112, 113, 125-127, 146, 158, 160, 188, 190
Information Systems Plan 15, 16, 112
Insertion 43, 63, 90
Installation and Maintenance 57, 90, 179
Instance . xxix, 1, 7, 10, 18, 22, 27, 28, 41, 42, 44, 61, 64, 66, 69, 70, 76, 78, 80, 87, 90, 94, 99, 100, 103, 104, 111, 141, 142, 152, 154, 156, 161-163, 166, 167, 169, 182, 189
Integrity ... 17, 19, 23, 26, 27, 31, 37, 39, 41-43, 54, 63, 67, 71, 74, 77, 83, 90, 104, 150, 153, 156, 163, 170-172, 181
Integrity Constraints (DBMS Enforced) 90
Internal Schema 91
Interrogation 8, 55, 56, 91, 155, 157
Inverted Access 58, 60, 91
ISO .... xxx, 2, 5, 22, 37, 39, 40, 56, 81, 91, 95
ISO 11179 .... 22, 37, 39
JDBC 1, 57, 130, 131
Job 91, 93, 94, 147, 154, 162, 179, 187
Job Title 91, 147
Job Unit 187
Join 43, 47, 51, 91, 131, 141, 153, 170
Journal File 19, 91, 94, 152
Justify 82, 91
Keeplist 92

Data Management's Concepts and Terms

Key . 4, 7, 8, 16, 17, 22, 25, 37, 40, 43, 44, 46, 48, 54, 59, 61, 64, 65, 68, 69, 71, 73, 75, 76, 80, 83, 85, 87, 88, 92, 93, 95, 96, 107, 108, 115, 116, 120, 121, 132, 135-137, 139, 141, 142, 145, 146, 154, 164-166, 169, 176, 177, 180-182
Key Value 43, 73, 92, 136, 165
Knowledge Worker 80, 93, 106, 122, 194
Knowledge Worker Framework 80, 93, 106, 122, 194
Language . 1, 4-6, 9, 14, 20, 21, 30, 35, 40, 43-46, 49, 50, 52, 53, 56-60, 66, 69, 71, 73, 76, 81-85, 87, 90-93, 97, 113, 130-133, 139, 142, 143, 145-147, 151, 153, 156, 161-163, 165, 167, 170-174, 177, 179-182, 187, 189, 192
Life Cycle 14, 15, 62, 74, 88, 112, 119, 122, 124, 145, 147, 150, 157-161
Line 9, 10, 18, 58, 71, 82-84, 93, 113, 131, 144, 147, 157, 171, 185
List 1, 18, 21, 77, 93, 94, 173
List Processing 93, 94
Lock 28, 70, 77, 80, 94, 146
Locking 10, 28, 145, 156
Log File 94
Logging 95
Logical Data Model 25, 26, 50, 95, 143, 144
Logical Database 55, 94, 144
Logical Database Reorganization 94
Logical File .... xxix, 4, 6, 29, 43, 48-50, 59, 87, 95, 170, 173-175, 178
Logical Record Facility 95
Logical Reorganization 95, 144, 156
Logical User View 95
Management Level 95, 118
Many-to-Many Relationship 95
Map 22, 33, 53, 61, 64, 67, 181, 191
Member ... 29, 30, 43, 45, 47, 51, 84, 90, 94-96, 131, 132, 138, 139, 142, 152, 155, 156, 161, 166, 167, 176, 178
Membership Rationale 61, 63, 96, 106
Message Processing 57, 96, 179
Messages 85, 96, 151, 185
Meta Category Value Type 96, 97, 109, 113, 114, 121
Meta Category Value Type Classification 96, 97
Meta Category Values   8, 23, 37-39, 65, 96, 97, 103, 109, 110, 113, 114, 117, 121, 122
Meta Language 9, 97
Metabase .... xxx, 12, 14, 18, 19, 22, 39, 77, 85, 89, 93, 98-101, 104-107, 111-115, 118, 119, 122-126, 128, 140, 143, 157, 184, 190

Metadata ... xxx, 7, 14, 15, 19, 20, 22, 23, 26, 36, 37, 39, 64, 71, 80, 81, 85, 86, 93, 100, 106, 122, 125, 126, 147, 183, 187
Metadata Management System ... xxx, 19, 26, 36, 71, 86, 93, 106, 122, 125, 126, 147, 187
Metadata Repository ... 20, 126
Metric ... 15, 126, 148
Mission . 7, 12, 16, 54, 74, 77, 80, 81, 88, 89, 93, 104, 107, 111, 114, 115, 118, 119, 122, 126-129, 143, 145, 151
Mission Assigned Business Term ... 126
Mission Assigned Database Domain ... 126
Mission Description ... 129
Mission Resource ... 129
Mission Versus Function ... 81, 129
Module ... 14, 92, 127-130, 143, 172
Multi-user Mode ... 130
Multiple Database Processing ... 28, 57, 130, 179
Multiset ... 1, 130
Multithread ... 130
Multivalued Dependency ... 130, 136
Natural Language ... 58, 60, 91, 130, 131, 163
Navigate ... 131, 188
NDL . 4-6, 21, 30, 43, 49, 52, 56, 60, 73, 81-83, 90, 96, 97, 132, 142, 156, 161, 167, 177, 181, 194
NDL Data Language ... 6, 21, 30, 52, 73, 90, 132, 142, 156, 167, 177, 181
NDL Data Language Standard ... 6, 21, 30, 52, 73, 90, 132, 156, 167, 177, 181
Nested Repeating Group ... 1, 44, 51, 78, 79, 132
Network ... xxix, 4-6, 20, 21, 45, 48-50, 59, 60, 81, 82, 90, 132, 161, 170, 171, 174, 175, 178
Network Data Language ... 5, 132, 161
Network Data Model ... 4, 21, 49, 82, 90, 132, 174
Next Key (Next Pointer) ... 132
NIST ... 81, 82
Non Procedural Language ... 133
Normal Forms ... 133, 136-138
Normalize ... 137
Normalized Data ... 135, 138
Null ... 19, 43, 138, 141, 173
O/S File ... 6, 53, 77, 87, 94, 138

Object ... 14, 15, 36, 54, 60-63, 70, 74, 90, 93, 96, 98, 104-106, 112, 119, 150, 158, 160, 163
ODBC 1, 57, 122, 130, 131, 138, 139
OLAP 89, 138
OLTP 138
One-to-many Relationship 31, 33
One-to-one Relationship 138
Open Database Connectivity 138, 139
Operating Systems 74, 174
Operational Data Model .. xxx, 19, 32-34, 37, 52, 65-69, 77, 79, 85, 115-117, 139-141, 143, 144, 149, 150, 180, 184, 185, 188, 190
Operational Data Model Relationship 141
Order . 9, 12, 22, 23, 34, 47, 71, 83, 88, 137, 138, 141, 144, 150, 153, 154, 158, 164, 165, 174
Ordered 15, 21, 34, 93, 141, 166
Organization .. 2-4, 12, 16, 20, 21, 28-30, 48, 51, 54, 59, 71-74, 77, 80, 81, 88, 89, 91, 93, 95, 107, 111, 118, 122, 126-129, 141, 143-145, 147, 150, 151, 176, 179
Outer Join 141
Overflow 142
Owner 18, 43, 45, 47, 51, 66, 83, 84, 90, 95, 131, 132, 138, 139, 142, 145, 152, 156, 166, 167, 176
Owner Key (Owner Pointer) 142
Owner-multiple Member 132, 142
Owner-single Member Relationship 142
Packed Decimal 142
Padding 142
Page 41, 131, 143
Parameter 143, 164
Password 143
Person .... ii, 31, 32, 44, 54, 63, 73, 77, 78, 118, 128, 143, 173, 178, 179, 187
Phone 21, 78, 143, 147
Phone Type 143, 147
Physical Attribute 143
Physical Data Model 25, 50, 143, 145
Physical Database 55, 56, 130, 139, 144, 145, 154
Physical Record 144
Physical Reorganization 144, 156
Physical Schema 53, 71, 87, 145, 179

Index

Pointer 18, 73, 83, 132, 142, 145, 146, 154, 161, 178
Position 12, 16, 29, 30, 81, 118, 122, 126-129, 143, 145, 155
Precedence Vector 145
Precision 34, 96, 97, 145, 194
Predominant User 14, 99, 113, 146
Primary Key . . 7, 8, 22, 25, 43, 46, 54, 64, 65, 68, 69, 71, 73, 75, 76, 80, 83, 85, 87,
88, 92, 96, 108, 115, 116, 120, 121, 135-137, 141, 142, 146, 154, 165, 169,
176, 177, 180-182
Prior Key 146
Prior Pointer 146
Privacy 1, 53, 56, 57, 125, 146, 164, 170, 179
Privacy Key 146
Privacy Lock 146
Procedural Language 133, 146
Procedure Oriented Language 56, 130, 146
Process Driven Methodology 36, 146
Program 14, 15, 24, 41, 58, 59, 94, 129-131, 147, 152, 162, 179, 189
Project . . 7, 9, 10, 15, 16, 22, 28, 29, 43, 51, 64, 70, 72, 91, 106, 131, 143, 146-150,
153, 157, 159, 162, 167, 170, 178, 182, 183, 193, 194
Project Management 7, 9, 10, 28, 29, 70, 72, 91, 143, 147-150, 157, 159, 162,
167, 178, 182, 183, 193, 194
Project Management Model . 7, 9, 10, 28, 29, 70, 91, 143, 147-150, 157, 159, 162,
167, 178, 182, 183, 193, 194
Project Template 147, 149, 150, 183
Project Template & Deliverable Template 147, 149
Project Template & Task Template 147, 149
Project Template Type 147, 150
Projection 150, 153
Projects 16, 30, 72, 75, 137, 149
Property Class 60, 150
Prototyping 15
Pure Alphabetic 150
Pure Numeric 150
Qualification 150
Quality Assurance 150
Query Update Language 151
Queue 151
RAM 151
Random Access 151

Range Value Tables 187
Ranking 111, 151
RDL 5, 81, 83
Record ... xxix, 9-11, 26, 28, 48, 51, 58, 59, 66, 70, 73, 80, 83, 91, 94, 95, 130, 138,
          142-145, 151, 154-156, 165-167, 170, 174, 179, 185, 188, 189, 192
Record Check 151, 192
Record Layout 151
Record Length 151
Record Structures 174
Record Type .... xxix, 151, 167, 179
Record-element 151
Recovery 2, 9, 10, 56, 64, 77, 151, 152, 161-163, 167, 179, 185
Recovery File 152
Recursive 7, 22, 45, 65, 68, 87, 92, 132, 141, 152, 156, 170, 175, 176, 182
Recursive Relationship 7, 22, 65, 68, 152, 182
Reference Data 30, 31, 34, 35, 146
Referential Integrity 42, 43, 63, 83, 153, 156, 171, 172
Relation . xxix, xxx, 4-6, 10, 17, 29, 45, 48-51, 59, 60, 70, 72, 81, 94, 137, 138, 141,
          150, 153, 154, 162, 170-172, 174, 175, 177, 180, 181, 183, 192
Relational Algebra 153
Relational Calculus 153
Relational Data Language 5, 81
Relational Data Model . xxx, 5, 6, 45, 49, 50, 59, 72, 137, 150, 153, 170, 171, 174,
                        175, 177, 180, 181
Relational Database 10, 153, 171
Relational Model 59
Relational Operators 183
Relational View 154
Relationships ... 1, 5, 7, 10, 21, 22, 25, 26, 30-33, 43-48, 52-54, 56, 59, 61, 64, 65,
          73, 76, 84, 85, 87, 90, 93, 94, 96, 109, 110, 116, 117, 132, 139, 141, 142, 144,
          145, 153-156, 158, 161, 165-170, 175, 176, 178, 179, 186, 188, 189
Relative Addressing 156
Reorganization 94, 95, 144, 145, 156, 179
Repeating Group 1, 44, 51, 78, 79, 132, 135, 156, 165
Report 4, 8, 17, 56, 57, 72, 88, 90, 110, 117, 122, 130, 131, 149, 157
Report Writer 4, 130, 131, 157
Repository 20, 74, 126
Representation 9, 11, 18, 25, 36, 38, 41, 76, 91, 142, 150, 157, 192

Resource . 14, 15, 25, 29, 52, 62, 74, 88, 90, 112, 119, 122, 124, 126, 129, 145, 147, 157-161
Resource Life Cycle 14, 15, 62, 74, 88, 112, 119, 122, 124, 145, 147, 157-161
Resource Life Cycle Analysis 74, 122, 157, 159-161
Resource Life Cycle Analysis Model 157, 159-161
Resource Life Cycle Analysis Node 159
Resource Life Cycle Characteristic: Basic 159
Resource Life Cycle Characteristic: Centralized 159
Resource Life Cycle Characteristic: Complex 159
Resource Life Cycle Characteristic: Enduring 159
Resource Life Cycle Characteristic: Shareable 159
Resource Life Cycle Characteristic: Structured 160
Resource Life Cycle Characteristic: Valuable 160
Resource Life Cycle Characteristics 159
Resource Life Cycle Node Database Object Assignment 158, 160
Resource Life Cycle Node Information Need Assignment 160
Resource Life Cycle Node Matrix 160
Resource Life Cycle Node Structure 119, 161
Resource Life Cycle Node Structure Type: 119, 161
Resource Type 119, 158, 161
Restore 77, 91, 161
Retention 43, 161
Retrieval 45, 46, 68, 69, 75, 130, 138, 154, 161, 170, 181, 188
Ring Structure 161
Rings 48
RJE 162
Robust 48, 162
Role 7, 23, 29, 30, 37-39, 59, 95, 97, 99, 127, 147, 162
Role Type 7, 162
Rollback 152, 162, 163
ROM 162
Root Segment 84, 162
Row . xxix, 6, 7, 10, 18, 21, 22, 24, 28, 30, 42, 43, 45, 47, 48, 53, 54, 64-66, 68, 69, 73, 75-77, 79, 83, 84, 87, 90, 92-94, 96, 131, 132, 135, 136, 138, 142, 146, 151-156, 161, 162, 164-166, 170, 172, 173, 176-178, 181, 182, 186, 189, 192
Run-unit 28, 70, 94, 96, 130, 131, 152, 155, 162, 163, 189
Save 9, 163
Savepoint 152, 163
Scale 4, 163

Schema .. 4, 22, 26, 27, 35, 41, 43, 53, 66, 67, 71, 85, 87, 91, 95, 98, 105-110, 115-117, 122, 125, 132, 139, 143-145, 163-165, 172, 179-181, 187-189
Schema Assigned Database Object 163
Schema Record 179
Screen 36
Second Normal Form 134, 136
Secondary Key 46, 69, 92, 115, 116, 164
Secretary 81
Security and Privacy 1, 53, 56, 57, 125, 146, 164, 179
Segment 63, 84, 162, 165
Selection 17, 41, 130, 136, 150, 153, 156, 163, 165, 170, 188
Semantics 7, 22, 26, 31, 34, 36-38, 77, 80, 86, 93, 97, 106, 108, 120, 121, 126, 132, 145, 164, 165, 168, 180, 189
Sequential Search 10, 165
Serial Search 165
Serial Storage 166
Serializability 166
Set . 1, 2, 6-12, 17-22, 24-27, 30-35, 37-39, 41-45, 47, 48, 53, 54, 56, 61, 63-65, 67-70, 72, 73, 75, 76, 78-80, 87, 90-94, 100, 108-111, 116-118, 120-122, 131-133, 138-141, 143, 144, 147, 149-151, 153-157, 159-169, 174, 175, 177, 179-183, 187, 188, 190, 192, 193
Simple Fact 51, 66, 77, 78, 92, 166, 177
Simple Record 189
Simple Row 166
Simple Table 166
Single Thread 166
Single User Mode 166
Singular Set 166
Singular, Multiple Member Relationship 166
Singular, Single Member Relationship 166, 167
Skill 7, 78, 147, 149, 165, 167, 178, 183, 194
Skill Level 7, 147, 167, 178, 183
Skill Level Type 147, 167
Snapshot 19, 167
Softvelocity 19
SPARC 3-6, 26, 27
Specified Data Model .. xxx, 7, 8, 19, 22, 25, 26, 30, 32, 34, 37, 39, 52, 75-78, 86, 87, 109, 110, 119, 121, 167-169, 179, 184, 185, 188
Specified Data Model Relationship 169

Specified Data Models .. 26, 27, 31, 37, 40, 41, 51, 85, 88, 122, 167, 168, 183, 184
SQL ... xxix, xxx, 1, 4-7, 22, 30, 43, 45, 46, 49, 50, 52, 56, 59, 60, 65-67, 69, 73, 76, 78, 79, 81-85, 87, 92, 95-97, 107-109, 116, 120-123, 130, 131, 139, 140, 142, 155, 156, 162-165, 167, 170-178, 180-182, 184, 192, 194
SQL Data Language 6, 30, 49, 50, 52, 69, 73, 76, 82, 156, 162, 167, 170, 172, 177, 180-182
SQL Data Language Standard 6, 30, 49, 50, 52, 69, 73, 76, 82, 156, 162, 167, 170, 172, 177, 180-182
SQL Data Type 52, 107, 108, 177
SQL: 2003 84
SQL: 2008 84
SQL:1986 .... 83, 92, 156, 162, 177, 178
SQL:1992 .... 83, 92, 156, 162, 171, 180
SQL:1999 .... 6, 22, 59, 65, 66, 82, 92, 155, 156, 162, 163, 170-177, 180
Staff 7, 9, 10, 15, 16, 29, 126, 147-149, 157, 167, 178, 182, 183, 194
Staff Skill Level 7, 147, 178
Standards Development Board 3
Standards Planning and Requirements Committee 3
Standards Policy Board 3
State . 1, 7, 28, 42, 44, 61, 63, 70, 78, 88, 90, 105, 106, 126, 147, 152, 155, 157, 159, 163, 173, 175, 178
Static Relationship 73, 94, 131, 154-156, 167, 178, 186
Status Type 147, 178
Storage Structure 2, 9, 23, 28, 41, 53, 56, 57, 59, 64, 66, 71, 94, 144, 145, 154, 179
Stored Procedure 56, 67, 143, 179
Subject .... ii, 7, 17, 30, 34, 35, 50, 75, 109, 110, 117, 120, 121, 126, 168, 179
Subschema 67, 71, 125, 132, 179, 187
Subschema Data Definition Language 179
Subschema Record Type 179
System . xxx, 1, 4, 10-20, 22, 26, 28, 36, 39, 41, 53-59, 61-64, 66, 70-72, 74-77, 79, 85, 86, 88-91, 93, 98-101, 104-107, 111-115, 118, 119, 122-128, 130, 138-140, 143, 146, 147, 150, 157, 158, 160, 162, 170, 174, 179, 183, 184, 187, 188, 190
System Control 55, 56, 179
Systems Analysis 20, 179
Table ... iii, xxix, 1, 2, 6, 7, 9, 17, 20-22, 24, 25, 28-30, 32-36, 42, 43, 45-48, 51-54, 59, 61, 63-71, 73, 75, 77, 80, 83-85, 87, 88, 90-92, 94-96, 105-110, 115-117,

Data Management's Concepts and Terms

        125, 132, 135-137, 139, 141-143, 150-155, 161, 162, 165-167, 170, 172, 173,
        175, 176, 178, 180-183, 185, 186, 188, 189, 193

Table Candidate Key Assigned Column 181
Table Foreign Key Assigned Column 182
Table Look up 182
Table Primary Key 69, 182
Table Primary Key Assigned Column 182
Task 7, 9, 20, 147, 149, 150, 162, 167, 178, 182, 183, 193
Task & Work Environment Factor 147, 182
Task Skill Level Requirement 183
Task Template 147, 149, 150, 183
Teleprocessing Task 183
Temporary View Table 183
Test Data 90
Third Normal Form 67, 85, 95, 134, 136-138, 168, 180
Time Charges 183
Topology 72, 185
Transaction 19, 30, 34, 138, 139, 152, 163, 170-172, 185
Transaction Backout 185
Transaction Processing Monitor 185
Transitive Dependency 185
Tree Structure 185
Trigger 19, 23, 68, 185
Truncate 185
Tuple 24, 141, 153, 162, 166, 186
Unload 9, 94, 186
Unordered 186
User ... 1, 14, 18, 20, 27, 28, 42, 54, 60, 73, 82, 91, 95, 99, 113, 125, 130, 138, 141,
        143, 146, 152, 154, 155, 164, 166, 172-174, 179, 182, 185, 187, 192, 193
User Interface 187
User Schema 91, 179, 187
User Schema (Subschema) 187
User View 95, 187
Valid, Invalid, and Range Value Tables 187
Value Domain 8, 23, 27, 37, 38, 40, 65, 100-102, 104, 108-110, 117, 121, 123,
        124, 141, 187, 188
Value Domain Data Type 108, 187
Value Domain Structure 27, 101, 123, 187
Value Domain Structure Type 27, 187

Index

Value Domain Value 123, 124, 187, 188
Value Domain Value Structure 124, 188
Value Domain Value Structure Type 188
Value Domains .. 27, 37, 39, 41, 79, 85, 86, 100-102, 104, 109, 110, 117, 121, 123, 124, 146, 184, 188
Value Sets 61
Value-based 155
Variable Length Data Element 188
Variable Length Record 188
Vector 145, 188
Vice Chair 81
View 2, 14, 19, 31, 34-37, 51, 53, 64, 67, 72, 73, 77, 79, 80, 88, 95, 98, 99, 112, 122, 124, 125, 131, 139, 154, 155, 157, 162, 164, 173, 179, 183, 185, 187-192
View Column 36, 64, 77, 79, 124, 157, 189, 190
View Column Assigned Compound Data Element 189
View Column Assigned DBMS Column 190
View Column Assigned Derived Data Element 190
View Column Structure 124, 190
View Column Structure Process 124, 190
View Column Structure Type 124, 190
View Data Model 37, 77, 79, 124, 139, 185, 189-191
Virtual Data Element 192
Virtual Relation 192
Volatility 53, 192
Warehouse Databases 35, 144
WG3 81
Where Clause 165, 192, 193
Where Expression 192
Work . ii, 5, 7, 9, 10, 15, 16, 28, 29, 31, 70, 74, 78, 93, 106, 126, 145, 147-149, 157, 158, 167, 178, 182, 183, 193, 194
Work Environment Factor 9, 10, 147, 182, 193, 194
Work Environment Factor Type 147, 193
Work Environment Multiplier Type 147, 193
Work Factor 183, 194
Work Period 183
Work Task 7
X3 .... 3-6, 26, 27, 81, 83, 84, 194
X3H2 .... 3, 5, 81, 83, 84, 194

215

X3J3 5
X3J4 5
X3J9 5
Zachman Framework 80, 93, 194

CPSIA information can be obtained at www.ICGtesting.com
Printed in the USA
BVOW081317290112

281596BV00004B/6/P